The Lived Experiences of African International Students in the UK

The Lived Experiences of African International Students in the UK

Precarity, Consciousness and the Law

James Marson, Mohammed Dirisu, and Katy Ferris

ANTHEM PRESS

Anthem Press
An imprint of Wimbledon Publishing Company
www.anthempress.com

This edition first published in UK and USA 2025
by ANTHEM PRESS
75–76 Blackfriars Road, London SE1 8HA, UK
or PO Box 9779, London SW19 7ZG, UK
and
244 Madison Ave #116, New York, NY 10016, USA

First published in the UK and USA by Anthem Press in 2022

Copyright © James Marson, Mohammed Dirisu, and Katy Ferris 2025

The author asserts the moral right to be identified as the author of this work.

All rights reserved. Without limiting the rights under copyright reserved above, no part of this publication may be reproduced, stored or introduced into a retrieval system, or transmitted, in any form or by any means (electronic, mechanical, photocopying, recording or otherwise), without the prior written permission of both the copyright owner and the above publisher of this book.

British Library Cataloguing-in-Publication Data
A catalogue record for this book is available from the British Library.

Library of Congress Control Number: 2024943623

ISBN-13: 978-1-83999-375-6 (Pbk)
ISBN-10: 1-83999-375-8 (Pbk)

This title is also available as an e-book.

CONTENTS

Preface vii
Acknowledgements ix
Legislation xi
Case Law xiii
1. Introduction 1
2. Methodology 11
3. Student Migration and Global Inequality 29
4. Migration as a Socio-Legal Phenomenon 55
5. The 'Student-Migrant-Worker' Meets 'Precarity' 95
6. The 'Utterly Transactional Worker' 123
7. Semi-Legal Working? 167
8. Conclusions 199
Bibliography 209
Index 239

PREFACE

There exist two interesting strands to the 'international student' stereotype reminiscent of the allegorical *'Schrodinger's immigrant'*.[1] On the one hand, it is often presented that such students are privileged actors with means. They pay substantial tuition fees, significantly higher payments than are levied against home students, and they withstand the costs associated with transnational mobility. Indeed, financial security is one of the conditions in the Student Route Points-Based System introduced in the Immigration Rules. Meanwhile, on the other hand, there is a lingering caution that some of these students may be committing to study abroad purely for the purposes of securing immigration and/or for immediate economic gain. While it is disingenuous to ignore the racial dimension present in this rhetoric, there are also inherent socioeconomic inequalities to account for these disparities in approach. The suspicion expressed in the latter sentiment becomes especially pronounced when the country of domicile of these students populates the bottom half of global wealth indexes[2] (see van Mol and Timmerman 2014).

The socioeconomic disparities between some of the world's wealthiest and its most financially deprived states have impacted the writings on the subject across the disciplinary spectrum, especially as these inequalities have been documented to impress upon the quality of life and opportunities available to its peoples (Faist 2016). To this end, 'migration', 'education' and 'employment' are probably three of the most touted routes to socioeconomic betterment for citizens of the world's disadvantaged regions (Slaughter and Cantwell 2012;

---

1. The term 'Schrödinger's immigrant' is a play on 'Schrödinger's cat' which describes a paradox in quantum physics in which a particle can exist in two opposite states simultaneously. Here the cat, having been sealed in a box, is both dead and alive until it is seen. https://blog.oup.com/2015/12/schrodingers-immigrant-investment-funds/.
2. Respondents to our study originate from countries in sub-Saharan Africa and are located in the lower-middle-income countries. See United Nations Department of Economic and Social Affairs, *World Security Report 2020. Inequality in a Rapidly Change World*, United Nations Publication, p. XV, available at https://www.un.org/development/desa/dspd/wp-content/uploads/sites/22/2020/01/World-Social-Report-2020-FullReport.pdf.

Castelli 2018; King et al. 2010). The empirical agenda set out in this study is one instance where all three of these factors intersect. In broad terms, we examine the employment experiences of student-migrants of sub-Saharan African descent in the United Kingdom, and critically question the socio-legal implications of this exchange.

ACKNOWLEDGEMENTS

We would like to first offer our sincere thanks and appreciation to the participants to this study and in particular for their patience, honesty and the access they gave willingly to the project. Without them, the narrative accounts and impact of their situations which underpin the discursive theories explored in this book would not have been possible.

We would also like to take this opportunity to thank Megan Greiving for taking on the project and for agreeing to publish the manuscript. Megan and all the staff at Anthem Press have been wonderfully supportive, offering suggestions and constructive criticism, while also providing us with the valuable feedback from the anonymous reviewers.

For James and Katy, we would like to thank Isabelle, Mia Rose and Lydia May for accepting our time away from them when working. They are by far our greatest achievement. We would also like to take this opportunity to formally thank Mohammed for all his work in undertaking the fieldwork and gathering the data upon which this book is based. His considerable efforts have made this book a reality and we hope he is as proud of the finished product as we are of him.

For Mohammed, I wish to thank Nassar, Asimau, Rukayat, Hassan, Hussein, Kevin, Uyi and Esowese. Indeed, this book would not have been possible without your unwavering support and encouragement. Also, special thanks to the study director and lead author, Dr James Marson, for overseeing the entire research process and more so for bringing this book to life.

LEGISLATION

Agency Workers Regulations 2010 (SI 2010/93)
Agency Workers (Amendment) Regulations 2019 (SI 2019/724)
Employment Rights Act 1996 ss. 94; 135; 230
Equality Act 2010 ss. 13; 66
Immigration Act 1971 s. 24B
Immigration Act 2016 Sch. 6
Immigration, Asylum and Nationality Act 2006 ss. 15–25
Immigration Rules
National Minimum Wage Regulations 1998 (SI 1998/2574)
Part-time Workers (Prevention of Less Favourable Treatment) Regulations 2000 (SI 2000/1551)
Public Interest Disclosure Act 1998
Trade Union and Labour Relations (Consolidation) Act 1992 s. 296
Working Time Directive (Council Directive 93/104/EC of 23 November 1993 concerning certain aspects of the organization of working time)
Working Time Regulations 1998 (SI 1998/1833)

CASE LAW

Bebbington v Palmer T/A Sturry News UKEAT/0371/09/DM
Brook Street Bureau (UK) Limited v Dacas) EWCA Civ 217
Cable and Wireless plc v Muscat [2006] EWCA Civ 220
Case (C-257/04) *Caulfield v Hanson Clay Products Ltd* [2006] ECLI:EU:C:2006:177
Cassidy v Ministry of Health [1951] 2 KB 343 CA
Hall v Lorimer [1994] 1 WLR 209
Hitchcock v Post Office [1980] CLY 1045
Lane v The Shire Roofing Company [1995] PIQR 421
Lee Ting Sang v Chung Chi-Keung [1990] 2 AC 374
Lee Ting Sang v Chung Chi-Keung [1990] UKPC 9
MacFarlane and Skivington v Glasgow City Council [2000] EAT/1277
Market Investigations ltd v Minister of Social Security [1969] 2 QB 173
Massey v Crown Life Insurance Company [1978] IRLR 31, CA
Morren v Swinton and Pendlebury Borough Council [1965] 1 WLR 576
Nethermere (St Neots) Ltd v Gardiner [1984] ICR 612
O'Kelly v Trusthouse Forte plc [1983] ICR 728
Pimlico Plumbers Ltd and another v Smith [2018] UKSC 29
Prest v Petrodel Resources Ltd & Others [2013] UKSC 34
Re Darby ex p Brougham [1911] 1 KB 95
Ready Mixed Concrete (South East) Ltd v Minister of Pensions and National Insurance [1968] 2 QB 497
Slaight Communications v. Davidson [1989] 1 SCR 1038
Stevenson Jordan and Harrison v Macdonald and Evans [1952] 1 TLR 101
Uber BV and others v Aslam and others [2021] UKSC 5
Walker v Crystal Palace FC [1910] 1 KB 87
Yewens v Noakes (1880) 6 QBD 530
Young and Woods Ltd v West [1980] IRLR 201

Chapter 1

INTRODUCTION

Undertaking study abroad is an important and often exhilarating experience, and certainly one to which prospective international students often look forward to. For some, the outlook is one of heightened excitement for the possibilities that lay await, yet for others, this excitement is tempered by anxieties regarding the associated financial expenses and how these are to be costed. This study centres on the experiences of the 'others' aforementioned, and from one of the poorer regions which sends relatively high numbers of students to institutions in the United Kingdom (UK). These international students of sub-Saharan African descent, and who undertake temporary employment while in full-time education to mitigate against the worst effects of the financial burden international study can impose, are the focus of the empirical and ethnographic evidence presented in this study. Studies from academics including Forbes-Mewett et al. (2009) have revealed many international students experience financial difficulties while studying abroad, and students from financially impoverished states are more given to these anxieties. A corollary matter, and central to this study's undertaking, is that international students are officially designated migrants and therefore subject to a suite of migration control in the UK, albeit of a different cadre. This is both a legal and sociopolitically charged designation and noteworthy particularly as it impacts on the students' employment experiences in the UK.

It is generally acknowledged that allowing international students access to temporary/part-time employment while studying can be beneficial for their personal and professional development, and indeed their overall experience in the host country (Creed et al. 2015; Park and Sprung 2013; Sanchez-Gelabert et al. 2017). In return, these students can provide a pool of nascent, contingent labour, capable of being engaged to fill employment shortages within local industries and at relatively low costs (Hawthorne 2010; Khadria 2009; Ziguras and Law 2006). However, as subjects of migration controls, legal conditions apply to their employment and the rights therein which affect approximately half a million international students that enter UK Higher Education Institutions (HEIs) every other academic year (Higher Education Statistics Agency 2016). These students (previously) entered the UK on a Tier

4 (study) visa[1] which generally restrict them to a maximum of 20 hours of employment per week during term-time, and also proscribed their taking of work autonomously as independent contractors or on a self-employed basis. These restrictions aimed at maintaining 'students as students', a sentiment underpinned by a number of rationales. The principal reasons, however, are first, there is the altruistic desire to protect students from the burnout that may result from having to juggle the demands of their academic study and extensive work commitments (Bradley 2006; Neill et al. 2004; Riggert et al. 2006). Second, there exists the politically underpinned object dually aimed at setting international students apart from other groups of economic migrants (which includes migrant workers), and the need to protect the indigenous workforce from undue competition in the labour market (Costello and Freedland 2014; Fudge 2018; Ruhs 2014).

Nonetheless, international students' lived experiences (in spite) of these employment restrictions have been underexplored in the existing scholarship; indeed, knowledge on this subject is scarce. Perhaps plausibly so, this being, after all, a very niche empirical data set within a still nascent scholarship on the everyday mobility of international students as migrants in their host state (see Adepoju et al. 2007; Kritz 2015; Nyland et al. 2009). Fortunately, this is the very lacuna which we intend to address in this study. Our study offers a contribution to the body of knowledge on student migration, socioeconomic inequity and socio-legal studies, in two principal ways. For the first part, we adopt a socio-legal paradigm where the empirical schema of 'semi-legality' in respect of student-migrant labour is centred. Semi-legality is used here in reference to students' employment contexts that violate the conditions outlined in migration rules (Kubal 2012a; Ruhs and Anderson 2010). As an analytical tool, the concept marks a middle ground between outrightly illegal/unauthorised and utterly legal/compliant student-migrant employment (Kubal 2013). They are legal in the sense that they are in possession of the right to gainful employment while studying, but illegal as they defy the conditions imposed

---

1. The Tier 4 (General) student visa was removed from the Immigration Rules on 5 October 2020 and replaced with the new Appendix ST: Student Route, as part of a wider change to migration and employment in the UK. The Student Route imposes new requirements on international applicants including possessing a minimum, and mandatory, 70 points (via the immigration points-based system) to be granted a visa to study at a UK university. The points are established through the applicant being in receipt of an offer of a place to study at a university, having proficiency in the English language, and being in possession of financial means to support themselves and to pay tuition fees.

on the manner in which they are expected to exercise this right (Kubal 2013). This insight is necessitated by the dearth in the literature surrounding the intricacies that exist within variations of legality and how this may come to impact the actors' relationship with the law. It is apparent that the manner of engagement with the law may differ between someone who is acquiescent to the law, and an 'outlaw' who habitually defies it (see Boittin 2013). This, however, begs the question as to what behavioural distinctions can be expected of actors that engage in processes that straddle the divide between spectrums of legality and illegality. To this end, we question the various devises of semi-legality as it impacts the students' subjective perceptions of the legal conditions that regulate their employment in the state (legal consciousness), and their claims-making behaviour as it concerns the intricacies of their engagement with the law and its institutions in response to injurious experiences in the workplace (legal mobilisation).

For the second, we explore the employment experiences of these student-workers through the analytical frame of precarity. Precarity is a concept that has been deployed by contemporary sociologists within the industrial relations scholarship to denote the spread of insecure, transient employment, and more so to interrogate the lived experiences of workers who are given to this manner of subsistence, that is, 'the precariat'. Here, the aim is to question the various ways through which the aforementioned employment restrictions may engender insecurity in the lived experiences of these students, and consequently examine their agency as they move to respond to, counteract and resist these erstwhile limiting legal structures. The pertinence of this empirical agenda is based on the scarcity in the existing scholarship to incorporate these students into the discourse surrounding precarious work, or indeed to contemplate them as a distinct subset of *precariat* subjects. We argue that this status quo defies the de facto and de jure circumstances surrounding their labour market participation, steeped as it is with the potential for manifold, intersecting forms of socioeconomic and legal insecurities.

Study Objectives and Justifications

The study originated due to the scarcity in the literature of informed and detailed scholarship with regards the student-migrant-worker population and their everyday mobilities, especially as it concerns the context of labour market participation. This study, at its most fundamental, examines the employment experiences of student-migrant-workers from sub-Saharan Africa in the UK and achieves this through two principal frames of analysis.

Precarity and subjectivities

Despite the potential for intersecting insecurities, it would be imprudent to assume the existence of a uniform representation of precarity across all situations and circumstances, or even to infer it as a phenomenon applicable to all student-migrant-workers. Indeed, even though we note this cohort as a collective, they are not a monolith, exhibiting a range of individualised variables including socioeconomic status, located in specific employment contexts and local labour market terrains, with nationality status and a relative position within the global economy. They do of course share commonalities too, not restricted to their gender, forms of study, familial and financial pressures which may cumulatively serve to enhance or pre-empt the manifestations of insecurities in their subjective experiences (Anderson 2010; Paret and Gleeson 2016). This construct is, however, not novel and has led to debate as presented in the literature. Scholars such as Standing (2011) make the case for the existence of a common precariat identity which would achieve a uniform end-state that makes for a more coherent understanding of the class of persons generally. This approach chimes with that of Neilson and Rossiter (2008) but who differ slightly against the assumption of a singular model to account for its variant manifestations, albeit accepting the consistency of the structural provisions that effect it as a processual. This is because in consonance with almost every other sociological phenomenon, the construct of precarity is inherently subjective. This ideation is especially relevant here as it leaves sufficient margin for the empirical acknowledgement of the migrants' agency and structural circumstance in the fashioning of their own reality in spite of the intersecting structural impediments that may engender insecurity (Neilson and Rossiter 2008; Paret and Gleeson 2016). This potential for agency and subjectivity is apparent in Wu's (2016) study where she contrasts two groups of domestic workers in the United States – one group was populated with migrant women of colour without college degrees, meanwhile the other was of native-born and college-educated white women. Although she finds that both groups experienced precarious working conditions including low-wages and uncertain working hours, the experiences of migrant women of colour were exacerbated by insecurities and inequalities at the micro or interactional level, including discrimination, disrespect and abuse. Sexsmith (2016), in an ethnographic study of social justice efforts within New York farmhouses, finds that precarity stems from the cumulation of porous labour regimes, state immigration enforcement and more notably, workers' physical marginalisation.

Consequently, nuanced by the convergent facets of socioeconomic inequities and precarity they are ostensibly prone to encounter, our second research objective is to assess the ways through which precarity manifests as a consequence of migration and employment structures, and how this may impact the experiences of student-migrants as individual actors.

Precarity and covert resistance

Furthermore, precariousness is not exacted within a vacuum, neither does it necessarily linger unchallenged. It is constantly bound with resistance in a relation of persistent entanglement, and the acknowledgement of agency, or at least its potential, can been seen to rally against the prevalent notions of migrant-workers as docile, precarious subjects. From exploitation at work, to exclusion from public services, to criminalisation and the persistent possibility of deportation and family separation, it is documented that manifestations of agency can elicit the potential for resistance, collective or individual, overt or passive, where disadvantage concurrently becomes a motivator and a constraint (Paret and Gleeson 2016, 286). Naturally, there will be distinctions in the forms of resistance against converging forms of insecurity dependent on the context.

However, a review of the literature reveals an imbalance in favour of more grandiose, highly visible collective forms of resistance to what can be conceived of as precarity, to the detriment of more covert, less apparent forms. For instance, studies including those by Gleeson (2010), Rodriguez (2004), and Waldinger and Lichter (2003) document how low-wage migrant-workers, as a collective, deploy various strategies to manage the risk and uncertainty of their legal and economic lives, including industrial action manifested through coordinated slow-downs, walk-outs or action short of striking (Hirsch and Macpherson 2015). Wheatley and Gomberg-Muñoz (2015), in an ethnographic study, note the patterns of collective resistance in a party of migrant-workers from Mexico headed to the United States. These scholars document how the actors contest antagonistic structures on their route – from enclosure and labour subordination, to threats of deportation and legal exclusion, by acts of communal solidarity including forging relations, sharing meals and pockets of information, offering protection to one another, and organising political opposition (Wheatley and Gomberg-Muñoz 2015). In an illustration of responses to precarity stemming from both employment and everyday mobilities, Neilson (2009) describes acts of political resistance during a protest by migrant taxi drivers mostly comprising international students who proceeded to blockade the city of Melbourne following the stabbing of a colleague. Nielson (2009) subsequently notes of the emergence of novel forms of political practice, experience and subjectivity in a society where the regulation of labour mobilities exceeds the machinations of transnational borders.

Indeed, Paret and Gleeson (2016), whose scholarly contributions in respect of precarity this book appropriates, advocate for more empirical emphasis on these collective forms of resistance. It is our position that these individual-level formations can also present with the potential for robust, relational insights worthy of scrutiny. While we concede for the most part that these visible acts of collective resistance can be critical and quite insightful from which to generate relational knowledge, they are also rarities and special occasions. These are not everyday occurrences, yet these grand events *are* the culmination of the everyday implications and resistance that for the most part occur on a much more intimate level. More so, the ability for workers to exert agency and/or resist inherently depends on their ordinary structural location (Abrego 2011; Gleeson and Gonzales 2012). Thus, situating these collective acts of resistance to the exclusion of more closeted insights by way of individual strategies deployed towards economic survival and well-being means that we miss out on the foundational arenas where the most critical battles are being waged.

Scholars including Anderson (2010), Boswell and Straubhaar (2004), Calavita (1998), Gleeson (2010), Paret and Gleeson (2016) and Piore (1979) grasp at this agenda in some measure while documenting how irregular migrant-workers act in connivance with employers to circumvent legal restrictions on migrant-labour. This is effected through evasive manoeuvres ranging from the receipt of wage payments in cash to the outright falsification of documents (Boswell and Straubhaar 2004). However, while precarity may well be contested, the value of contestation for the individual ought to be accounted for, and in what ways the forms of resistance deployed by actors to counteract precarity can serve to undermine or reinforce it. For instance, it is subsequently noted how these arrangements can significantly alter the dynamics of the employment relationship to the detriment of the worker. These forms of contestation can heighten the worker's dependency on the one employer for subsistence, predispose them to labour exploitation and exacerbate their already precarious and, in some instances, dire condition (Boswell and Straubhaar 2004; Calavita 1998; Gleeson 2010; Paret and Gleeson 2016; Piore 1979). The culmination of such scenarios makes it increasingly apparent that the scholarship would be better served with phenomenological accounts centring on the subjects themselves, less of momentous or highly visible collective mobilisations, and more of the mundane as the student-migrants act in the everyday as autonomous social actors.[2] This must then be combined with a critical interrogation establishing the connexions in the collated responses across various case locations.

---

2. See 'Methods Design' in Chapter 2.

These reviewed insights consequently inform this study's overarching objective which is to critically analyse the ways through which these student-migrant-workers respond to and/or resist the implications of these intersecting forms of precarity brought on by a culmination of their subjective circumstance on the one hand, and temporalities associated with migration and employment structures on the other. More so, we examine how this process may contour the everyday experiences, or even the lack thereof of the student-migrant-workers. Through a centring on the individual actor, not only can we interrogate the mediums adopted towards resistance but we may also vicariously discern the implications and intricacies of other actors' involvement in this process.

Finally, in a bid to render the individual migrant-student-worker as the idiosyncratic actor they are, this empirical undertaking assumes a socio-legal turn by attending to the ways through which precarity and patterns of resistance that follow therefrom may impact their subjective perceptions of the law, that is, their legal consciousness. Consequently, we consider how this exchange may impact their agency in deciding if and how to seek redress for disputes and injurious experiences in the workplace, that is, their claims-making behaviour. These issues are the focus of the discussion in the substantive chapters presented in this book.

Structure of the Text

The book is divided into eight chapters, the first chapter providing an introduction to the topic of international student migration and how it affects the UK, the empirical agenda centred in this study, and the book's structure and objectives. This introduction and outline are built upon in Chapter 2 where the methodology for the empirical (35 participants involving in-depth semi-structured interviews) and ethnographical (9 participants observed over a one-year period) data are presented, as is the methodical design, along with the frameworks which underpin the discursive elements in subsequent chapters.

Chapter 3 presents a 'sending and receiving countries' outlook to student migration. Here we present a review of the literature surrounding international student mobility through the lens of global inequality, in particular highlighting student flows from sub-Saharan Africa. In so doing we focus on mobility trends, the individual and institutional drivers of student migration, and the inherent consequences for the relevant parties and states involved. Meanwhile, the sociopolitical reception surrounding student migration and employment in the UK, with international students' admission into the country as a microcosm of the broader discourse regarding contemporary migration, allows for a discussion of the tinges of protectionism which have come to contour the bureaucratic structures regulating same. We discuss the state's 'whole government' and 'degrees of harm' approach towards combatting forms of unauthorised migrant labour.

Chapter 4 addresses the socio-legal theoretical paradigm adopted for this study. Here, we review the existing scholarship surrounding migration as a socio-legal phenomenon and the various readings that have been proffered to account for migrants' relationship with the legal provisions of the host state, while noting their inherent shortcomings. This segues into a discussion of the predominant analytical framework adopted for this study, legal consciousness (per Ewick and Silbey 1998), which is deployed to account for the subjects' perception of the legal rules that dictate the terms of their labour market participation, and legal mobilisation, as it concerns how actors invoke and make claims of the law in response to problematic experiences and disputes at work. This chapter subsequently introduces the concept of semi-legality (Kubal 2009), which we adopt to account for student-migrant employment. We also identify the gap in the corpus of knowledge on the various designs through which semi-legality with regard to migrant labour may be achieved, and more so how this may potentially affect actors' relationship with the law. Significantly, we discuss the ways through which this study aims to rectify the discerned dearth in the body of literature.

Chapter 5 provides more context to this book's empirical agenda by reviewing the literature on the employment experiences of international student workers through the framework of precarity. These subjects are portrayed as a distinct category of the broader migrant workforce who are often subject to multiple reinforcing avenues for socioeconomic and legal vulnerabilities within employment spaces. Thus, we examine the structural underpinnings of their situatedness within the secondary labour market and participation in atypical work forms. Furthermore, we adopt a more sentient, localised approach by zeroing in on one such atypical employment relationship – temporary agency work (TAW), due to its sheer prevalence in the sourced data. We consequently review the legal indeterminacies surrounding the categorisation of workers' employment status in the UK and identify how this may potentially affect the experiences of student-migrant-workers, especially in light of the aforementioned work restrictions. The concluding findings of Chapter 5 lead to the assessment of the legal structures and policies through the lens of therapeutic jurisprudence (TJ) in Chapter 6. TJ is an emerging philosophy which can not only help to identify problematic aspects in the legal system and its operation but also help to present alternative views or mitigating strategies to minimise the law's negative effects. It is in this chapter where we critique the existing law, but also note the TJ-esque approach taken by members of the community that make positive and therapeutically compliant changes for the benefit of a marginalised but important sector of the economy.

In Chapter 6, we begin the presentation of the findings from the empirical data collection. Here, we situate the employment experiences of the respondents through the frame of precarity. The presented findings are divided into three main sections; for the first, we address students' prevailing vision of temporary employment while studying pre-mobility, which is then compared against their de facto employment station post-mobility. We also account for their pathways into paid work, and their employment profiles; including the sectors within which they worked, for how long, and the relationship with their respective employers. We conclude this part by emphasising the inherent structural and socioeconomic vulnerabilities they are beset with while working on a student visa. For the second part, we attend to the role of employment intermediaries by way of temporary work agencies, in categorising these students in paid employment as recent migrants and new jobseekers. We discuss the various reasons for the concentration of international students in TAW, its consequent allure and, conversely, the inherent disadvantages this employment form presents for the study participants. The third part of this chapter specifically addresses the detrimental conditions experienced by students during employment. This includes accounts of low pay, exploitation, discrimination and abuse; we also interrogate how the participants respond to these conditions. This chapter closes with a summary of findings, and some actionable recommendations towards bettering international students' outlook in respect of employment while studying.

Chapter 7 centres on the socio-legal empirical objectives of the study and draws from ethnographic observations involving two distinct cohorts of student-migrant workers. This chapter is presented in three sections; the first considers the students' lived accounts of their 'semi-legal' employment. Here we identify the distinct devises employed by the participants in service of achieving and evading detection for working practices which violate study visa conditions. This section subsequently turns to the intricacies of each stratagem – the underpinnings, parties involved, the benefits and consequent vulnerabilities they engender for subjects. The second part of this chapter attends to the implications of semi-legality through the subjects' legal mobilisation and claims-making efforts as they respond to potentially justiciable experiences and disputes in the workplace. Meanwhile the third section focuses on the relationship between the various formations of semi-legality and legal consciousness. Here, we argue that semi-legality in student-migrant employment operates as a mediated, less dire form of illegality regarding migrant labour. While outrightly illegal migrant workers are increasingly documented to present with an 'against the law' strand of legal consciousness (see Calavita

2007 and Gleeson 2010), the respondents to this study who engage in semi-legality act increasingly 'with the law'. This much is apparent in the discourses with the participants to justify their 'sometimes' aberrant behaviour. We discuss these under the auspices of victimhood, the subjects' perception of the legitimacy and flexibility of the aforementioned rules, and their attitude to potential reform. This segues into a discussion of semi-legality as a form of resistance towards the law and its institutions, and as a contestation of legal hegemony, albeit an ineffective one.

In Chapter 8, the key findings are summarised before potential areas for further research and concluding remarks are presented.

Chapter 2

METHODOLOGY

Introduction

This chapter outlines the methodical design, theoretical framework, data collection method, researcher situatedness and the analytical process used in the empirical data presented in this book. We also explain the ethical considerations, and the inherent justifications, strengths and limitations of the adopted approach.

Methods Design

For this study, we chose a qualitative, case study design, drawing from both ethnographic observations and in-depth interviews. The selection of a purely qualitative paradigm is informed by this book's ambition for a holistic, fluid account of subjective behavioural patterns, experiences and the consequent meaning-making process of the actors within the study population. This objective pre-empts the viability of quantitative methods due to their rigidity (Creswell 2009). Yet, qualitative methods are especially appropriate here for three principal reasons. The first being that interpretive methods provide the researcher sufficient latitude to adapt to emergent patterns in real time (Creswell 2009; Yin 2017). For example, the aims of this study began with a focus on students' engagement with temporary or part-time employment. However, this focus was corrected at the midway point of the project to place the emphasis on TAW, precarity and semi-legality due to their frequent manifestations during the early stages of data collection and analysis. This adaptation would not have been possible with quantitative measures. Second, the empirical socio-legal frames deployed, including semi-legality, legal consciousness, mobilisation and precarity, are innately idiosyncratic and subjective, this nuance being well captured by interactive methods but lost in numerical approaches (Creswell 2009; Hull 2016). Last, this selection is also informed by the contemporary socio-legal scholarship that has since moved on from the use of quantitative surveys so to statistically gauge the perceptions and use of law within a population, in search of a more rounded and layered interpretive rendition of law as it exists in everyday social locations (Harrington and Yngvesson 1990; Hull 2016; Silbey 2005).

Adopting a case study approach meanwhile amplifies the intensity of this research design as it allows for the collation and analysis of data through the combination of methods deemed necessary by the researcher (Bryman 2016; Creswell 2009; Yin 2017). More so, in acknowledgement of the fluidity of what actors may perceive as law and legality, the multiplicity of empirical perspectives involved in a qualitative case study allows for the integration of methods in a way that improves the overall understanding of the phenomenon of empirical interest (Creswell 1998; Hakim 2000; Ritchie and Lewis 2003).

The researcher as an 'insider'

The researcher's position as either an outsider or an insider, relative to the phenomena of empirical interest, is an epistemological issue that speaks directly to the quality of knowledge being generated (Griffith 1998). Succinctly, an 'insider' can be identified as a researcher who personally belongs to the group under study (based on characteristics such as ethnicity, sexual identity, gender, etc.) whereas an 'outsider' is not (Saidin 2017). Importantly for this study, one of the team, Mohammed Dirisu, was the researcher who conducted the data collection. Mohammed would be considered an 'insider looking in'; he was a student-migrant and therefore a member of the population under study, and he shared many of the participants' structural qualities. These included the same distinguishing demographical attributes including ethnicity and nationality. The participant student-workers also experienced commonalities in exposure to the system of rules and normative institutions that dictate the terms of their participation within specified realms of UK society including residency, employment and relationship with the welfare state, to mention but a few. The researcher being an insider, therefore, lent credibility to the findings, not just because it helped establish the trust between the researcher and population, and thereby honesty of the contributions by the participants but also because it was a factor integral to facilitating the research (LaSala 2003; Watts 2006). Indeed, the benefits of conducting *insider research* are well documented. Bonner and Tolhurst (2002) assert that conducting insider research provides a more profound understanding and familiarity with the study context that might not be readily accessible to outsiders (Smyth and Holian 2008). In addition, having an established intimacy with the study context has been adjudged to ultimately enable the researcher to better appraise 'the telling' and 'the judging of truth', and thus amplifies the study's internal validity (Hayfield and Huxley 2015). These features cumulatively situate the researcher to a position where they are best able to 'appreciate the full complexity of the social world being studied and result in a potentially accurate portrayal, rather than a simplistic caricature' (Healey 2017; Hockey 1993; Unluer 2012).

However, it is also important to acknowledge that the expediency of insider research has been subject to critical commentary, especially on the premise that a degree of commonality does not necessarily correlate with the insider having a more profound understanding of participants' perspectives, at least any more than would an outsider. This is especially because their lives and experiences may be just as dissimilar as they are similar where there are other circumstances that overshadow the shared attribute(s) (Bridges 2001; Huxley and Hayfield 2015). It is further argued that the intimacy associated with insider research can introduce sentimental values into the study, for instance, where an insider researcher may struggle with polarising emotions, an outsider is better able to distance themselves from the study context.

In response to these critiques, while it is conceded that the idiosyncrasies that set apart the researcher and the researched can potentially eclipse any apparent commonality, we insist that the quality of insider research does more than imply a degree of 'camaraderie'; it also informs the researcher on pertinent empirically rooted issues, the most critical of which is *how* and *where* to look. This is even more pertinent where the study centres are marginalised, the participants' closed off voices from hard-to-reach populations and who tend to be distrustful of outsiders through years of disenfranchisement and social violence and exclusion, being overcome (Hayfield and Huxley 2015; Tang 2007). Mohammed, in being the 'insider' researcher on this project imparted a foreground exposure that helped present a profound portrait of the experiences, values, anathemas and power structures inherent in this distinct subset of the migrant population (Coghlan 2003; Herrmann 1989; Rooney 2005). In response to concerns that an insider's intimacy with the population under study may have adverse effects on the quality of data elicited, it is pertinent to state that this was managed during this project. The researcher conducting the data collection ensured to remain a distanced observer of the respondents during this period. The assessment instruments were carefully constructed and assessed by the project team, and the ethnographic accounts were carefully scrutinised, examined over a period of months to ensure consistency and veracity of the materials collated, and subject to detailed examination to mitigate against any researcher bias or influence in the materials collected.

Succinctly, our research reflects the position that insider knowledge has great value in developing more nuanced and complex accounts of a social phenomenon. The intimate insights and familiarity afforded by being an insider not only helped develop the research objectives and theoretical paradigm, but aided in establishing intricate aspects of the methodological design including the sampling technique, research locations and sites, and modes of data collection.

Study sites

The choice of the location for a study raises issues about its specificities, and in particular the generalisability of the results (Creswell 2003). It is doubtful that insights generated from any one location can be exhaustively representative of the entire population, or transferrable to other locations (Büthe et al. 2015). Such a limitation was readily identified in this study, yet the group under examination were inherently interesting and the detailed narrative accounts provided, along with the ethnographic observations possible allowed us to make claims regarding this cohort, while extrapolating the results where sufficiently reliable to do so.

The study was conducted in house-shares occupied by student-workers within two UK cities which we term Location A and Location B to preserve the anonymity of the participants. This is warranted because of the intricate nature of the topics broached during data collection, which includes behaviour that is conceived, by some participants at least, as semi-legal if not illegal or criminal. Indeed, when negotiating access to the study populations, anonymising the study sites as far as possible was a prerequisite to assuage concerns of potential reprisals and targeted enforcement from a range of actors, from state institutions including the Home Office and Her Majesty's Revenue and Customs, to private actors including employers and university authorities.[1] These fears are only reified by the current political climate in respect to immigration, and the participants' vulnerabilities as foreign nationals susceptible to removal, especially as some admit to breaching visa rules pertaining to employment. There are no reasons to believe that the location details are either relevant or that its omission negatively impacts on the quality of data presented.

The choice of the study locations was informed by various considerations. The first of which was that although both cities have a high student population, each hosting multiple HEIs, they nonetheless complement each other within socioeconomic contexts. Being intentionally vague, Location A is situated in the North-East of the UK, a region with a more modest economic profile where income levels fall within the lower half of national thresholds.

---

1. The logic behind this is that naming these sites effectively creates a signpost towards this study cohort especially as there are, for the most part, but a few higher education institutions per UK city.

Location B is a city in the South-West with a higher economic output, and with income levels above the national average. These sites complement each other by enabling an in-depth comparison of divergent yet somewhat parallel lived experiences, while noting any discernible disparities and similarities that exist across both locations.

Fieldwork progression

The fieldwork was conducted between October 2017 and June 2019. This period included the recruitment of participants to the completion of the fieldwork, the bulk of this time was spent located within different student house-shares at Locations A and B. These house-shares were inhabited by international students of sub-Saharan African descent.

A challenging aspect of the study was in negotiating access to a pool of willing participants across both locations. The adoption of an invasive design involving ethnographic observations in residential settings, coupled with the very precise selection criteria[2] and sensitive nature of the study themes, cumulatively meant that negotiating access to a not only suitable but also amenable study population and setting was a protracted process involving months of intricate and rigorous planning. Timing was also of importance as we intended to run both study locations in synchrony, so insights from both locations could develop in tandem and inform each other in real time. It soon became clear that this was infeasible due to practical constraints and difficulties in facilitating effective research programmes which would perfectly overlap. Thus, fieldwork commenced in Location A some three weeks before it did for Location B, and the fieldwork phase subsequently continued for a longer period than first envisioned.

Sampling strategy

The study adopts non-probability sampling by way of convenience and a snowball design.[3] Convenience sampling is a type of non-probability sampling in which participants are sampled simply because they are 'convenient' sources of data for researchers (Lavrakas 2008). Snowball sampling is one form of convenience sampling that involves identifying initial research participants who subsequently refer the researcher to other potential respondents who meet the selection criteria (Biernacki and Waldorf 1981; Cresswell 2012; Vogt 1999).

---

2. International students of sub-Saharan African descent with experiences of temporary employment in the UK.
3. Also known as referral or chain sampling.

Thus, the metaphor of the 'snowball' is used in allusion to the evolving and accumulative form of this sampling technique, that is, one subject gives the researcher the name of another subject, who in turn provides the name of a further participant, and it goes on up until data saturation or the target sample size is met (Noy 2008; Vogt 1999). These approaches are widely acknowledged as particularly useful in accessing participants from underserved and marginalised communities, where members maintain low visibility due to the moral, legal or social sensitivities of the time, and in instances where the researcher anticipates complications in creating a representative sample (Morgan 1996; and Petersen and Valdez 2005). More so, it has been adduced that convenience and snowball sampling are most effective in granting access to such populations where a degree of trust is required to initiate contact and recruit participants. Trust between the researcher and participants is better developed here especially as contact is facilitated by acquaintances and peers rather than other more formal or direct methods of communication (Valdez and Peterson 2005).

The convenience sampling was most effective during recruitment for the ethnographic aspects of this study. The design for this phase was intensive; for Location A, in addition to leaving adverts about the study on web-portals and in the house-shares occupied by international students, potential participants were also contacted at events hosted by student bodies including the Black and minority ethnic groups and broader international student societies at two local universities. This presented an opportunity to directly brief representatives and attendees about the research, and led to the recruitment of the first cohort of four students (aged between 24 and 28 years).

At Location B, recruitment was less onerous because of an existing contact, a colleague and long-time resident of the city who we are calling 'Awo'.[4] Awo not only had substantial knowledge of the inner city but was also familiar with much of the African international student population. He effectively acted as gatekeeper and facilitator for this study site, directing us to suitable research locations and a cohort of willing participants. This location provided us with access to five international students from sub-Saharan Africa all aged between 25 and 33 years. The participants were initially, and understandably, somewhat hesitant yet very curious at the outset of the project, but they provided their informed consent after in-depth briefings about the study objectives, data management protocols and extensive guarantees of utmost anonymity and confidentiality. Through these participants the snowball sample design allowed for the recruitment of further student-migrants. We intermittently alternated

---

4. An alias to protect the source.

between both study locations as the study progressed in real time, spending no more than 28 consecutive days at any one location for each fieldtrip episode.

Data Collection Methods

Data was sourced through ethnographic observations and interviews.

Ethnographic observations

The house-shares made for the respective observation sites and the housemates featured as recurrent participants. The observation episodes were often sporadic and intermittent, as this was dependent on participant availability and willingness to interact. Nonetheless, the episodes were most effective in the evenings when participants would enter communal areas of the residence. The activity of empirical interest was set to document mundane, unstructured interactions the participants had with one another, acquaintances from the outside and with the researcher where he assumed the dual role of participant and facilitator. This observation technique may be most accurately described as the 'observer as participant' which is a method particularly suited to instances where the researcher is a member of the group being observed as it allows for idiosyncratic views to be exchanged in a more fluid, true-to-life manner (Kawulich 2005). More so, this approach, complemented by the 'insider' status, ensured the researcher was neither disruptive nor out of place, and perhaps even more relatable to the participants (Ritchie and Lewis 2003).

These observation episodes involved interactions with the participants, either through striking a conversation anew or picking one up from where it had previously been left, and the documenting of information or prompts that would be offered by the participants which were relevant to the portrayal of their realities as student-migrants. In particular, this included information which might signify potential spaces for law and the reproduction of legality (Ewick and Silbey 1998).

Although the nine inhabitants across both house-shares featured as the main characters in these observations, we occasionally had the opportunity to observe their interactions with acquaintances.[5] A considerable amount of time was also spent in public spaces outside of these house-shares. The immersion in the everyday realities of the participants meant that we sometimes accompanied them outdoors when requested, including visits to grocery shops, bars and even a house party on one occasion. For these excursions, a digital journal

---

5. This happened very infrequently, and special permission was sought from all participants prior to these observations.

was maintained to make note of any pertinent and interesting interactions. The consequence was that a significant volume of data were collected through these observations, the pool of information garnered was broad and varied, touching on everything from mundane topics including the cost of living, employment, academic life, backgrounds and future aspirations, to social issues including race relations, discrimination, politics and corporate greed. We limit the discussion of the data themes explored during these observations to the issues pertinent to the topic investigated in this book.

The empirical worth of these observations was, in our view, particularly valuable. In addition to being one of the primary modes of data collection, these observations more so informed the interview themes and overall research trajectory. Witnessing how the participants behaved and interacted within in their own spaces provided a source for data triangulation as we were able to compare insights gleaned from these observations against the content from the interviews (Boittin 2013). An illustration of this occurred during the fieldwork episodes which involved some participants' hesitance to discuss the exact extent of their labour market participation, especially when in breach of the restrictions imposed per their student visa terms. However, through contextual clues gleaned from sitting in on otherwise everyday 'off-the-record' conversations and noting the frequencies of their 'coming and going' while donning their work uniforms, we were able to deduce from patterns of behaviour the employment extents of the participants.

It is clear that being thoroughly immersed in the social context of a study can provide to the researcher an understanding or appreciation of the relevant lines of empirical inquiry and how to articulate these in terms relatable to participants. The result is a more rounded insight into the subjects' lived realities and gives a voice to their holistic experiences. More so, while the contemporary legal consciousness scholarship has relied on interviews as its principal data collection method (Abrego 2011; Boittin 2013; Hull 2016; Young 2014), this method is barely sufficient for interrogating the underlying structures that ground one's manifested consciousness (Hull 2016). It is not exactly novel to forward the theory that the way social actors come to experience, think and act as it pertains to the law is greatly nuanced, indeterminate, transient, circumstantial and subjective (Ewick and Silbey 1998; Hull 2016; and Young 2014). Ethnographies best allow the socio-legal researcher to take in all of these inchoate manifestations as it presents the opportunity to witness commonplace interactions rife with imbedded, albeit easily taken for granted, socio-legal meaning.

Finally, these observations provided vital context that developed our understanding of the participants' lived realities, and this nuance is apparent in the depictions of their experiences and socio-legal meaning-making presented later in this study.

Interviews

Interviews feature as the second method of data collection. The theoretical underpinning of this study's interview design is informed by the legal consciousness framework conceived by Ewick and Silbey (1998). In this formation, not only is there a shift in focus from legal actors, and those who formally invoke the machinery of the law to 'lodge their complaints, voice their grievances, seek their rights, or demand justice' towards ordinary actors in common social locations, but there is also a decentring of the law and legal institutions in the design of the research instruments (Ewick and Silbey 1998).

To this end, semi-structured questions were utilised, and more importantly formal, legalistic verbiage usually associated with the law and its institutions were avoided. Specifically, terms that directly correlate with 'rights talk' and dispute resolution processes – including abstract notions of justice and equality, substantive and procedural fairness, and more technical employment lexicon such as 'zero-hour' and 'independent contracting', 'working time regulations', 'substitution rights' and so on, whilst pertinent to the study – were omitted in the interview design. In its stead, more relatable, casual wording was adopted in framing questions. However, this does not mean these themes were not broached. Interviewees were encouraged to describe their experiences in their own words and comprehension, without the need to expressly name the legal themes being implicated. In fact, in consonance with Ewick and Silbey's (1998) original methodology, when these legal phenomena did arise, it was at the participants' behest, and the researcher's task herein was to educe and analyse if, why and how the interviewees incorporated these notions. This approach afforded the opportunity for assessment of the participants' subjective knowledge and understanding of relevant legal frameworks without the imposition of formal constructs. This more so allowed participants to express idiosyncratic understandings in acknowledgement of the legal pluralist notions concerning the subjectivity of what makes for law and legality (Ewick and Silbey 1998).

Interviews were integrated in this study design in two ways: as a feature of the ethnographic design for which it assumed aspects of a longitudinal study and as a standalone mode of data collection following the snowball sampling strategy.

Ethnographic interviews

For the first part of this aspect of the study, nine individuals who had featured in the ethnographic observations were interviewed, on a number of occasions, over the course of the fieldwork in a format similar to a longitudinal study, albeit with less formality. This phase built on and supplemented insights discerned from the participant observations. Save for the opening and closing rounds, these were mostly spontaneous and unstructured sessions, conducted on an ad hoc basis. These came by way of prompting questions, interjections and follow-up enquiries all aimed towards instigating and capturing qualitative content in depth and detail. The opening and closing rounds of these interviews mirrored each other and more so correlated with the beginning and end of fieldwork activities for each site.

The first round of this batch of interviews occurred two weeks after we assumed fieldwork duty and were mostly exploratory. Participants were encouraged to start with casual narratives about their newly found realities within social domains of their discretion, including the neighbourhood, work and family. This was followed up with more probing questions as participants revealed particularly insightful occurrences that broached structures catered to by socio-legal precepts, as broadly defined. The final round of these interviews built on insights gleaned from preceding data collection episodes, and the line of inquiry was adapted to suit the context of the interviewee who was already familiar to the study. This intensive design not only provided a further means of data triangulation and validation, but it also facilitated the conclusion of previously incomplete events, charted the socio-legal development of actors and captured the transient processes and sentiments that diminish with time. We found this to be an effective way to unravel and gauge the (ir)relevance of law and its constructs in everyday contexts. At the close of these sessions, the data were recapped, and participants debriefed.

Snowballers

The second deployment of interviews was themed more around atypical employment and was predicated on the snowball sample design which consequently meant that we could access and recruit more participants by exploiting personal networks as the fieldwork progressed. The selection criteria were as follows: participants should be international students of sub-Saharan African descent, resident in both locations and with first-hand employment experiences whilst in full-time study. We conducted 28 of these as one-off, 13 in Location A and 15 in Location B, thus bringing the sum of participants to this study to 37. These interview sessions lasted between one and two hours, with the interviewees being postgraduate students on study visas, within a 25–35 age range, all of whom were actively undertaking employment, for the most part, through temporary work agencies. The location of these interviews varied and were contingent on the respondents' convenience.

For this phase of interviews, there was a greater structure adopted, with the questions increasingly centred around the participants' employment experiences. The interview design as such deviated slightly from Ewick and Silbey's (1998) template of a strictly unstructured approach. This was because this second phase interviews were tailored to elicit more information about the work experiences of a broader group of international student-workers beyond those who participated in the observations, and thus adopting a similar unstructured approach may mean that relevant themes are not covered in-depth, especially as these were one-off interviews. Although the interview guide was sparsely structured around employment themes and concerns, interviewees were nonetheless afforded the liberty to express personal concerns and to introduce topics and expand upon themes as they deigned fit while the interview progressed.

Consequently, the questionnaire was developed with a number of broadly themed questions to best allow for the idiosyncratic views of the participants to be expressed and explored with minimal interference while guaranteeing the satisfaction of the participants to the trajectory of the interview (Creswell 2012). Interviewees were encouraged to begin their contribution by describing the circumstantial antecedents behind their entry to the job market upon arrival in the UK. This segued to an enquiry regarding their present employment contexts, discussed in chronological order, including any noteworthy incidents/concerns associated therewith. These casual narratives were intermittently followed up with more probing questions where the participants highlighted issues that touched on the law or issues of legality, or issues we judged as particularly insightful. The findings from the data collated during the standalone interviews are presented in Chapter 6: 'The "Utterly Transactional Worker"', where we discuss the employment experiences encountered by study subjects. Meanwhile findings following the ethnographic observations are presented in Chapter 7: 'Semi-Legal Working?', where we specifically discuss the lived experiences of the employment restrictions in respect of the student-migrants.

Data Coding and Analysis

As noted above, a significant volume of data was collated in the form of notes and audio recordings, these were transcribed into raw word files, uploaded and subject to qualitative data analysis through the programme

Nvivo. This began the coding and analysis process to ensure the analytical reliability of the data on which our conclusions are based. The methodology adopted for this process chimes most with the phenomenological analytical approach, which is primed on describing the lived realities of actors through the phenomenon of interest (Creswell 2012; Silverman 2017). The overarching aim was to produce nuanced descriptions that captured the phenomenological essence of not only what was experienced, but more so how it was being experienced (Moustakas 1994). Similarly, a socio-legally underpinned phenomenological approach generally aims to uncover and describe how the law and its institutions shape everyday lives and practices, and conversely how the law is shaped by everyday lives and practices, from the bottom up per the study subjects' respective presentations (Blandy 2014). Respondents were each categorised into individual cases and arranged per study site; Location A or Location B. A multi-level thematic analysis was adopted in line with fulfilling the distinct, albeit related, objectives of this study, and the overarching themes were drawn directly from the data collated from the empirical research. Meanwhile the thematic arrangement was informed by the existing literature on topics relevant for this study (Glaser and Strauss 1967).

Three sets of open thematic parent nodes were created, centred around the relevant empirical frames. The first node was informed by legal consciousness theory, here three sub-nodes marked as with, against and for the law in consonance with Ewick and Silbey's (1998) archetypal dispositions regarding legality were generated. The second set of nodes were created in reference to the legal mobilisation and the transformation of disputes, this node being classed according to the three steps on the dispute pyramid hypothesised by Felstiner et al. (1980) 'Naming' 'Blaming' and 'Claiming.' The third node was more experiential and contextual, and themed around employment experiences, especially through the lens of precarity and semi-legality. Sub-nodes were created to represent potential openings for law including potentially justiciable experiences, grievances and dispute resolution attempts. In total over fifty different thematic nodes were generated for this process.

The analytic process began with broad-themed queries representing the objects of empirical interest, each element of data reviewed for commonalities and dissimilarities to note how each fit into the grander portrait. Once the thematic arrangement was completed, we proceeded to code the data in an open and inclusive form, after which the resultant data was fashioned into thematic groups for presentation. This analytical process enabled the thematic arrangement and discovery of manifested patterns within a large data pool. Analytical data triangulation was also employed wherein the interview data were compared with the observations to identify potential conflicts or contrasts, and to ensure the consistency and veracity of the data. The findings are presented and discussed in the chapters that follow.

Ethical Considerations

Here we confirm that a University Research Ethics Committee provided the necessary clearance for us to conduct the research project, having approved the background, the methodical approach selected, the guidelines towards ensuring the safety of all parties involved, and the storage of the data, thereby ensuring anonymity of the participants. Of course, the nature of this study warranted a strict and thorough ethical assessment. The data collection was carried out in residential spaces and, coupled with the sensitive nature of the issues contemplated, it was apparent that we would need effective safeguarding strategies in place. This concern was even more poignant considering the insider status of the researcher conducting the data collection and the convenience sampling technique adopted, both of which approaches are associated with a high degree of intimacy between the researcher and participants. It has been reported that research using such a method can result in creeping complacency and the subsequent blurring of ethical standards (Ulnuer 2012). Indeed, best practice suggest that insider researchers become increasingly aware of 'the potential repercussions that professionalizing the personal may have' (DeLyser 2001, as cited in Chavez 2008, 483). Mindful of this meant that the overall welfare of the participants and the researcher were of utmost concern and framed the study's design and execution. The steps taken to assuage these ethical concerns were manifold; perhaps the most important was creating a transparent and safe process. This meant ideals of anonymity, confidentiality, discretion and fully informed consent were reiterated throughout this study's execution. In seeking informed consent, participants were informed of the aims of the study, ethical standards, and were asked for permission to document each data collection session. Participants were also briefed about how the data collected would be stored, presented and used, and informed of their rights to withdraw from the study. The transparency of the design ensured that covert methods were not utilised at any point. An effective data management protocol was adopted and we confirmed to the participants how the entire data pool for this study was pseudonymised and hosted on a university encrypted cloud drive.

Critique of Methods

Here we discuss the inherent strengths and limitations of the methodical design.

Strengths of methods

The design of this study intentionally incorporated an immersive qualitative paradigm which is particularly suited for interactional and in-depth explorations of social phenomenon (Creswell 2014). An interpretive paradigm such as this allows the researcher sufficient flexibility to adapt in response to emergent issues or themes which present themselves during the study. This is particularly pertinent as empirical social research will involve an element of the unknown if it does not merely set out to replicate previous knowledge (Pole and Lampard 2002). This flexibility was manifested through the adoption of an open, reactive and interactive fieldwork design, primed in anticipation of the unanticipated during data collection (Maxwell 2012). For instance, our original proposal was established on the basis that the gathering of data from interviews was the primary mode of data collection. When the scope for research was broadened following interactions with the original participants, it allowed us to amend the method to incorporate ethnographic observations, which proved to generate a meaningful source of data.

A further strength of the methods used is in the robustness of the sourced data. The wealth and depth of data that we were able to access and to incorporate into the empirical frame provided for an unabridged expression and rendition of subjective realities of the participants. This included all complexity and nuances of their lived experiences without the need to confine or reduce the data for standardisation per frequency of occurrence. This reverberates throughout this methodical design; the ethnographic case study allows for the combination of methods that facilitate a detailed and in-depth understanding of the phenomenon of interest (Creswell 2014). The semi-structured interviews incorporated a series of open-ended questions which afforded the participants an opportunity to discuss a variety of experiences and perceptions associated with working on a student visa. This would not have been possible through the use of more rigid approaches that limit the range of responses to scales and/or predefined statements, with the consequence of impairing the quality of individualistic data (Seidman 2006). The immersive nature of our fieldwork meant that every other day was a potential data collection exercise. More so, the researcher's absolute immersion in the study context, the extensive period spent in the field, the comprehensive descriptions and analysis provided, and the increased intimacy between the researcher and participants in the study are considered as particularly advantageous for the validity of insights generated (Creswell 2014). The unstructured participant observations and the choice of research site allowed us to capture interactions in their most naturalistic environment, more so in a spontaneous form, free from premeditation. The experientially rooted phenomenological approach adopted in the analytical phases also contributes to the vigour of the study, centring as it does on the lived reality of subjects as authored by them (Creswell 2012; Flick 2014).

Furthermore, the multiplicity of data sources incorporated in this design allows for data triangulation. As data is generated via a combination of sources (including interviews and participant observations), there are increased opportunities for 'triangulation of sources' wherein corroborating evidence garnered from several sources are utilised to substantiate and validate research findings. An example in this regard is the use of participant observations to complement and validate the data obtained from the interviews for the cohorts and thus curtail, to an extent, the reporting biases inherent in many qualitative studies (Denzin and Lincoln 2011). As a strategy towards validation, the use of a variety of data sources helped to confirm and enhance the precision of the study findings (Ritchie and Lewis 2003). It also proved beneficial during our analysis stage as it contributed to the credibility of the findings and strengthened confidence in our conclusions being as representative of the lived experiences of our participants (Patton 2002).

Study limitations and mitigations

The principal limitation to the methods used in this study, as with the bulk of qualitative studies, has to do with the intrinsic biases that impair the generalisability of study findings to other contexts. This is in part due to the non-probability sample which is inherently prone to recruitment biases as participants are not being selected at random. This limitation is exacerbated by the snowball sampling strategy adopted; the researcher's dependence on individuals with relationships will often result in the concentration of respondents from specific social network circles, to the exclusion of subjects who are 'isolates', that is, individuals not connected to any network that the researcher has tapped into (Cohen and Arieli 2011; Van Meter 1990).

Another impediment with the use of snowball sampling is 'gatekeeper bias' (Cohen and Arieli 2011) where the gatekeepers are intermediaries who are in the position to facilitate contact between the researcher and further potential respondents (Cohen and Arieli 2011; Tushman and Katz 1980). The gatekeeper may have subjective motives for referring (or not referring) the researcher to potential respondents (Cohen and Arieli 2011; Groger et al. 1999) although the majority of studies that involve negotiating access to potential participants through gatekeepers will suffer some degree of this bias.

In addition to these structural biases, the insider researcher method adopted also presents concerns for the de facto impartiality of the researcher. Simmel (1950) argued that greater familiarity can lead to a loss of objectivity by way of unconsciously making flawed assumptions due to prior experience and knowledge of the study context (DeLyser 2001; Hewitt-Taylor 2002). Meanwhile Schuetz (1971) argued that the insider researcher might be heavily influenced by past experiences as compared to an outsider researcher who has no prior background information about the topic, and may thus render a more objective report from the data. It must be stated that these concerns consequently make it so that the study findings cannot claim to be accurately representative of the entire study population nor does it account for any experiences beyond those of the participants (Atkinson and Flint 2001).

In response to these acknowledged limitations, this study is not attempting to present the findings as being representative or generalisable. Rather, the generalisability strongly associated with quantitative methods is relinquished in favour of unravelling a critical, in-depth account of the phenomenon under study for all its complexity and nuances (Ritchie and Lewis 2003). Furthermore, although the insider researcher may be more prone to inherent biases, it is also that an outsider may fail to fully appreciate the intricacies present in the study context, which may similarly make for a flawed study (Merton 1972). Even then, any information divulged by a study participant is often dependent on their subjective perception of the researcher and the project (Drever 1995; Porteli 2008), thus, such situations where the researcher and 'researched' share a common value system, experience or identity, not only eases the research process but also makes for a conducive environment for 'truth telling'. While we unavoidably had pre-established notions going into the research, we were nonetheless amenable to having any predetermined ideas challenged by the data, as is the essence of qualitative research which is primed on capturing subjective realities for all their idiosyncratic distinctions (King 2004; Waring and Wainwright 2008).

Conclusions

It is our belief that the use of an insider researcher in accessing the data underpinning the analysis and discussion presented in this study provides a unique advantage over those data collected by an outsider. An outsider would likely have struggled to convince two cohorts of Black, international students with a distrust for authoritative symbols to participate in an ethnographic study set on their everyday lives and in spaces they consider home. Further, this feature was exacerbated when requesting these participants to give access to their similarly situated colleagues to participate in the study.

More so, it was always anticipated that the sensitive nature of this inquiry may cause participants to be cautious in participating and disclosing what is sensitive information. Therefore, creating a relatable, empathetic space where trust could be fostered was of utmost importance if candid views were to be exchanged. Being amenable helped to circumvent this apprehension. This included conversations being held off the record, and sometimes not recorded for that particular fieldwork episode. The researcher collecting the data was an open figure throughout the field process, being candid about the purpose of the research, his background, how the participants' data would be used and especially how it would not. We also offered reassurance and transparency throughout the data collection phase. We allowed the participants to review the notes and audio recordings taken whenever they were so inclined, and indeed, we even found it warmly amusing when someone would express curiosity about the data collection process and comment: 'You are always writing … what are you always writing? We didn't even say anything important.'

As time went on, the researcher and participants became accustomed to each other, with the participants freely expressing themselves and communicating sentiments of humiliation, reprieve, delight, grief and fears, without reservations. This was a truly insightful experience and we feel humbled that the participants chose to share their stories. In all, we believe the methods adopted for this study are appropriate and sufficient to fulfil the study objectives, to accurately tell the participants' stories, and this is reflected in the following chapters where we report and discuss the findings.

Chapter 3

STUDENT MIGRATION AND GLOBAL INEQUALITY

Introduction

> Unfortunately, despite their importance as a distinct migrant population, and also in terms of the topic's potential for enriching our understanding of contemporary forms of mobility, there has been relatively little research on international student mobility in comparison to other forms of migration. (Riaño and Piguet 2016, 1)

International students make up the bulk of migrant flows into most Organisation for Economic Co-operation and Development (OECD) states. Therefore, it is perhaps surprising that the prevalence of this distinct cohort is not paralleled in the body of scholarship on migration (IOM 2018, 105). The literature is quite fragmented and inherently dependent on the discipline concerned; economists for instance tend to focus on the fiscal impacts of this group, sociologists interrogate their societal implications, geographers highlight mobility trends, meanwhile pedagogues situate them within educational institutions for didactic intents. While definitions may vary, international students are generally understood as having left their country of origin and moved to another country for the purpose of study[1] (Riaño and Piguet 2016). More so, as student migration essentially involves the transnational mobility of students outside their country of birth or citizenship for study, international students can easily be portrayed as part of the migrant population (King and Raghuram 2013; Riaño and Piguet 2016;

---

1. For descriptive purposes, international students are usually divided into two groups: those who move abroad to complete a degree (degree mobility), and those who move for a short-term study exchange (credit mobility). This study is centred on the former category.

Spring 2009). Within this niche scholarship, emergent interpretations have sought to account for, and explain, international student mobility patterns and the implications for the sending and receiving states (Hawthorne 2010; Waters and Brooks 2010; Xiang and Shen 2009). Centring on the individual, the socioeconomic and cultural capital students require for, as well as acquire through, the process of transnational mobility has also garnered attention (Baláz and Williams 2004; Brooks and Waters 2009; Findlay et al. 2006; Waters 2006). In an era marked by heightened globalisation, international students have been portrayed as global citizens and as coparticipants in higher education as a transnational enterprise (King and Raghuram 2013, 127).

In this chapter we consider international student mobility through the lens of global inequality, with a focus on student flows from sub-Saharan Africa. We examine student mobility trends, the inherent individual and institutional drivers that underpin this and the consequences for the relevant parties involved.

International Student Mobility Trends

Recent decades have borne witness to a steep growth in the volume of student-migrants worldwide, rising four times as fast as other forms of transnational migration. International student numbers more than quadrupled between 1975 and 2008, with recent figures estimating approximately 5.3 million student-migrants, a rise from 4.5 million in 2012 (de Wit 2008; IOM 2008; King and Raghuram 2013; and see UNESCO 2018).

As far as mobility trends go, the results have been predictable and reflect a well-known axiom in migration studies: people tend to go where they know (Dreher and Poutvaara 2005). More than 50 per cent of the international student population is enrolled in educational institutions within five OECD countries: Australia, France, Germany, the UK and the United States of America,[2] meanwhile prominent sending countries include China, India, Nigeria and Saudi Arabia (UNESCO 2019). The reasons for this growth and the stratified distribution of students are manifold, yet from which we can distil distinct elements including institutional factors and individual-level factors influencing this behaviour. We consider each in turn.

---

2. Meanwhile prominent sending countries include China, India, Nigeria and Saudi Arabia.
    See http://uis.unesco.org/en/uis-student-flow.

Institutional Drivers of Student Migration

First, the internationalisation and commercialisation of higher education as subsumed within a broader globalisation agenda is often identified as a principal driver for growth in international student numbers throughout the industrial world (de Wit 2011; Gupta 2015; Shumar 1997). Indeed, the high demand for international students has seen relevant players mostly composed of developed states, with the higher education institutions in these territories competing intensely for students within a truly global market. This occurs both for the talent of the students and, especially, for their fiscal contributions to the host state's economy by way of tuition fees and living expenses (Migration Advisory Committee 2018). International students now form part of a sizeable migration industry, encompassing prospective students, recruitment teams, international education agents and other institutions selling an international education (Beech 2018; Bilecen and Van Mol 2017).

Studies including those of Agarwal et al. (2008), Clark and Sedgwick (2005), de Wit (2008), Hira (2003), Kritz (2006), Lowell and Khadka (2011) and Tremblay (2005) have all, to varying degrees, written about the mounting competition between the usual student migration destinations, emphasising the way policies and socioeconomic factors may serve to either entice or deter prospective international students. It is well illustrated how universities increasingly assume an entrepreneurial approach towards student recruitment and adopt strategies that specially appeal to prospective international students. These strategies have seen learning content increasingly developed with an international appeal and education institutions consistently building transnational partnerships with relevant stakeholders (Agarwal et al. 2008; Clark and Sedgwick 2005; de Wit 2008; Hira 2003; Kritz 2006; Lowell and Khadka 2011; Tremblay 2005). These efforts are often supplemented on the state level. Some countries have considerably relaxed bureaucratic provisions for student migration, just as some go the lengths of providing bursaries to entice prospective international students (Kritz 2006). Such concerted efforts are often not altruistic, seen through the benefits of international student mobility for universities, and the states within which they are housed, in the academic scrutiny on the topic (Chen 2007; Findlay 2011; Mulley and Sachrajda 2011; Neilson 2009).

International student admissions are a significant source of income for universities and, in some cases, this cash injection helps lower the cost of higher education for the local population,[3] just as their recurrent living expenses help

---

3. In Sweden, for instance, international undergraduate students have been charged tuition fees whereas home students are being granted free tuition. Meanwhile in Australia and the UK, international and home students are segregated for the purpose

stimulate local economies (McBurnie and Ziguras 2003; Brown et. al. 2010; Marginson 2007; Slaughter and Cantwell 2012). Universities and states more generally also stand to benefit from the cultural capital that foreign students bring with them from their home states (Findlay 2011, 164; Hall 2011). In addition, some states view international students as prospective highly skilled migrants with the potential to make tangible socioeconomic contributions and thus enact policies that encourage them to remain following the completion of their studies (Riaño and Piguet 2016), and for others, it is seen as a means to strengthen foreign relations and project soft power (Kritz 2006).

Meanwhile, the benefits of international student mobility for the sending states include financial inflow through scholarships and remittances, and intangibles by way of cultural capital and international relations (Knerr et al. 2010). Spilimbergo (2009), for instance, asserts that foreign education promotes democracy in the origin countries of the students, especially when education has been acquired in democratic countries.

Individual-level drivers

Some traditional accounts attempt to explain the drivers of international student mobility as strictly being in pursuit of human capital: students are proactive and intentional actors in pursuit of capital advantage (Waters and Brooks 2010, 218). The student will only migrate if this culminates in socioeconomic betterment in some way, for example, a degree as a means to improve job prospects and future earnings. In a push/pull model,[4] the educational facilities and career prospects in their home country are compared against those available and possible in another, and the student decides to move per the outcome of this calculation (Parvati 2013; and Madge et al. 2014). Mazzarol et al. (1997) sought to condense the factors that underpin the students' decision-making in study destinations into six considerations: the first has to do with the familiarity of the host country in the students' home state, including the quality of its educational institutions and qualifications, the accessibility of information on the potential destinations, and cultural factors including language commonalities and historical ties. The second is socioeconomic factors including tuition, living and travel expenses, and availability of employment privileges while studying, career progression and future

---

of tuition fees, the former being charged an 'overseas fee premium' meanwhile the latter benefiting from subsidised home-status fees (Cantwell 2015).

4. Push factors include the reasons why the students leave their respective home states, and pull factors are those reasons why they decide to move to a specific region to undertake study at a specific institution.

earnings, along with social concerns including crime and discrimination rates, the presence of kinfolk and security of citizenship. The third factor involves referrals and recommendations by other actors within the students' social network. The fourth encompasses environmental factors including the climate and lifestyle possible in the potential destination. The fifth factor is geographic proximity, and finally the sixth factor is the availability of established social networks in the country of destination (see Baas 2010; Baláz and Williams 2004; Beine et al. 2014; Bessey 2012; Choudaha and de Wit 2014; González et al. 2011; Hazen and Alberts 2006; Mazzarol et al. 1997; Neilson 2009; Perkins and Neumayer 2014; Riaño and Piguet 2016; Rosenzweig 2006; van Mol and Timmerman 2014).

From a consumerist perspective, students must also take into account the actual context within which they will undertake study as it is yet the case that the extent to which an international education provides individuals with socioeconomic leverage may very well depend on the 'quality' of the institution attended (Baláz and Williams 2004; Findlay et al. 2006; Waters 2006). This assumption is actively fed by notions of social stratification which reify the exclusivity of the degrees from specific institutions in the global hierarchy; for instance, attending a prestigious university such as either of the 'Oxbridge' universities, Harvard or Nanjing University may well translate to better job market prospects (Alberts 2007; Olds 2007; Pandit 2009).[5] Institution-specific 'pull' factors for students in this sense may include the quality and accessibility of the university, including the range of courses provided, institutional partnerships, staff expertise, research facilities, information technology adeptness, resources, alumni base and its market profile and promotional efforts (Mazzarol 1998). A further consideration is that student mobility can also be culturally insightful; it offers students the opportunity for novel experiences in terms of exploring new places, languages and peoples, and indeed, per Waters and Brooks (2010), tourism can be a principal driver of student migration.

Student migration from sub-Saharan Africa: Developing states and inequities

Despite the continent's intimate history with the subject, there is an inescapable meagreness in the contemporary scholarship on transnational migration

---

5. It is, however, the case that 'world-class' universities that sit atop league tables represent only a meagre proportion of the total number of tertiary education institutions, both nationally and internationally. They are also largely inaccessible to the majority of international students due to the limited availability of study places and their highly selective entry policies. For detailed discussion, see Perkins and Neumayer (2014).

centring on sub-Saharan African actors, let alone of the specific student population. Even then, whenever migration is the focus within contemporary academic discourse with respect to Africa, it is less likely to be about student mobilities as a phenomenon in itself, and more likely to be about more *exigent* contexts of international mobility and in particular the human rights issues they present (Adepoju and van der Wiel 2010; Appleyard 1988; Oucho 2008; Tienda et al. 2006).[6] The literature on student migration is populated with empirical accounts that centre students, institutions and mobilities from and within a selection of regional contexts, and especially from European, North American and South Asian regions (Bessey 2012; de Wit 2008; OECD 2013; Ruiz 2014; Teichler et al. 2011; van Mol and Timmerman 2014; Wächter 2014). Nonetheless, as the region's gross domestic product per capita ranks amongst the lowest in the world,[7] the sub-Saharan continent can be subsumed within the broader literature on student mobilities from developing regions, where there is minimal industrial and economic activity and a pervasiveness of low wages and equally low standards of living (International Monetary Fund 2019). Further, and in respect to global inequities, a concept primed on the inherent inequalities in income and living standards between states, and how this may come to affect the opportunities and lives of actors, is a continued theme (Roser 2013).[8]

A marked trend in international student mobility more recently has been the steep rise in the numbers of international students from developing countries, especially from Africa and Asia, for which Nigeria and India feature prominently (Kritz 2015). Cumulatively, developing to developed country movement currently accounts for more than half of the total volume of the overall student mobility flows, whereas the reverse, that is, student flows from developed to developing country flows are near negligible, averaging less than 5 per cent of the total volume (UNESCO 2018). These wealth disparities can be found to contour students' migration outcomes, as Perkins and Neumayer (2014) poignantly note that the determinants of student migration will broadly vary between 'developed' and 'developing' countries. McMahon (1992), adopting a 'push' model and an 'pull' model in a study of international student flows

---

6. The prevalent literature often touch on human rights concerns associated with migration including asylum-seekers, trafficking in persons and forced labour. Further, there exist broader developmental agendas including diasporic remittances, 'brain drain/gain' and regional growth.
7. Only second to that of Antarctica.
8. Global inequality is measured through indices of wealth including capita gross domestic product, life expectancy, access to infrastructures including health care and social inequalities and so on (Roser 2013).

from 18 developing countries to developed countries between the 1960s and 1970s, documents the outbound student flow as highly dependent on the relative economic wealth of the sending/developing country, its participation in the world economy, and the priority placed on education and the availability of educational opportunities in the home country. Meanwhile the pull model similarly highlighted students' allure to a host country as being mostly influenced by the size of its economy, the availability of financial bursaries for international students and the socioeconomic links between the home and host country (Mazzarol and Soutar 2002; McMahon 1992).

Concentrating on sub-Saharan Africa, while it was previously the case that the trajectory of international student mobility usually flowed from countries in the South to those in the Global North, recent trends have revealed how the African subcontinent has become an active regional player in international students' mobility, albeit that outward movements far exceed inward flows (Kritz 2015). While it remains that the substantial costs associated with an overseas education far exceed the budgetary capabilities of the bulk of the population, the documented broadening of the middle class within this region has effectively facilitated international study becoming increasingly accessible for more families, if only just so. The heightened acknowledgement within this class education is seen as a proven pathway for upward socioeconomic mobility (Kritz 2006). There are also demographical factors to account for the heightened exodus of student-migrants from sub-Saharan Africa. This region happens to be densely populated, and with youth, with a median age of approximately 19.7 years (Berthélemy 2006). This, coupled with the continent's rising levels of secondary education completion, effectively means that a substantial proportion of its population is primed for tertiary education at any given point. Unfortunately, it is yet the case that despite the recent influx of investment,[9] most African states do not possess the requisite capacities to cater to this demand indigenously, hence the outward flow of students (Kritz 2006). Thus, it is unsurprising that socioeconomic inequalities litter the dynamics surrounding student migration, from recruitment to students' post study mobilities. Studies by Abuosi and Abor (2015), Efionayi and Piguet (2014) and Dako-Gyeke (2015) have demonstrated that African students (from Ghana, Senegal, Ivory Coast and the Niger) tend to emigrate in pursuit of better employment opportunities, an improved standard of living, established networks and, more generally, because of a lack of confidence in the future direction in their home

---

9. Including greatly increasing their number of universities in recent decades. Countries in the region now spend an average of 18 per cent of their budgets on education; a higher amount than most OECD countries spend (World Bank 2010, xxvi). African households also spend a significant proportion of their budgets on education.

states.[10] More so, the context within which students from this region select between study destinations has evolved quite considerably. The push factors have been identified to include predominantly the inability to access equivalent educational structures in the home country – with scholars, including Brooks and Waters (2010), Hall (2015), Mazzarol and Soutar (2002), Syed et al. (2007), finding that young people in this region often consider universities at home to be of inferior standard and attending them may consequently detract from their career profile. There are also disparities apparent in the quality and acclaim accorded to foreign and domestic degree awards. In some cases, academic qualifications from developing states are either downgraded or outrightly disregarded in more developed contexts (Gordon and Jallade 1996; Szelenyi 2006). Furthermore, these inequities have even been seen to affect early decision-making for the child's educational development, where choices on matters such as what language to study and which subjects to take are made in a way so to facilitate migration for further study (Bullough 2007).[11] As it concerns post-migration patterns, Rosenzweig (2006)[12] suggests two archetypes to explain the transnational mobility of students from developing to developed states. The first is the school-constrained model which posits that this exodus takes place because of a lack of educational facilities in the home country which causes students to migrate in the quest of human capital. They return home to reap the benefits of the differentiation an overseas education provides in the home state. Meanwhile on the second part, it is adduced that migration under a student visa could well be a strategy into discovering more permanent forms of residency in the host country (Findlay 2011; Güruz 2011; Macready and Tucker 2011; Mazzarol and Soutar 2002; Robertson 2011).

Consequences of international student emigration: Sub-Saharan Africa

There are important consequences for consideration of student mobility from this region, especially as this is seen to further exacerbate inherent

---

10. This may be contrasted with the main motivations for English students to leave for school abroad. Reasons include the exclusive admissions from the more reputable universities in the UK, course specialties and, quite simply, a desire for adventure; see Brooks and Waters (2011).
11. More so, it has been found that in some cases, the expectation of undertaking study in a foreign, developed country has become so endemic that it assumes cultural significance as a 'coming of age' marker for some peoples (Ali 2007).
12. The only slight critique of this model is that it stops short of accounting for students who may be driven to study abroad as it grants them easier access to the broader international labour market, not just of the host state.

socioeconomic inequities (IOM 2020). From a macro-institutional vantage point, it has been asserted that an increasingly laissez faire approach to higher education will enable the wealthiest states and their academic institutions to take ever larger shares of the market, to the exclusion of less well-off states. The result is an undermining of domestic educational structures (Ross and Gibson 2007). In addition to the direct loss of potential financial capital in the sending country by way of tuition and mundane expenditure, there is also a trade off in human capital that follows from student migration which can be portrayed through 'brain gain-drain' frames (Dodani and LaPorte 2005; Ross and Gibson 2007). These frames are premised by notions that the process of migration, especially of students, essentially involves the emigration of human capital stock from the origin country, that is, the brain drain effect (Boeri et al. 2012; Chiswick 2011; Docquier et. al. 2009). Further, some students may never return home to make direct contributions and may instead continue and become permanent residents in the respective host countries, or even migrate somewhere else for better opportunities (Beine et al. 2014; Docquier and Rapoport 2012).

Student migration can also lead to steeper socioeconomic disparities amongst citizens in less wealthier regions, especially as the bulk of the population will increasingly struggle to afford study abroad. Per Bourdieu, those who already have an advantageous socioeconomic background are likely to continue to hold these positions in their later life as they dispose of the necessary capital progress through acts of mobilisation, including higher education and migration, and will maintain their differentiation and higher status in relation to the rest of the society (Bourdieu 1984, 1986, 1993). In this way, student migration can exacerbate the already dense social disparities that exist between the rich and the poor in developing states (Beine 2013). Then for the student, in addition to the inherent socioeconomic disparities and financial burdens associated with transnational mobility, their situation may well conclude with a lack of tangible and significant benefits following this transaction into international education. Haugen (2013) demonstrates this while noting how Chinese institutions proactively recruit from Africa as a means to generate revenue and strengthen foreign relations, objectives which, for the most part, they achieve. Yet, as a negative result of such initiatives, the students to Haugen's study often indicated dissatisfaction with the quality and value of the education and degree received (Haugen 2013).

Moving on from trends, towards charting everyday mobilities

Despite the fragmented and scant body of knowledge on the subject, there is burgeoning interest in developing empirical accounts of the implications of these structural inequities as they impact students' everyday mobilities in the host state as an ongoing spatio-temporal process (see Findlay 2011; Findlay et al. 2012; King and Raghuram 2013; Lejeune 2002; Madge et al. 2014; Raghuram 2013). To this end, a number of empirical agendas have been proffered; Findlay (2010) and Findlay et al. (2012) advocate social stratification theories as a means for interrogating student migration within broader structures of international class reproduction, and the socioeconomic pressures brought forth by states, higher education institutions and individual actors including students and their families. Meanwhile Murphy-Lejeune (2002) propose that international students be analysed as a new migratory 'elite within an elite' considering it is one of the more capital-intensive forms of transnational mobility. Within pedagogical fields, Raghuram (2013), King and Raghuram (2013) and Madge et al. (2014) proffer global knowledge theories towards situating international students not simply as individuals moving between physical locations, but as key agents in transforming and constituting new spaces within an increasingly knowledge-based global economy. As far as experiential accounts turn, studies including Chiang (2014) and Gunawardena and Wilson (2012) have sought out students' cultural adaptation in the host state, studies by Collins (2012) and Malet Calvo (2018) examine students' routine strategies adopted for life in a foreign country, meanwhile Guissé and Bolzman (2015), Khan et al., (2015) and Waters and Leung (2013) address the challenges that international students encounter during their studies and career paths.

Nonetheless, and beyond these instances, there are relatively few accounts that capture the implications of these socioeconomic inequities for the students' experiences, especially beyond mobility trends, stocks or pedagogical precepts. King and Raghuram (2013) especially note this lacuna in the existing scholarship and call for further in-depth qualitative and especially ethnographic research into accounting for the experiences of international students while in the host state within sociological frames. This is pertinent because interrogating the experiences of students abroad allows for not only better predictions to future mobilities but more so to critically gauge the efficacy of existing education, immigration, and employment structures (Riaño and Piguet 2016). This knowledge becomes even more critical when nuanced by insights that this seeming inequality and its accompanying implications do not simply go away or cease upon cross-national mobility; just as student migration can present a medium for socioeconomic mobility, this process may yet present with implications that at the same time reify these unequal structures.[13] There is a plethora of avenues for socioeconomic inequities to

---

13. For instance, migrant labour studies document how migrants from less affluent countries are often disproportionately represented in the atypical, lightly regulated labour

creep into the student-migrant experience in real time. For example, study abroad is an expensive endeavour and the bulk of these costs are being carried by students' and their families' drawing from private savings domiciled in their home countries. As such, relative differences in wealth between states may well come to matter during their study overseas (Brooks and Waters 2011a; Findlay et al. 2006; Khadria 2006; Lee and Tan 1984; UKCISA 2018). Consequently, given the economic disparities between the world's states, it is often the case that the cost of living and currency value in the destination/developed country will be significantly higher when compared with that from the sending/developing country, and thus financial reserves held in the latter may depreciate once introduced into that economy (Macready and Tucker 2011). After all, there are accounts of students and their families having to take out loans or sell properties so to afford study overseas, or indeed for the express purpose of this study, having to undertake employment in 'low status' jobs and having to work beyond the mandated limits of their visas (Guisse and Bolzman 2015; Neilson 2009; Nyland et al. 2009). Neilson (2009), for instance, highlights how the commodification of education in Australia and the financial burdens associated with student migration effectively forces students into the labour market, just as Nyland et al. (2009) finds for multiple, reinforcing vulnerabilities in a study of the working conditions encountered by international student-workers. This is not limited only to direct fiscality, it is increasingly the case that academic qualifications and proficiencies from developed states are not formally recognised in developed states. This structural disparity may reverberate at several levels, from student enrolments to employment prospects. Guissé and Bolzman (2015) in a qualitative study of the living conditions encountered by international students of African and Latin-American decent in Switzerland find their circumstances increasingly precarious within legal and socioeconomic contexts, especially as the students encounter significant hindrances in accessing the Swiss labour market and struggle to find suitable jobs. Khan et al. (2015) in a study primed on the migratory experiences of international medical graduates to the UK identify that they often encounter significant impediments in training and career progression while having to deal with psychosocial strains and cultural and academic difficulties.

Yet it is intellectually lethargic to premise that the resultant portrait of global inequalities in respect to student migration is monolithic. Neither is it a given that actors from low-income states will be prone to experience the

---

market often characterised by fewer employment rights, occupying low-status, lower-skilled jobs, often susceptible to exploitative, and less desirable working conditions (e.g. Favell and Recchi 2011).

difficulties previously outlined. Just like any other social phenomenon, notions of inequality cannot act as a template as its manifestations are intrinsically relative and dependent on the social circumstance of the specific actor. Faist (2016), for instance, insightfully reflects on how for South Asian migrant-workers in the Gulf states, mobility and agency is often constrained, whereas the elites and oligarchs enjoy far wider latitude in their access to urban amenities and goods, 'if sometimes (self-)limited to specific (immobile) enclaves in global cities and luxury resorts' (10). Meanwhile, albeit that student migration is deemed as a route to socioeconomic betterment, this process is ironically associated with means and privilege; migration, especially for study, is for the most part only accessible to the world's upper quintile (Korzeniewicz and Moran 2009).[14] The bulk of studies confirm this insight while noting that international students tend to fall within the middle and upper classes of their respective states (Findlay et al. 2012; HEFCE 2004, 2009; Waters 2006; Waters and Brooks 2010). Indeed, the bureaucratic framework in relation to student migration in most developed states including the UK, is established to screen prospective students that lack the requisite financial means. These are the reasons why it has been argued by the likes of King et al. (2010) that study abroad effectively engenders elitism.

Succinctly, it is apparent that the implications of these socioeconomic disparities are essentially subjective and contextual and this somewhat woolly juncture sets the pace for our study's trajectory, underpinned by notions that perhaps the most apt way to interrogate the socioeconomic implications of transnational mobility for students is to collate what could very well be intensely subjective phenomenological accounts of how they may react to these structural disparities, especially beyond the classroom. This is predicated by ideas that, albeit study is marked as the explicit purpose of migration, international students are never just that, they are multidimensional actors whose subjective experiences are key to further understanding student migration with regards to everyday inequalities, and more so equalising these inhibitive and lopsided structures (Neilson 2009). Per Baas (2010), international students often must assume multiple identities in the everyday; they are students just as much as they can be workers, kinfolk, migrants, tourists or settlers (Geddie 2013; Mosneaga and Winther 2013). Meanwhile, Findlay et al. (2012) highlights inequities with regards the importance of privilege and wider processes of class distinction surrounding student migration, and calls for empirical accounts to explain the intersecting identities and structures mediated by student-migrants. The evidence presented in this book answers this call and

---

14. This sentiment corroborates the argument presented by Murphy-Lejeune (2002) that international students can be framed as 'elites within elites'.

seeks to build on these notions in entirely subjective dimensions by empirically isolating the experiences engendered by three of these structural identities, that is, the student-migrant-worker. How they respond to the highlighted socioeconomic pressures, especially nuanced by notions of social inequities and precarity[15] on the one part, and the socio-legal frames of legal mobilisation and consciousness on the other.[16] Yet, it is pertinent to address the specific sociopolitical terrain surrounding students' reception in the employment field within which this book is set – the UK.

Between student-migrants and the UK state

Introduction: The international student-migrant amidst political tensions

> Even the majority of those sympathetic to the overall aim of reducing migration believe that student migration is a good thing, both economically and culturally. So long as students are genuine. Mark Fields MP (2014).

The UK is home to a vibrant student-migrant population, a position it has held for some time. During the 2018/19 academic year, there were some 458,490 international students studying across UK HEIs, accounting for 19.6 per cent of the total student population in the UK (indeed, 14 per cent of all undergraduates and 35.8 per cent of all postgraduates were international students). This marks a 20 per cent increase within the past decade, figures bested only by the United States (Migration Advisory Committee 2018; Migration Observatory 2020). While there is currently no cap on the number of international students being admitted into the UK for study, they are nonetheless included in the net migration calculations for policy intents. Net migration figures dictate the administrative agenda for migration, and the political ambition is to see it effectively reduced to the mere tens of thousands in post-Brexit Britain[17] (Owen et al. 2019). To this end, it has been argued that it is counterproductive to include international students within these figures, especially as they make for a distinct class of migrants the state should be keen on admitting, due, if for no other reason, than the immensity of their contributions to the UK economy. International students

---

15. See Chapter 5.
16. See Chapters 6 and 7.
17. Net migration figures represent the difference between the number of people who migrate to the UK for a year or more, and the number who emigrate elsewhere for the same period.

are reportedly worth £22 billion to the UK economy annually in addition to any intangible cultural capital they present with (BBC 2018; *Financial Times* 2018; *The Independent* 2018).

This designation is underpinned less by profound political rationales and more by the methodology adopted in the delineation of who and what makes for both an 'international student' and a 'migrant' for official policy purposes in the UK. For immigration, international students are defined as students who are not of British or EU nationality (pre-Brexit at least) and who do not have the right to permanent residence (Home Office 2017a). Meanwhile for the purpose of tuition, they are classed as overseas students, that is, 'those whose normal residence prior to commencing their course of study is outside the EU'[18] (HESA 2016). Albeit the inexistence of a uniform delineation, official UN policy defines a migrant as an individual who moves to a country other than that of their usual residence for a period no less than a year (United Nations 1993). Thus, nuanced by the fact that the majority of full-length Higher Education programs run for at least a year at postgraduate level and up to four for undergraduate study, it would seem that these students are aptly designated as migrants and indeed any subsequent alteration may mean the UK's approach would be inconsistent with international standards. More so, beyond these de jure constructs, following the process of transnational mobility, international students can be conceived as de facto migrants for most mundane intents and thus subject to immigration control (Biene et al. 2013; Doan 2015).

These descriptions are neither abstract nor without consequence, international students being conceived as de facto and de jure migrants presents with far-reaching implications especially for the students themselves. This consequently sets the template for the seeming hostility that contours the contemporary policy trajectory on international students in terms of migration, which has been described as adverse on its worst day, and contradictory on its best (Riaño et al. 2018). This sentiment is expounded upon in the ensuing section where we review the sociopolitical terrain surrounding student migration and the implications of the resultant exclusionary structures for the student. This is followed by a discussion of the UK's outlook on international students as nascent temporary workers, as seen through the employment restrictions to which they are subject, and the state's efforts to enforce the distinctions that ostensibly set them apart from the broader migrant-worker population.

---

18. In this regard, overseas students can pay from 50 to 100 per cent higher tuition rates than their home-based counterparts.

The political terrain: Student migration and the UK

For Foucault (1971), the representations produced in public and political discourses create systems of signification that may acquire the status of 'truth' and subsequently are reflected in public policies. In the UK, similarly with many other states, the regulation of student migration is subsumed within the broader bureaucratic structure and policy discourse of migration. There are two discernible approaches to this; 'closed' policies, which are legitimised by security issues as well as the fear that foreign students might crowd out natives from graduate programs and ultimately become competitors in the labour market (Biene et al. 2013; Kim and Kwak 2019; Tomusk 2004). Alternatively, there exist 'open' policies which aim to increase the numbers of highly skilled workers and which follow the impression that student migration promotes entrepreneurship, international trade and investment (Biene et al. 2011; Riaño and Piguet 2016).[19] These approaches, albeit contradictory, are not mutually exclusive as some states, including the UK, effectively straddle both (Levatino et al. 2018). Levatino et al. (2018) demonstrate this in an analytic review of the evolution of student migration policies since the late 1990s, in France, Spain and the UK. Levatino contends that although attracting international students is the affirmed objective in these states, country-specific factors – including a peoples' history with migration, and the political party at the helm – more crucially explain inconsistencies between the broadcasted intent and policy implementation, in respect to student migration.

Insofar as it applies to the UK, Lomer (2018) divides political trajectory into a sequence of changes spanning the course of two decades. The dawn of this coincided with early efforts to commercialise higher education, and more so the decision to charge international students full-cost tuition in 1979. Per Lomer (2018), the foremost tranche of reforms was brought on by the 1997-Labour Government which launched a Prime Minister's Initiative to recruiting more international students. This lasted from 1999 to 2004, wherein, motivated by economic, political and cultural incentives, the government expressly set out to attract some fifty thousand more international students within a six-year period (Blair 1999). This objective was implemented through a range of policy measures, from easing the visa processes and requirements, to financial incentives including scholarships and intensified marketing drives (BBC 2004; Lomer 2014). More notably, a post-study work (PSW) scheme was introduced between 2004 and 2008 to allow new graduates to seek work in the UK for

---

19. The Canadian and Danish systems, aimed at creating economic and cultural advantage by attracting and admitting more student-migrants, have been presented as examples of an 'open' approach (Mosneaga and Winther 2013).

12–24 months. In 2009, the Tier 4 visa process[20] that is still in effect, was launched with the aim of simplifying the visa application process for all.

During this period, the sociopolitical climate was hospitable, international students were perceived as valuable additions to the cultural landscape and indeed were considered prized contributors to the domestic labour market (Hall 2015; Lomer 2018). This *honeymoon phase* only lasted until 2010 when political power changed hands and the Conservative-led coalition government moved to undo the more flexible, open migration structures adopted by the previous Labour administration in a bid to tame a migration flow what was deemed 'out of control' (Lomer 2018). Meanwhile, student-migration policies drew intense scrutiny as a result of the public outrage following revelations that a handful of colleges were found to be operating sham student recruitments, and essentially served as fronts for unauthorised economic migration (UKBA 2010; Lomer 2018). This culminated in a bevy of policy proposals aimed at regulating admission and residency of student-migrants in the state, ranging from the pragmatic – for example, calls for more stringent monitoring, and increased responsibility for university administrators to ensure compliance with student-migration policy – to the seemingly overbearing, for instance, suggestions to legally mandate prospective international students to pay a bond of up to £2,000 a year, only refundable upon completion of their course of study and subsequent exit from the country (*The Independent* 2010; Lomer 2018).

The resultant changes were phased in as follows: first, in 2010 those studying below degree level (except for those on a foundation degree course) had their work privileges halved to 10 hours work per week during term time. The student visa process was tightened, the bar was raised for English-language proficiency tests, and in-person interviews at border entry points were introduced to establish 'student credibility'. HEIs were mandated to increasingly monitor student engagement, in collaboration with the Home Office, and furthermore, a five-year time limit was introduced for bachelor's- and master's-degree level study, and the amount of time students were allowed to spend on work placements was truncated (Lomer 2018; MAC 2018). The

---

20. Tier 4 Points Based System (PBS); Students from outside the European Economic Area could apply to study in the UK under the provisions of the PBS for Managed Migration, or under the short-term study provisions. There were two types of Tier 4 visas for international students – a Tier 4 (Child) student visa and a Tier 4 (General) student visa. Those on a Tier 4 visa needed to be sponsored by a licenced institution and meet minimum English-language requirements, have a place on a course and be in possession of sufficient funds for subsistence during their time studying. (Note the changes to this system per fn 1 Chapter 1).

most critical of these changes was the elimination of the PSW visa in 2012. Subsequent years brought even more stringent policies; while maintaining that the UK remained welcoming of international students, the government set out to prune the student visa numbers by 80,000 following its pledge to cut net migration (Cameron 2011; Lomer 2018). This policy trajectory was sustained by significant increases in the cost of a student visa application – including the imposition of a £250 annual health surcharge, restrictions which prevented international students from securing private accommodation prior to their arrival in the country, and the introduction of a requirement for the student to demonstrate academic progression (Geddie 2015; Home Office 2013; Lomer 2018). Meanwhile in 2015 came the imposition of a maximum length of study time, where term limits for Further Education was cut from three to two years, and the financial maintenance thresholds for a study visa was increased. Following the Brexit referendum in 2016, the home secretary at the time, Amber Rudd hinted that student visa numbers might yet be further restricted (Travis and Weale 2016).

The rationale for these changes was to bolster the selectivity of student recruitment into UK HEI to include only those who would be making the highest economic contribution, to weed out those 'who do not deserve to be in the country', and curtail potential abuse of the study visa as a route to economic migration (Robertson 2011).

> The reduction in post-study work opportunities, mixed with a more stringent application of Tier 4 regulations, as well as harsher government rhetoric around migration more generally, has had a particularly deleterious impact on some markets, such as India. (Million Plus Group as quoted in Migration Advisory Committee 2018, 38)

The negative consequence of these policies was seen in the volumes of international students to the UK. Overseas student numbers fell by 1 per cent between 2012 and 2013, defying growth trends maintained since the 1980's (Marginson 2014), meanwhile South Asian student numbers fell by more than 20 per cent, citing the lack of employment opportunities following the removal of the PSW route (Marginson 2014). These findings were subsequently corroborated by Hobson's (2015) analysis of the responses of 17,000 prospective international students who had considered studying in the UK. A third of students polled indicated they eventually chose to study elsewhere, the most prevalent reason for this being the lack of PSW options.

> The classification of international students as immigrants is at odds with public perception. Recent polling conducted for Universities UK

revealed that only 24% of British adults think of international students as immigrants. (Migration Advisory Committee 2018)

Nonetheless, it has been argued that the sum of public opinion tilts only so slightly in favour of these students; this is mostly attributable to the treatment of international education as akin to any other industry in the country for which the state has an interest in promoting. The transaction summary follows that the students are seen as consumers and an international degree, the commodity. Meanwhile, the likes of Lomer (2018) and Nyland et al. (2009) contend that this market-based logic is inherently flawed as it oversimplifies this relationship and rids international students of any meaningful agency by limiting them to the status of end-consumers as opposed to partners in the co-construction of higher education as a social institution (Lomer 2018).

Personalising the political discourse: The brightest and the best

As these debates raged on, it is easy to gloss over the fact that it is the students themselves for the most part that have to navigate and bear the brunt of this hostile, contradictory policy landscape. Student-migrants have to oscillate between these simultaneously exclusionary and inclusionary discursive constructs – they are in the same breath both desired and unwanted, both commodified and under surveillance (Collins 2012). They are effectively caught in between the motions that espouse their financial and cultural desirability, on the one hand, and on the other, immigration discourse that has increasingly seen ideals of national security and protectionist sentiments percolate the contemporary discourse regarding migration – one where borders and ports of entry are increasingly treated as potential vulnerabilities to be strengthened by ever more stringent policies (Jürges and Schneider 2004). This is just as the motivations behind students' transnational mobility is frequently being called to question: *are they really students or are they covert migrant-workers seeking backdoor access to the labour market and permanent residence under the guise of a study visa?* (King et al. 2010).

This hostility may yet come at a high social cost for these students' time in the UK as it goes without saying that there are dire implications of this portrait. There has also been concern regarding student safety in the UK, as this group are increasingly susceptible to politically charged acts of violence, discrimination, racism and other structural inequalities (Mazzarol and Soutar 2002). Perhaps the gravest of this was the murder of an Indian postgraduate student in 2011, which was officially ruled a hate crime by Manchester City Police. Meanwhile on a psychological level, this sociopolitical discourse may be internalised and breed self-subjectification that can hamper students' self-esteem and progression. Adopting ideations of 'otherness' associated with the works of classical sociologists including Durkheim, Marx and Weber,[21] it is asserted that 'living in an environment in which individuals are assimilated to a category of undesirable subjects by virtue of their residency, citizenship, or, covertly, race, may affect individuals' lived experiences within the classroom and beyond.' (Lomer 2018). This template more so dehumanises and reduces students to very monochromatic boxes that play one part against the other – as between deserving and undeserving, genuine and bogus, those who 'contribute' versus those who take, the 'brightest and the best' and 'those seeking 'backdoor' access to the UK's socioeconomic resources reserved only for her citizens. Perhaps Lomer (2018) best articulates this while asserting that in negotiating and creating their own subject position, students must engage with, resist, or opt out from this structural framing of their legitimacy and identity, in an enactment of 'bounded agency' (p. 320).

In response, in our study we intend to interrogate the intricacies of the subjective manifestation of the agency and identity of student-migrant-workers, especially as they navigate the structures that bind their employment capacities while studying. Thus, we turn to address the ways through which political structures engender enforced demarcations aimed at keeping student-migrants from effectively transgressing the confines of this identity and veering into the terrain of economic migration through employment as a social institution.

The student-migrant-worker and the state: Keeping students as students

'Politically, this erosion of the boundary between study and work has been troubling as there has been a vilification of student migrants who are also working' (Raghuram 2013, 141). Gainful employment for all its socioeconomic proceeds is often central to peoples' lives and experiences, regardless of citizenship, but an argument can be made that this is even more so for the population of recent migrants for whom studies have increasingly portrayed as highly eager workhands as well as subsistence wage earners (Dadush 2014; Dustman et al. 2013; Manacorda et al. 2012; Ruhs and Vargas-Silva 2020). The evidence albeit scant, certainly suggest that student-migrants are no different. From the onset, speaking of the extent to which financial factors play a critical factor in determining student mobility, studies likewise identify that the work privileges offered during study is often a key consideration in prospective students' decision-making of their study destinations (MAC 2018; UKCISA

---

21. Durkheim (1933) in his Division of Labour, Marx (1887, 1931, 1968) in his theories of the labour process and alienation and Weber (1978) in his conceptualisations of bureaucracy and social closure.

2018; see also Adepoju et al. 2007; Beine et al. 2014; Knerr et al. 2010; Kritz 2013; Nyland et al. 2009; Riaño and Piguet 2016).

The sociopolitical discourse on student-migrants and temporary employment can be rendered as yet another front for the broader discourse with regard to immigration and the labour market in Britain. This subject in popular discourse often broaches the vilification of migrant-workers as posing a threat for the domestic workforce by 'taking jobs away from honest citizens' and 'driving down wage levels' (Ruhs and Vargas-Silva 2012, 4; Dustmann et al. 2005).[22] Nonetheless, we seek to interrogate the employment experiences of international students *because* they are a migrant group whose labour market participation is easily understated, especially as the express purpose for their cross-border mobility and admission into the country is for academic pursuits. Here economic activity, if anything, is meant to take the backseat.[23] However, just like migrant-workers, their presence within employment spaces presents poignant sociopolitical implications that transcend simply the individual. A number of countries recognise the value of students as nascent skilled migrant-workers who could serve the domestic labour market at relatively low wages, meanwhile others are not keen on the prospect of 'student-migrant-workers' and this manner of identity multiplication (Hawthorne 2010; Khadria 2009; Ziguras and Law 2006). Where the UK falls within this divide is subjective, as an argument can be made either way, but what remain, however, are the structures put in place to pre-empt international students from effectively becoming economic migrants under the auspice of a study visa (Mezzadra and Neilson 2008; Madge et al. 2014). Concerted efforts to curtail the potential for these muddled identities is tacked on to the bureaucratic structures regarding student migration in a number of ways – from the early stages where pre-mobility in the student-visa application process, where prospective students must demonstrate evidence of adequate financial means to cover tuition fees and living costs, referred to as the 'maintenance requirement'. Further, once admitted, there are rules in place that

---

22. To this end, it is yet the case that relational inequalities may mean that some migrants are only too eager to take on jobs with wages and conditions that many UK nationals will refuse. Recent research findings have shown that migrant-workers have near negligible effects on wage determination and unemployment rates in the labour economy, this instead being attributable to more structural considerations that have little correlation with immigration. More so, their labour market participation contributes directly towards economic growth that in turn goes to fund the welfare state to which they have limited access.
23. Even then, when the subject of employment with respect to student-migrants is usually raised in the mainstream, it is often on the basis of 'post-study' employment options (or lack thereof) rather than students as workers.

mandate HEIs to routinely monitor students' course engagement. More pertinently for the express context of this book, there are restrictions over how many hours and in what contexts students can undertake paid employment.[24] International students in UK Higher Education have been generally restricted to a maximum of 20 hours of work per week during term time, prohibited from taking up full-time or permanent job roles, and from engaging in economic activity as independent contractors or the genuinely self-employed.

Although PSW options are less generous than those offered by a number of competitors, the UK nonetheless offers similar rights to work while studying as do other countries. Canada, New Zealand and the United States[25] allow international students to work for up to 20 hours per week, meanwhile the Netherlands only allows up to 10 hours of work per week (MAC 2018). The public policy rationales for these restrictions are conceivably underpinned by sentience on the one hand, and notions of protectionism on the other. These restrictions are sentient of the need to protect students from the burnout that may follow from attempting to balance academic commitments with extensive work responsibilities. Although the readings on the effects of paid employment on both the academic performance and long-term wellbeing of full-time students may differ (Bradley 2006; Riggert et al. 2006), scholars including Neill et al. (2004) assert that 15 hours of work per week is the critical point beyond which students' studies and wellbeing are prone to suffer (Lingard 2007).[26] Meanwhile notions of protectionism can be read from the state's express agenda to protect native workers from undue competition in the labour market, especially as migrant labour is (wrongly) hypothesised to negatively impact wage levels for the indigenous workforce (Migration Observatory 2020).

Enforcing these distinctions

> We remain open to those foreign students who want to come to the UK for legitimate study – they remain welcome. But those who are not

---

24. Changes to UK immigration law commencing from 2015 resulted in Tier 4 students at further education colleges no longer being permitted to work during study.
25. The United States is the most restrictive with most students only allowed to work on campus while studying. An exception exists for those who qualify with the Department of Homeland Security as having 'economic hardship'.
26. Meanwhile, some universities sternly discourage its enrolled international students from undertaking employment outside of campus in any form, whereas others advise students not to work beyond 10 hours per week during term time. See https://www.cambridgestudents.cam.ac.uk/your-course/graduate-study/your-student-status/working-while-you-study.

seriously interested in coming here to study but come primarily to work – they should be in no doubt that we will come down hard on those that flout the rules. Alan Johnson MP (Gabbatt 2010)

The enforcement of the aforementioned employment restrictions is subsumed within the broader agenda of anti-illicit migrant labour. Illegal migrant labour in the UK is quite a sensitive subject, for one, it raises pertinent questions concerning the state's ability to enforce its own migration rules, just as it presents socioeconomic, humanitarian and legal consequences concerning the living conditions, protection and social integration of migrant-workers in the underground economy (Fudge 2018; Migration Watch 2019). This reiterates assertions that illicit migrant labour may be culpable for driving down wage levels[27] (Migration Watch 2019), a circumstance that has also been associated with labour market abuses including tax evasion, statutory wage violations, exploitative and inhumane working conditions, essentially modern slavery (Fudge 2018; MAC 2018).

The legal provisions with regard to illegal migrant labour are set out in ss 15–25 of the Immigration, Asylum and Nationality Act 2006 (the 2006 Act), s. 24B of the Immigration Act 1971 and Sch 6 of the Immigration Act 2016. These statutory provisions are aimed at workers and employers alike.[28] The Immigration Act 2016 deems it an offence to work illegally in the UK, the offence occurring when an individual who is subject to immigration control undertakes employment cognisant of the fact that they lack the requisite immigration status, or have been disqualified from doing so. Thus, student-migrants who undertake employment while studying may be caught within the remits of this provision. In addition to potentially having the proceeds of illicit work confiscated, 'illegal' workers may also be prosecuted and can be imprisoned for a period of up to six months. This conviction may also be taken into consideration in any future immigration applications the individual may make (Fudge 2018; Home Office 2020; Migration Watch 2019).

Meanwhile the 'whole government approach' represents the state's collaborative agenda on purging illegal or unauthorised migrant labour (Fudge 2018). This approach emphasises greater levels of cooperation and coordination across government arms and agencies,[29] so to ensure the effective

---

27. Albeit that most of these detriments have been contended. For example, there is scant evidence to show that illegal migrant-labour negatively impacts wage levels of indigenous workers (Ruhs and Vargas-Silva 2020).
28. As well as including those working illegally under a contract of employment, the offence also applies to work undertaken by those who are self-employed. The offence covers both informal and formal working arrangements.
29. Including the police, Her Majesty's Revenue and Customs and the Home Office.

detection and prosecution of illegal migrant labour. The risk of detection can only be exacerbated by the backdrop of the legally mandated National Insurance social security system and subscription to Her Majesty's Revenue and Customs's (HMRC's) taxation frameworks as prerequisites for undertaking work and receiving due wages. This system creates a paper trail that can lead to the unravelling of the true nature and extents of the individual's labour market engagement. Furthermore, employers are mandated to perform 'right to work checks' before making hiring decisions to ascertain the applicant has the legal right to perform the job being considered or is not disqualified from carrying out the work in question by reason of their immigration status[30] (Boswell and Straubhaar 2004; Fudge 2018; Home Office 2020; Migration Watch 2019). Some universities, including the University of Cambridge, require international students to obtain a formal document from their employer such as a 'contract of employment', 'worker's agreement' or some other written statement expressly confirming their employment status is not that of an independent contractor (University of Cambridge 2014).

However, it is pertinent to note that active enforcement of the aforementioned rules that proscribe unauthorised migrant labour may not be easy to obtain or be cheap to acquire. Efforts towards maintaining tighter border controls, stringent internal checks and other routine forms of detection all make for capital- and time-intensive endeavours (Fudge 2018). More so, it has been argued that intensifying these efforts may very well interfere with civil liberties and engender undue discrimination against legal migrants (Cornelius et al. 1994; Costa and Martin 2018). From a market-based standpoint, it has been argued that the optimal number of illegal migrant-workers in the UK is definitely above zero, and in acquiescence of this, pro-business leaning governments have been willing to accept a degree of illegal labour as it benefits the UK economy in very cogent terms (Baldwin-Edwards 1998). More so, firms have been ingenious in their efforts to circumvent these rules, from labour market manoeuvres including subcontracting and devising novel employment arrangements, to more attractive practices including payment of wages in cash in order to eliminate

---

30. Section 15 of the Immigration, Asylum and Nationality Act 2006 provides, inter alia, that a contravention exists following the employment of an individual who is subject to immigration control in contexts that breach the conditions of their leave to remain. Penalties for contravention are as follows: a civil penalty of up to £20,000 per illegal worker (in more serious cases), a criminal conviction carrying a prison sentence of up to 5 years and an unlimited fine, the closure of the business and a compliance order issued by the court, disqualification of responsible persons as a director, restrictions of permissions to sponsor migrants, and seizure of earnings made as a result of illegal working.

any paper trail, or even outright falsification of employment records. All of these factors can reduce chances of detection of illicit migrant labour and result in the enforcement of the rules proscribing same a particularly arduous exercise.

Even then, there is a seeming laxity from state institutions especially as it concerns unauthorised student-migrant labour. There is a relative 'degree of harm' protocol in effect where contexts of illicit labour are ranked according to severity of their impacts on the socioeconomic interests of the UK state, and consequently a 'harm reduction system', where enforcement is targeted at instances of more grievous violations (Home Office 2007, 10). In this spectrum, international students enrolled by accredited institutions, who work beyond the terms of their immigration permits, are deemed to be relatively low harm, compared with say those who are enrolled in 'bogus' academic institutions, and have neither the intention nor will to undertake any form of study while in the UK, and student visa overstayers. All of these in turn wane in comparison to contexts that involve more cogent elements of criminality, say for instance forced migrant labour and trafficking (Home Office 2007, 10). Here, 'harm' is delineated as 'all the potential negative consequences' and the risk for unauthorised student-migrant employment is chiefly the subversion of legally constituted immigration structures, which is mostly ideological in itself (Home Office 2007, 13). Notwithstanding the relativity of this frame, it is useful to conclude this section by reiterating that it is yet the case that governments may stand to lose legitimacy and moral capital if they are seen to be apathetic towards enforcing their own laws.

Towards centring the student-migrant-worker

In sum, the reviewed findings reinforce the notion that employment can be manifestly relevant to the socioeconomic subsistence of student-migrants. There is ample basis to speculate that the de facto implication of the regulatory systems may well exceed a simple restriction to 'keep students as students', but more so extend to impede or amplify their agency within socioeconomic and legal contexts. While it is mostly acknowledged that students can survive through part-time employment while studying, especially with respect to income and experience, it is easily understated just how critical the former is for some. The UK Council for International Student Affairs (UKCISA 2006) reports that over 70 per cent of international students in the UK are individually responsible for paying their fees and subsistence, wholly or in part, and for some 79 per cent, these expenses came from their own or familial resources. More so, over 50 per cent of the students polled were actively engaged in the labour market and had admitted to encountering financial hardship while studying (UKCISA 2006). Neilson (2009, 425) in theorising the deconstruction of political arenas during a protest of 'student-migrant-workers' in Australia, highlights how the commodification of education, coupled with the substantial expenses associated with migration, effectively leads to the multiplication of student subjectivities where they take up paid employment in a bid for subsistence while studying. Studies have since found that international students tend to work more hours than domestic students (Anderson 2014; Nyland et al. 2009; UKCISA 2006). Meanwhile studies including those of Anderson (2010), Kubal (2013) and Nyland et al. (2009) each report that a significant proportion of international students indeed work more hours than their visas permit. Anderson et al. (2006) find that as much as 75 per cent of the international student-worker population polled admitted to working in excess of 20 hours per week in term time, and of this, a little over two-thirds acknowledged working more than 30 hours, thus in violation of work restrictions inscribed on their visas.

Concluding Observations

As far as legalities go, there are inherent temporalities associated with circular, transient forms of migration to contemplate. These employment provisions and any consequential violation thereof may well engender precariousness into the residence of these international students for the temporary migrants that they de facto are. Although susceptibility to removal/deportation is much steeper for the undocumented migrant whose residence is proscribed de jure, it is also often the case that even non-citizens with other forms of unsettled or transient legal status may yet well be subject to removal orders, especially following violations of the host state's legal framework and its immigration precepts. More so, these restrictions are not simply about conditions of entry, they are also the terms of continued residence, and thus, blatantly breaching this divide between 'student' and 'worker' by working outside of the prescribed visa terms can be perilous for their rights to remain in the country. For instance, a handful of international students found working in excess of the 20 hours a week during term time had their visa extension or renewal applications denied by the Home Office applications on account of this, and one of such instances resulted in legal action (*Telegraph* 2010).

For Neilson (2009), the fact that student-migrants are not recognised as 'workers' effectively means they 'exist neither inside nor outside the construct of the national labour market and its attendant juridical schemes. Their working lives are carried out in a zone in which internality and externality mix and borders proliferate within the space of the nation-state once imagined as unitary and homogeneous' (Neilson 2009, 439). The sentiment, in sum, reifies notions of precariousness that follow from an allegorical axe that hangs over the head of non-citizens who are forced to skulk around the political demarcations that exist between student migration and economic migration as they navigate the UK labour market.

Nonetheless, while the current political trajectory gives cogent grounds for one to speculate, the experiences engendered by and especially in spite of these constraints have for long gone un-interrogated in the literature, and in this book we set on rectifying that. For if we are to ever truly gauge and critique the efficacy of these provisions, the burgeoning student-migration literature is in need of an empirical agenda that explicitly seeks out the de facto implications of these juridical structures and political discourse. This insight can only be achieved by empirically situating the experiences of student-migrants in the British workspace, in forms that transcend the abstract formations that populate the extant scholarship. To this end, it is relevant to review the extant literature on the socio-legal constructs on which we will test the empirical data presented in Chapters 6 and 7, that is of legal consciousness, legal mobilisation and semi-legality.

Chapter 4

MIGRATION AS A SOCIO-LEGAL PHENOMENON

Introduction

The reception within the territory of a state to migrants, and indeed to migration generally, is influenced by the zeitgeist of the time and this political stance is matched by regulation and law-making. The subject of migration is just one of the several instances where there is a real-time interpolation of the social and legal orders, and it helps that the socio-legal scholarship is seemingly not intent on drawing (to distraction) theoretical distinctions between these two disciplines (Albiston 2005; Cotterrell 2002; Nelken 2009). This understanding apparently defies the positivists' view of the law as neatly extractable from the social structures and interpretive schemas that mediate everyday lives (Banakar 2015).

This chapter begins with an examination of the intricacies of socio-legal studies and migration as an empirical undertaking. This includes a review of the socio-legal schemas deployed to account for the relationship migrants have with the law in the host state, including legal assimilation and adaptation, while noting their inherent flaws. This segues into a discussion of the empirical framework of legal consciousness (Ewick and Silbey 1998) which we use as the principal schema for this aspect of our study. However, our approach has been adapted to incorporate notions of legal pluralism and second-order consciousness so to make it more relevant for the nature of this study. In the second part of the chapter we review the concept of legal mobilisation and migrants' claims-making behaviour. This includes a discussion of the 'naming, blaming, and claiming' dispute transformation pyramid as introduced by Felstiner et al. (1980). In the final substantive aspect of the chapter, the migrants' relationship with state bureaucratic structures is considered. Here, we deconstruct and critique the subject of migrant legal status as an empirical object. Further, we review the concept of semi-legality in respect of student-migrants, which is being deployed as an indeterminate (perhaps halfway point) between legality and illegality of migrant labour. We close the chapter with a discussion that ties the three frameworks – legal consciousness, legal mobilisation and semi-legality – and consider how these cumulatively inform socio-legal scholarship and migration.

Part One: Socio-Legal Studies

It is beyond the scope of this study to condense a scholarship as broad and varied as SLS into a singular statement. However, a discernible denominator is of a staunch rejection of both the analytical positivist thesis which views the law as exclusively resident within its articulation by duly constituted authorities and institutions, and the Austinian proposition, where the law can simply be rationalised as an expression of the sovereign's wills and commands that are sanctioned with the threat of force (Freeman 2008). Here, there is an understanding that to fully unravel the law empirically will entail a review of the social, cultural and political precepts and discourses that underline its machinations within society; that is, the constitutive theory of the law (Banakar 2015; Nielsen 2000):

> The focus is no longer on the legal system, known and accepted, but on understanding the nature of social order through a study of law […] the goal is not to primarily improve the legal system but rather to construct a theoretical understanding of that legal system in terms of the wider social structure. (Campbell and Wiles 1976, 134)

In its critical dimensions, the SLS scholarship is underpinned by agendas posed by Roscoe Pound (1910) and the American legal realists of the early twentieth century where scholars began to empirically explore the processes and consequences associated with implementing and administering the law (Kalman 2016; Schlegel 1995). The emergent scholarship consistently found what might be described as the ineffectiveness of law and a persistent gap between the law 'on the books' and the law 'in action' (Pound 1910; Sarat 1985). The developing body of literature from the law and society tradition explained that despite law's egalitarian ideals of equality and due process, the 'haves' habitually and methodically 'come out ahead' when compared to the less privileged members of society (Galanter 1974). Consequently, by way of highlighting gaps between the law on the books and the law in action, and in identifying how social organisation and legal procedures propagated systematic inequalities contrary to equal treatment, law and society studies generated a significant critique of the justice conceivable through the instrument of the law (Freeman 2008).

Meanwhile, and as an empirical undertaking, proponents of this tradition acknowledge that several jurisprudential queries exceed strictly theoretical dimensions and are amenable to social-scientific research methods, wherein law must be situated as a phenomenon subsumed within social structures (Gibbs 1968). This has, however, drawn criticism, and scholars including Banakar (2000), Freeman (2006) and Nelken (1998) have since questioned the compatibility of legal reasoning and sociology, more precisely assessing the extent to which legal notions can and should be transformed into sociological categories, and vice versa, sociological frames into legal concepts (Freeman 2006). Nelken (1998) in particular cautions that the introduction of sociologically rooted schemas into legal scholarship threatens the integrity of legal reasoning and the sanctity of the values they embody. This position is adopted because, it is argued, the law cannot be grasped from a sociological perspective as legal phenomenon are autopoietic and as such assumes a course distinct from other sociological schemas (Samek 1974). Reiterating law's exceptionalism, Banakar (2000) similarly asserts that the sheer institutional power of the law pre-empts any effort to accessorise sociological notions for legal studies. Nonetheless, this study subscribes to the defences mounted by ardent proponents of the socio-legal scholarship including Cotterell (1998), Ewick and Silbey (1998), Felstiner (2001), Griffiths (2017) and Sarat and Garth (1998), who each have advocated for the pliability of both disciplines. In particular, Cotterell (1998) argues that the merger of both approaches can deliver a more nuanced understanding of law's functioning in society, and the myriad ways social actors may come to construct their realities in the legal sphere, and conversely, how legal precepts are received and reproduced within social locations. In this way, the resonance of SLS is operationalised in its ability to transform legal reasoning by reinterpretation through social precepts in carefully measured, viable empirical directions that mirror the de facto co-dependence of both disciplines (Tamanaha 2001). It is this understanding that reverberates through the theoretical framework used in this study.

A Socio-Legal Approach to Empiricism

To reiterate, it is almost impossible to offer a fixed or consensus depiction of the essence of SLS or its core methodological assumptions. This is due to the existence of several, often incompatible interpretations of its empirical tenets and scope (McCrudden 2006). Per Cotterrell (2002, 2), SLS is composed of a 'rich, almost anarchic heterogeneity and […] consistent openness to many different aims, outlooks and disciplinary backgrounds'.

Notwithstanding SLS's lack of a definite body of methodical assumptions, there are some themes that reverberate throughout this approach. Thomas

(1997) emphasised that a key tenet underpinning SLS is the commitment to a fully fledged 'law in context' approach to legal studies. He further asserts that in this empirical view, 'law is a component part of the wider social and political structure, is inextricably related to it in an infinite variety of ways and can therefore only be properly understood if studied in that context' (Thomas 1997, 3). Here, empirical analysis of law is directly linked to the social context to which it applies and its role in the creation, maintenance and/or change of the status quo (Schiff 1976). This approach assumes all forms of law and legal institutions broadly defined, and endeavours to further the understanding of how they are constructed, organised and operate in their social, cultural, political and economic contexts (Hilyard and Sim 1997). In its critical dimensions, this approach contemplates the effect of law on attitude, behaviour, institutions and organisations in society, and vice versa the effect of attitudes, behaviour, institutions and organisations in society on the law (Cowan 2004; Schiff 1976).

A further theme apparent in all works adopting this approach is a deviation from pure doctrinal analysis or 'black-letter law'; a jurisprudential tradition that espouses the view of the law as an internal self-sustaining set of principles that can be accessed through an evaluation of court rulings and statutes with little or no reference to its social context (Salter and Mason 2007). SLS scholars have long criticised the narrow doctrinal tradition as limited in its scope and application for what is considered as an overbearing reverence for case law and legislation to the exclusion of other contextual factors (Salter and Mason 2007). This sentiment has been iterated by several SLS scholars who have deemed the doctrinal tradition an 'intellectually rigid, inflexible, and in-ward looking' approach of understanding law and the operation of the legal system (Cotterrell 2002; Vick 2004). This critique of the black-letter approach of understating the social policy aspects and other ideological dimensions of the legal process is integral to the theoretical underpinning used in this book and a justification for its selection as this study's principal paradigm.

Another recurring theme in the SLS methodology that informs this study's theoretical focus is its commitment to the study of 'law in action'. Socio-legal scholars have long noted a distinction between the 'law in the books' and the 'law in action' (Allison 2015). This disparity or gap is rationalised as between the rules and institutional protocols preserved in legal provisions, and the reality of the law as it is (discriminately) experienced and enforced against specific groups in society (Rutherglen 2006). Jolly (1997) asserts that through a critical study of the actions and omissions of legal actors, it is often possible to detect a substantial disparity between the legal form of a measure and its actual effect and practical force, thus illustrating a tension between these 'paper' rights and the options individuals have in a realistic sense. Socio-legal research thus aims to unravel this gap, on an empirical basis, and, perhaps more ambitiously, explain the reasons behind it (Greene and Alys 2016).

A final underpinning of SLS which informs its selection here is its respect for interdisciplinarity. This entails the study of law through a combination of the theories, methods and research techniques from a range of disciplines that are subsequently integrated and synthesised during analysis (Vick 2004). Although the lack of a definite methodological approach has often been identified as a significant weakness of SLS, the advantage of this may be reflected in this inter/multidisciplinary feature which affords the researcher flexibility to adopt the techniques and methods of law and other social science disciplines best suited to the study. This interaction of methods subsequently serves to produce a distinct form of analysis that would not otherwise be possible from the application of disciplines in isolation (Vick 2004). Consequently, such a methodical approach is appropriate for use in this study for several reasons. First, it promotes an inquiry into the law's intricate workings within society and consequently makes space for the inclusion of the accounts and interpretations of experiences of the law in action from non-legally trained actors, including student-migrants in specific reference to this study. It affords to the researcher flexibility to consider the broader context of how policy underlying the application and enforcement of legal rules affects groups in society (Rutherglen 2006). Furthermore, adopting an SLS approach allows for the critical examination of the relationship between these state-established rules and other, less formal, operating norms and standards within a society/group, and more importantly to capture the study subjects' reactions to these constructions (Sandfeur 2015). Further, this approach enables the critical exploration of the subjects' narratives of their subjective experiences of the law as it applies to their employment context which are subsequently measured against the regulatory framework of rights, obligations and restrictions that dictate the terms of their labour market participation. Holistically this permits us to draw conclusions and understand why disconnects exist between the substance of these formal legal rules and the actors' lived experiences of them.

Unravelling Migrants' Relationship with the Law

Migration is one social phenomenon that is replete with potential for socio-legal meaning-making. As transnational migration involves mobilising from one nation-state's jurisdiction into another's, the law as an assemblage of a peoples' normative ideals is especially pertinent for this relocation process. To this end, a range of empirical schemas have been presented to account for migrants' relationship with the law. The concept of legal assimilation which explicitly centres on migrants' understanding of the host states' legal ideology features as perhaps the earliest (Kubal 2012b). This approach highlights legal assimilation as a prerequisite for 'whole' civic enfranchisement, which can only be attained following an apprenticeship phase where the individual demonstrates sufficient judgement and subservience to the host state's legal structures. Upon successful completion of this 'apprenticeship phase', they become naturalised as *wholesome* socio-legal subjects (Borrie 1959; Castles 2000; Cronin 1970; Kallin 2003; Kubal 2012a).

Closely associated with the above is the concept of legal adaptation. This approach is designed to question migrants' interactions with the host state's formal legal structures and is construed as 'the adjustment process which enables international migrants to proactively participate in the host society's legal system to seek redress for grievances' (Hein and Beger 2001). This focus is founded on the premise that migrants who act as claimants in civil proceedings are the most apparent indicators of successful attainment of functional legal adaptation. This is because they are demonstrably making claims under the law via the legal channels facilitated by the host state's dispute resolution provisions and institutions (Faris 1995). Per both these scholarly accounts, migrants as socio-legal actors proceeding individually or as a collective will need to either adapt or assimilate pre-existing behaviours and norms so as to conform to the socio-legal norms and institutions that prescribe social relations and the distribution of rights and resources in the host state. These new legal structures may be intrinsically distinct from the structures obtainable in their home-states (Kubal 2013). An illustration is presented by Hein and Berger (2001) in their study of the legal adaptation patterns among Vietnamese refugees in the United States. They report how this group increasingly made use of official legal institutions for the purposes of dispute resolution, just as their claims-making behaviour underwent profound and rapid changes. Catalysed by these legal processes, members of this group effectively transformed into more proactive actors.

It is Okay to be Different?

Both migration and legal adaptation are inherently plagued by their very restrictive expedience. For one, legal assimilation theory is apparently of limited resonance for scholarly endeavours that centre on more temporary or transient migrant groups and patterns, where initial mobility across state borders is not essentially primed on resettlement ab initio (such as student-migrants). Meanwhile, similar limitations follow from legal adaptation's central focus on migrants acting within formal legal channels. This, evidently, precludes an analysis of the vast range of social locations migrants may assume outside of the legal sector, law offices and courtrooms. This is especially important given the relative scarcity of cases that enter formal dispute resolution channels, and that even fewer proceed to litigation (Sarat and Felstiner 1997). More so, in both these frames, the scope of understanding is prescribed and measured entirely on the terms of the host state's legal structures, thus subverting migrants' integral agency as idiosyncratic actors. These theories are reminiscent of the more conservative agenda towards a singular cultural identity that espouses nationalistic values, say for instance 'core British values'. This ambition ignores the range of cultural substructures and subjectivities that may well be of importance in moulding the migrants' relationship with the law, the bulk of which potentially eludes the top-down agenda associated with both theories of legal assimilation and adaptation. This makes even more apparent the need for an empirical agenda that acknowledges migrants as self-reflexive, complex actors with the potential to maintain pluralistic ideologies that differ from those provided by the host state's superstructures (Kubal 2013).

These considerations inform this study's deviation from legal assimilation/adaptation to, instead, adopting the schema of legal consciousness (Ewick and Silbey 1998) as its predominant analytical frame.

Legal Consciousness

Legal consciousness, as an intellectual sub-enterprise, presents a unique illustration of the interdisciplinarity typical of the broader socio-legal scholarship, drawing as it does from law, sociology and anthropology. Similarly to observations made previously, it is difficult to present a unanimous definition of legal consciousness and its theoretical extent. This is due to its inherent conceptual fluidity. For Silbey (2005), intellectual schemas including legal consciousness are inherently subjective and open to varied interpretations. This mutability is well illustrated in the literature. Trubek (1984) defines legal consciousness as 'all the ideas about the nature, function, and operation of law held by anyone in society at a given time' (p. 592), meanwhile for Merry (1990) it is the unassuming conception of 'the ways people understand and use law' (p. 5). Whereas in more abstract terms, scholars including Young (2014) have situated legal consciousness as a reproduction of legal ideology that actors absorb from the prevalent culture and institutions within their social orbit. Others including Engel and Munger (2003) have developed legal consciousness with profound regard for individual activism, engagement with and resistance to legal structures. Finally, readings from Abrego (2011) and Boittin (2013) go further by illustrating how perceptions of law are transformed into action and/or willingness to mobilise the law or invoke legal discourse, effectively correlating it to claims-making.

Similarly, empirical contributions have situated legal consciousness within a vast array of social groups and locations including the workplace (Albiston 2005; Hoffman 2003; Marshall 2003, 2005, 2006), in stock markets (Larson 2004), to social movements (Kirkland 2008; Kostiner 2003, 2006) in public spaces (Nielsen 2000, 2004); and within legal institutions including judges, lawyers, clients and juries (Fleury-Steiner 2004; Sarat and Felstiner 1989). There also exists a considerable body of work dedicated to socially marginalised/disadvantaged actors including the welfare poor (Sarat 1990), ethnic minorities (Bumiller 1987), sex workers (Boittin 2013), same-sex couples (Hull 2003), persons with disabilities (Engel and Munger 2003) and sexual minority groups (Connolly 2002; Harding 2006, 2012; Hull 2006, 2016; Richman 2006, 2010, 2014). Notwithstanding the dynamism and range of the contemporary legal consciousness scholarship, we can, nonetheless, highlight how the concept is deployed for this study and place it within the existing body of literature.

Legal consciousness and the reproduction of legality

An agenda that resonates within the majority of the works from contemporary legal consciousness scholarship is the ambition to seek out the law as embroiled in the everyday social transactions involving ordinary actors (Merry 1985; Silbey 2005). This trajectory was set in motion in response to Ewick and Silbey's (1998) seminal work *The Common Place of Law*. This work marked a notable shift from the scholarship's prior fixation on merely accounting for the levels of legal knowledge and awareness within specific populations, to a research agenda primed on unravelling a more critical and layered understanding of law in otherwise mundane and easily taken for granted contexts (Blandy 2014; Ewick and Silbey 1998).

Per Silbey (2005), the concept legal consciousness is deployed:

> To name analytically the understandings and meanings of law circulating in social relations. Legal consciousness refers to what people do as well as say about law. It is understood to be part of a reciprocal process in which the meanings given by individuals to their world become patterned, stabilized, and objectified. These meanings, once institutionalized, become part of the material and discursive systems that limit and constrain future meaning making. (p. 1)

The focus on mundane social transactions is justified as the 'commonplace operation of law in daily life makes us all legal agents insofar as we actively make law, even when no formal legal agent is involved' (Ewick and Silbey 1998, 20). Ewick and Silbey (1998) subsequently construct the schema of legality which they delineate as 'the meanings, sources, authority and cultural practices that are commonly recognized as legal, regardless of who employs them or for what ends'. In this sense, legality is constantly being (re)produced by social actors as they make meaning of their everyday experiences, 'it manifests itself in diverse places and serves as both an interpretive framework and a set of resources with which and through which the social world (including that part known as law) is constituted' (Ewick and Silbey 1998, 23). Legality in not exclusively ideational, instead, it is grounded in social and cultural practices and more importantly must 'be continually produced and worked on – invoked and deployed – by individual and group actors' so as to sustain its cognitive resonance (Ewick and Silbey 1998, 43; Sewell 1992). This is because while legality wields the capacity to colour the meanings derived from everyday transactions and restrict the opportunities for agency, actors nonetheless retain the capacity to conversely reconstruct legality and challenge those constraints in response to novel insights and experiences (Ewick and Silbey 1998).

Last, a distinction must be drawn between legality and the provisions of official, state-backed law, as unlike the latter which is transmitted top-down from lawmakers to the public, legality presents with subtler yet unremitting manifestations as it resides in the cognition and behaviour of ordinary actors in the everyday. Thus, actors may engage in practices that reflect and produce legality without necessarily ascribing any legal meaning to the practice or recognising them as remotely legalistic (Ewick and Silbey 1998). Consequently, by enacting and/or engaging legality, ordinary actors flesh out and render meaning to what may otherwise be considered as 'humdrum' events (Habermas 1996). Legal consciousness is thus rationalised as the individual's 'participation in this process of constructing legality' as they navigate an arena suffused with law (Ewick and Silbey 1998, 45).

The shifting forms of legal consciousness and legal hegemony

In *The Commonplace of Law*, Ewick and Silbey outline three predominant forms of legal consciousness; 'before the law', 'with the law', and 'against the law'. These forms each correlate with a distinct range of actions, perceptions and/ or behaviours towards law and legality (1998, 47–49). First, actors presenting with a 'before the law' disposition will typically conceive law as autonomous, objective and authoritative, and more so retain stock in and acquiesce to duly constituted legal structures (p. 47). In stark contrast to this is the 'against the law' strain of legal consciousness; here actors perceive law as a powerful, unaccommodating and overbearing force that permeates their everyday lives. In this orientation towards the law, 'legality is characterized as something to be avoided. Because it is a product of arbitrary power, legality is seen as capricious and thus dangerous to invoke. Rather than conditionally appropriate or useful, in this form of consciousness, legality is condemned' (p. 192). Actors against the law will typically set out to employ evasive manoeuvres or exploit cracks in the system 'to avoid, if only for that moment, the law and its costs' (p. 4). The third form of legal consciousness is 'with the law' where the law is 'played' as a game that can be manipulated for personal advantage (Ewick and Silbey 1998, 48). This 'game' is set in a morally neutral terrain riddled with contestation, where socio-legal actors as the players strategically deploy resources 'to win in competitive struggles for social position, wealth, and power' (p. 227). In this orientation, there is reportedly 'less concern about the legitimacy of legal procedures than about their effectiveness for achieving desires'. Actors with the law are documented to be increasingly aware of their rights and are likely to make claims for redress or inclusion, whether misplaced or not (p. 48). However, each form of legal consciousness does not remain static, rather these dispositions are 'forged in and around situated events and interactions' and are in this way 'plural and variable across contexts' (p. 50). Although these legal consciousness templates may loosely correlate with specific social locations, for instance, socially marginalised groups are reported to typically be against the law, they are neither mutually exclusive nor determinately charted (p. 235). The shifting and contingent orientations towards law renders it only to be expected that a specific actor may express varying forms of legal consciousness at different times and in different situations, or even manifest all three within the same event sequence. The potential for complication is all too apparent in the main character in Ewick and Silbey's work, an African American woman in New Jersey, Millie Simpson. They illustrate her varying countenance in engagements with the law and legal institutions, and especially note of how she fluctuates between conformity and acquiescence to the law, to resistance and strategic mobilisation, albeit to serve individual objectives. In addition, an individual's legal consciousness is for the most part a sum product of interactions past and present, just as past experiences dictate an individual's disposition regarding law, novel insights may well serve to dislodge existing conceptions of law and create new ones (Nielsen 2000). This is illustratable by Merry (1990) in her legal consciousness study of the litigation experiences of working-class Americans, who found that her participants' attitudes towards the law was significantly altered by making court appearances and partaking in formal legal processes:

> Lived encounters with the law re-shape consciousness, offering a sense of dynamism. It is precisely the contingency of the law, produced by people's engagements with it, that is at the core of the legal consciousness work. (Pieraccini and Cardwell 2016, 28)

The critical agenda of the legal consciousness framework of Ewick and Silbey (1998) is aimed at explaining the durability and ideological power of law, that is legal hegemony (Silbey 2005, 358). In this sense, the complexities presented by the transience, variedness and indeterminacy of legal consciousness culminates in a way for law to endure, come what may. This is because the law is ideally amenable to all of these variations, and this inspires a cumulative sense of coherence and consistency that serves to maintain its hegemonic dominion over social structures (Ewick and Silbey 1998; Silbey 2005). Legal hegemony is not habitually derived from a specific social arrangement but rather is experientially produced and reproduced in those everyday transactions that often go unnoticed, uncontested and are seemingly non-negotiable; these transactions are rarely ever overt or seismic, and subordinate actors appear normally socialised and unexceptional as subservience is not explicitly required of them.

However, despite law's sheer institutional/cultural immensity and propensity to suffuse everyday interactions, this normative conditioning is neither absolute nor perfectly naturalised.

'At any moment, the stabilized, historical legal fact can reappear, perhaps becoming a matter of concern, debate, or resistance. The iceberg cracks and hits a passing ship' (Silbey 2005, 333). This means that socio-legal actors may at any time stray off the confines of legally sanctioned behaviour, and effectively transgress the law's normative ideals. The legal consciousness project is thus primed on interrogating the submerged proportion of this iceberg towards the unravelling of a nuanced understanding of the durability and ideological power of law, thereby deconstructing legal hegemony (Silbey 2005, 358). Legal consciousness thus accounts for the forms of participation and interpretation socio-legal actors construct, sustain, reproduce and amend in the circulating structures of legality, albeit through contestation or hegemony, acquiescence or resistance (Silbey 2005).

The Critiques

Legal consciousness, resistance and marginalised actors

The theme of resistance is of considerable interest to the legal consciousness scholarship. According to Ewick and Silbey (1998), resistance to law may be collective or individual, and may assume an assortment of forms, albeit not always effective. The principal features of resistance consciousness are as follows. First, resistance involves a 'consciousness of being less powerful in a relationship of power' (Ewick and Silbey 1998, 1336); second, a 'consciousness of opportunity' recognises that a situation can be exploited for personal gain (p. 1336); third, resistant acts 'make claims about justice and fairness [...] but usually don't announce it as such', which is manifested by the actors as their subjective experiences being unjust and inequitable, and individuals or institutions wielding more power are culpable for injustices meted on them; and fourth, resistance is often 'institutionally indecipherable'; that is, there are few 'rules' or 'standard operating procedures' for handling the ways in which people resist (Ewick and Silbey 1998, 1337).

The authors go further by outlining a typology of resistance which includes the 'masquerading (playing with roles), rule literalness (playing with rules), disrupting hierarchy (playing with stratification), foot-dragging (playing with time), and colonizing space' (Ewick and Silbey 2003, 1350). In terms of this theorisation of resistance to legal hegemony, these acts signal a momentary reversal of power within spatial and temporal parameters, where often taken for granted social structures are exposed or at least temporarily undermined (Hull 2016; Silbey 2005). In this way, these acts of 'foot-dragging, wilful omissions, ploys, small deceits, humour, and creating scenes are typically more accessible forms of defiance for those actors up against the law' (Ewick and Silbey 2003, 1350). Furthermore, a resounding proposition within the scholarship is that that members of historically marginalised or disenfranchised groups hypothesised to be acting 'against the law' tend to exhibit a consciousness of resistance towards the law and legality (Ewick and Silbey 1998; Nielsen 2000).

However, there is yet an admission that legality could provide a formidable means for resistance, where despite law's propensity to infiltrate everyday life and the vicious cycle of oppression and inequality it often perpetuates, actors may nonetheless invoke legality by making claims of the law in everyday social interactions (Merry 1995; Sarat and Felstiner 1995). There is an apparent inconsistency here; this proposition implies that, for the *powerless*, on the one hand, legality can serve as an intuitive schema for opportunity and resistance, meanwhile on the other, they are typically 'against the law' and thus seek to evade legality which they deem to be capricious. This begs the question, are socially marginalised actors acting 'against the law' also intuitively apprehensive of resistance to law by way of enacting legality? Ewick and Silbey (1998 and 2003), for all their significant contributions in this area, stop short of a concise synthesis of the relationship between the forms of legal consciousness, resistance and marginalised actors.

This critique is corroborated by emergent readings including Munkres (2008) and Hull (2016), who especially note the inaptitude of Ewick and Silbey's conceptualisation of marginalised actors with regard to resistance and 'against the law' strand of legal consciousness in certain scenarios. For example, same-sex couples as study subjects, as opposed to seeking to avoid legality for its arbitrary and perilous effects in their lives, instead mostly embraced legality as a cultural reservoir of power. Hull (2016) concludes by tasking the legal consciousness scholarship as to whether resistance consciousness should be redefined to account for actors who may generally be predisposed to be 'against the law' yet simultaneously embrace legality as an accessory for their resistance.

Susan Silbey's critique

One of the more poignant critiques of the legal consciousness tradition has come from a progenitor of the contemporary scholarship, Susan Silbey, who decries the state of the scholarship and its sustained expedience (Silbey 2005). For one, Silbey asserts that the contemporary legal consciousness project has lost its critical edge and become conceptually tortuous. This, it is asserted, is mainly a result of the emergent works which have deviated from its core agenda 'to address issues of legal hegemony and more precisely at unravelling the ways which the law sustains its institutional power despite a persistent gap between the books and the law in action' (Silbey 2005, 267). For Silbey, the contemporary legal consciousness scholarship stopped short of accounting for how law and legal institutions impart and sustain a hegemonic consciousness within society (Silbey 2005, 267).

For the second part, Silbey decries the inattention to the underlying processes that influence consciousness. She impugns the descriptive laded focus which, she argues, is being undertaken to the detriment of more vigorous theoretical analysis towards unravelling the cultural underpinnings that ground the documented variability of legal consciousness orientations. Thus, Silbey concludes that as opposed to clarifying

> how the different experiences of law become synthesized into a set of circulating, often taken-for-granted understandings and habits, much of the literature tracks what particular individuals think and do '[...] as the correlations between consciousness and processes and hegemony often go unexplained, legal consciousness as an analytic concept is domesticated within what appear to be policy projects; making specific laws work better for particular groups or interests'. (Silbey 2005, 324)

However, it is somewhat bemusing to note that while Silbey pens her critique as a eulogy for the retirement of the legal consciousness scholarship to the 'storage closet of academic fashion' (Silbey 2005, 352), she contemporaneously makes an impassioned call for nascent legal consciousness scholars to 'recapture the critical project of explaining the durability and ideological power of law' (Silbey 2005, 353). This book harkens to the latter call, and shares Hull's (2016) optimism that it is perhaps a little premature to present obituaries for the scholarship, considering that critiques even as damning as Silbey's should be taken as an intellectual stimulant for a renewed vision of legal consciousness, reinvigorated with a more profound regard for its critical demands (Hull 2016).

It is well documented in the literature that legal consciousness is susceptible to transformation and reconfiguration in synchrony with the individual's lived experiences (Ewick and Silbey 1998; Nielsen 2000). Thus, there may exist a plethora of social processes with the potential to influence conceived attitudes towards law and reproduction of legality, and in this study we examine one, student-migration. Here we aim to unravel a profound understanding of (student)-migrants' relationship with the socio-legal structures that mediate their presence in the UK, and in so doing to generate empirically based insights on the trajectory and pliability of legal consciousness as a processual formation. Where it does or fails to undergo a transformation, what substructures may influence this process, and the implications of these transitions or the lack thereof?

Empirical Adaptations

It must be stated that the legal consciousness framework as utilised here differs slightly from its use in the bulk of the current literature. The approach for this study is supplemented by notions of second-order legal consciousness (Young 2014) and the concept of legal pluralism.

Second-order legal consciousness

A pertinent development in the contemporary legal consciousness scholarship occurred in Young's (2014) rendition of second-order consciousness which she advances when considering the relational qualities of the concept. Young defines second-order consciousness as individuals' beliefs about the legal consciousness of any individual or group beyond themselves (Young 2014, 502). Young then proceeds to question second-order legal consciousness as an intermediating variable that may serve to shape the individual's disposition towards the law. As it centres ideas and meanings that are developed and come to circulate within specific groups, second-order consciousness reifies the expressive power of law as inherent in its focus on the collective and relational aspects of law's sphere of influence. This study underlines Young's position that individual and group-level methodical approaches are not mutually exclusive;

groups' and individuals' attitudes may be salient in shaping legal consciousness within a specific location in symbiotic fashion.

Towards a more in-depth understanding of the relational aspects of legal consciousness, an important point to note is that it is acknowledged in the literature that the individuality of legal consciousness means that no two actors are likely to share the same legal consciousness orientation, even within broad social identity groups (Ewick and Silbey 1998; Hull 2016; Young 2014). Allegedly, this is to the exception of situations where individuals interact proximately and (re)construct legality intimately (Silbey 2005). While this may well be the case, a review of the literature reveals that there is little to no empirical evidence to buttress this hypothesis. Consequently, our study sets out to position the legal consciousness of two separate groups of similarly situated subjects (student-migrant-worker housemates), divided along regional lines, albeit within the broader coverage of the UK legal system. This study's situatedness within domiciliary contexts inter alia provides a fitting site to critically examine this proposition and expand the existing scholarship by interrogating actors' (re)construction of legality in perhaps the most common place of all.

Although this study, just like that of Young (2014), seeks out the ways in which individual and relational legal consciousness dispositions might intersect and inform one another,[1] we intend for a more mundane, holistic reading. The situatedness of Young's study in cockfighting events does indeed present a rare opportunity for profound relational insights; however, these events are exceptional circumstances and not necessarily the most ideal site to gain a true representation of a subject's socio-legal reality. Locations such as that in Young's study leaves little flexibility for the interrogation of meaning-making outside of the spectacle of the event, and thus restricts the empirical purview. This informs our study's drive to go beyond an issue-specific methodology and broaden the empirical scope to include an examination of the dynamics of actors' relationship with the law and legality stemming from *commonplace* transactions in *everyday* lives (Merry 1990).

However, it is noteworthy that while we consider its relational undertones, the objective here still remains a 'self-centred' account of the participants' understanding of legal consciousness within their everyday lives. Such an emphasis on the individual permits the questioning of the variations in legal consciousness among actors, but further how this affects others similarly situated (Ewick and Sibley 1998; Nielsen 2000). Hence, we aim to capture

---

1. That is, how group-level processes may come to affect the individual's understanding of law and more so the converse, how individual meanings and experiences may in turn affect the relative legal consciousness dynamics of a specific group.

meanings as they are developed through everyday experiences, derived in both the first-, and second-hand. It is not contrived to insist that even when we aim to capture group-level or collective legal consciousness formations, a 'bottom-up' approach which centres the individual-self can then be succeeded by group-level analysis. This method may prove theoretically expedient if we are to achieve a more nuanced understanding of second-order legal consciousness and how it may impact the individual's legal consciousness disposition.

Succinctly, this study provides a *selective* diary of the subjects' recurrent struggle of interpretation between the symbols and systems of legality in operation within these house-shares as its occupants individually set out to 'inhabit' and make sense of a somewhat unfamiliar socio-legal terrain.

The concept of legal pluralism

The second adaptation to the legal consciousness framework from Ewick and Silbey (1998) is the interpolation of notions of legal pluralism. Legal pluralism simply refers to the existence of multiple 'legal' systems or normative frameworks, networks and orders coexisting within the same spatio-temporal location (Merry 1988). Griffiths (1986) makes an early distinction between what he deems as 'juristic' and sociological legal pluralism. The juristic account of legal pluralism is a direct consequence of imperialism, 'in the contemporary world which have resulted from the transfer of whole legal systems across cultural boundaries' (Hooker 1975, 1), where the sovereign commands different bodies of law for different groups of the population varying by ethnicity, religion, nationality or geography, yet dependent on the state legal system for legitimacy[2] (Griffiths 2011). On the other hand, the sociological depiction of legal pluralism is founded on the coexistence of plural normative orders within societal subgroups, neither ascribed to a definite 'system', backed nor recognised by official state mechanisms. According to Pospisil (1971), 'every functioning subgroup in a society has its own legal system which is necessarily different in some respects from those of the other subgroups'[3] (p. 107). This

---

2. An easily apparent example is the Constitution of the Federal Republic of Nigeria, a former British colony which provides for three different civic and penal systems operational within specific regions in the state; indigenous customary law in the South, Sharia Islamic Law in the North, and the common law as handed down from the British colonialists at the federal level.
3. Legal system in this sense is broadly conceptualised to include the system of courts and judges reinforced by the state, and, more importantly, other extra-legal forms of normative orders and codes that may sometimes, but not always, replicate the structure and symbolism of state-enforced law. Meanwhile, subgroups in this context are construed in allusion to social units and sub-communities that constitute an integral aspect

study incorporates this approach, as it broadly seeks to assess the interactions between dominant and subordinate normative structures, primed on an understanding that unofficial legal frameworks may regulate actors' conduct in modes not so different from duly constituted legal structures sanctioned by the state (see Dupret 2007; Macaulay 1987).

While this strand of reasoning provides the broad umbrella for this study's approach, more contemporary, what can be termed as 'neo-legal pluralist', theorisations more aptly inform this study's template. In this rendition, legal pluralism is centred on individual socio-legal actors (relatively and individually), who are deemed as embodiments and manifestations of normative pluralism; thus the empirical torch is directed on their subjective interpretations, of the intersectionality of these alternative *legal* structures exogenous to the state's brand (Moore 1973). Neo-legal pluralism not only suggests the existence of manifold normative spheres that exceed state law, it also hypothesises the dynamics of their intersection in the everyday life of social actors, especially noting the mediums through which these extra-juridical principles are mediated, entrenched and come to be circulated in commonplace social processes (Merry 1988). Furthermore, this approach also assumes a critical agenda that seeks to deconstruct the state's claim to absolute hegemony and its central role in prescribing *the rule of law*, and a stark contestation of the more juristic hypothesis that *real constituted law* must be enforced by the institutional machinery of the state for its legitimacy (Dupret 2007; Griffiths 1986).

This approach is, however, not devoid of critiques. Tamanaha (2000) in particular argues that if the subjectivity of what makes for law is conceded, as social interactions are in turn subject to informal regulation, how then may formations of 'indigenous law' be disentangled from routine social interactions, succinctly, and what norms should be considered as legal and which are simply social conventions with minimal normative value? (Freeman 2014). In response, the critical legal pluralism argument is seemingly not so much hinged on the disparities between 'state law' and, for instance, 'ethnic minority customs', as it is on the variant normative frameworks, for which should be recognised and prioritised as 'law' (Menski and Rahman 1988). This tradition effectively accords a similar reverence for official state law as it does for other normative frameworks that jurists may tend to under-emphasise as pseudo-legal frameworks of minimal legitimate value.[4] This

---

of the social fibre and hierarchical structure present in every heterogeneous society (see Henry 2015; Macaulay 1987).

4. In this regard, proponents of this scholarship including Snyder (1999) have since cautioned against drawing monotonous demarcations between official and non-official normative ordering. The assertion being that they are ingredients of, and processed

position is buttressed by the fact that these various normative social structures are rarely ever mutually exclusive or completely autopoietic, neither are their intersections always determinately chartered. It is indeed the case that these systems influence each other through a variety of media. Thus, while these coexisting normative systems may sometimes appear inconsistent, they may well in other instances sustain or reinforce one another. The empirical agenda is thus set to unravel the terms under which this intervention is operationalised.

The Hybrid Approach: Legal Consciousness and Pluralism

The inherent compatibility of these socio-legal approaches is underpinned by a number of similarities, the foremost of which is the rejection of the legal centralist argument which hypothesises that the state, its institutions and officials, retain an exclusive preserve as the sole legitimate source of normative order in a given society (Twining 2009). The neo-pluralist account, for instance, rejects this notion especially because it emphasises the non-hierarchical arrangement of coexisting normative structures, and more so abjectly rejects both the legal centralist claim to absolute hegemony over other 'unofficial' structures, and the legal positivist assertion that *real* law can only be performed in the arena of courts, law offices, parliaments or other symbolic institutions associated with legal authority (Hertogh 2004; Kubal 2015). Here, the account of law disseminated by these institutions matter just as much as those cultural precepts that bind the everyday lives of actors. It follows that the law in society is conceived more as a fluid system of ideologies engraved and reproduced in social structures, and less in the form of a finite set of rules or normative structures delineated per the state's authority and reinforced by its duly constituted institutions (Mather 2011). There is neither a unitary delineation of what makes for law nor its discursive constructions including notions of justice and fairness, but instead a move towards a historically sourced understanding of the law as a socially subjective variable enmeshed and negotiated by actors over time. In this view, underpinned by a conception of the law as an idiosyncratic social construct, it also follows that the cognitive frameworks deployed by actors in making sense of the *socio-legal* are inherently pluralistic, often in indeterminate ways, and more so prone to transformations in response to novel social transactions (Hertogh 2004; Kubal 2015).

The use of legal pluralism and consciousness in a study effectively personalises the empirical query beyond an emphasis on just codified law, but instead looks to unravel subjective notions of what makes for law and its

---

within, the same cognitive structure and are historically intermediated within the same social micro-processes (Griffiths 1986, 17–18).

constructions in acknowledgement of actors' capacity for integral plurality (Hertogh 2004, 474–75; 2009; and Young 2014). This more so reinforces the view of 'legality' which Ewick and Silbey (1998) conceive of as an idiosyncratic, subjective schema. In this arrangement, while legal pluralism as a framework informs on the potential for intrinsic normative frameworks and value systems deployed by migrant subjects that may be cognitively distinct from the constituted legal ideology of the UK, legal consciousness provides the overarching schema towards charting the ideological, expressive and behavioural transformations effected by actors' everyday engagements in a novel socio-legal terrain. This aptly enables an understanding that how a people may come to rationalise law and its precepts, including order, justice, and equality, is dependent on the perspective from whence it is viewed, and perhaps more pertinently, the social situatedness of that actual individual.

Although such an approach is far from pervasive within the classic literature, some of the more contemporary legal consciousness studies have begun to incorporate notions of pluralism into their empirical design, one such is Young's (2014) *Everyone Knows the Game: Legal Consciousness in the Hawaiian Cockfight*, an ethnographic study of an illicit cockfighting ring located in rural Hawaii through legal consciousness. In this work, Young reports of a pluralist relationship between her subjects; those arranging the fights and the law and its enforcers (i.e. the police). She documents how the fight organisers, albeit perpetuating illegality, nonetheless managed to self-identify as upright citizens by delegitimising anti-cockfighting laws, while simultaneously viewing the police as legitimate even as they seek to stop the cockfighting activities and effect arrests. This pluralistic ideology consequently meant that actors could run afoul of the law while acknowledging and preserving the ideals of law and order upheld by the state. She surmises that while ostensibly it may seem that these actors are in violation of the law's provisions, their holistic reality is one where official law is but one layer and thus the participants were only acting in accordance with their subjective hierarchical social structures.

Cowan (2004), in a legal consciousness study primed on the experiences of unsuccessful welfare applicants in the UK, reports of what can be conceived as a Pandora's box of pluralistic, subjective precepts of what makes for 'law in society' as opposed to a singular or uniform interpretation within this particularly underprivileged group. A further study that combines legal consciousness and pluralism is Hull's (2003) study of same-sex couples partaking in public commitment rituals as a stand-in for formal marriage ceremonies, prior to official recognition of same-sex marriages in the United States. Here, Hull demonstrates the hegemony of state law as it seeps into the affairs of the members of this socially stigmatised and marginalised group, even as they seek alternatives to official law by way of engaging in these public commitment ceremonies so to protest its adverse cultural implications for their efforts to form familial ties of their own. However, while they resist official law for its consequent denial of marital rights, several of these same-sex couples nonetheless appropriate its verbiage and practices to define their relationships. Thus, in this way, there is a somewhat complementary interplay between normative spheres that coexist within the same social group.[5]

However, it is yet the case that only a handful of emergent studies have sought out actors' orientations towards law in excess of official legal provisions and institutions (Hertogh 2009; Kubal 2015). This limitation inherently betrays established findings from the socio-legal scholarship that even where the object of empirical interest is strictly restricted to recognised legal provisions and structures, 'one still finds a significant dependence on unofficial or customary rule structures' (Cowan 2004, 140). This, we believe, has consequently led scholars including Engel (1998) and Hertogh (2004) to advocate for an empirical situatedness of legal consciousness 'from below', especially in acknowledgement of actors' pluralistic socio-legal tendencies.[6] Our study does not stop here, however, as we investigate further to delineate how these subjective renderings of the law may serve to impact the individual's recourse to the law in negotiating everyday problems, in particular matters of legal mobilisation and the resolution of disputes.

Part Two: Legal Mobilisation and Dispute Resolution

It is acknowledged that the law goes beyond mere ideological values and instead provides a discursive and practical resource for the resolution of disputes and

---

5. Some other noteworthy legal consciousness readings that adopt this approach include Pieraccini and Cardwell (2016) and Hertogh (2009).
6. Hertogh (2004) for one impugns the scholarship's preoccupation with forms of official state law as it inadvertently preordains the substance of law as an autonomous variable precluded from empirical evaluation in itself. Meanwhile, Engel (1998) reiterates these sentiments while critiquing the classic legal consciousness methodology for its exclusive emphasis on the state's conception of law and formalised normative structures. Engel makes a compelling case for a legal consciousness methodology that adequately reflects the lived reality that 'different groups have different kinds of law' and thus scholars must seek to unravel law as it lives and breathes within the fibre of social structures. In other words, scholars ought to seek out 'living law'. Engel forwards this argument in allusion to the demarcations between the American legal realist 'law in action' project and the European conception of the 'living law'. For Engel, while the former scholarship at its core seeks out the efficacy of officially constituted legal provisions (law on the books), the latter is set on normative structures and values irrespective of whether they have been sanctioned by the legal institution. Engel thus advocates for a realignment of empirical objectives that fixates on the latter.

assertion of rights. While there is no single overarching definition of the concept of 'legal mobilisation' (Lehoucq and Taylor 2020), it is deployed in its strictest in reference to litigation efforts geared towards or against effecting social change, whereas in its broader conception, it is conceived more intrinsically as the processes through which actors individually or collectively invoke legal norms, discourse or symbols to influence policy or behaviour (McCann 1994).[7] A conceptualisation that is fit for purpose here is Zemans' succinct proposition that 'the law is mobilized when a desire or want is translated into a demand as an assertion of one's rights' (Zemans 1983, 700). Legal mobilisation is thus understood as the processes through which actors employ law and legal institutions so to seek redress for 'justiciable' problems – problems for which a remedy can potentially be obtained through legal processes (Genn 1999, 12). Classic legal mobilisation readings often proffered actors' socio-economic circumstance as the principal culprit for the disproportionate use of law and uneven distribution of legal resources amongst groups in society (see Carlin and Howard 1965; Domingo and O'Neil 2014; Kessler 1990; McCann 1994; Zemans 1983).

Carlin and Howard (1965) chart the disparity in the use of lawyers as divided along socioeconomic class while implicating relevant variables to include the appreciation of a problem as a legal issue, the will to pursue action (including prior contact, experience with law and fear of reprisal) and access to legal services, or lack thereof. The authors surmise that this effectively culminates in the poor disproportionately being denied redress and access to justice. Understandably, the poignancy of such findings catalysed a move for the determination of the legal needs of the poor, and more so to provide them affordable, sometimes even free, legal services where feasible. The resultant situation means individuals

> with greater resources of education, income, or familiarity, which is often a consequence of education or income, are more likely to use the law as a means of dispute resolution. Because minority populations command and deploy disproportionately fewer social resources of education, income, status, and power, they are less likely to turn to the law or the courts with their troubles. (Silbey 2005, 373)

---

7. Perhaps McCann (1994) surmises best the essence of the scholarship in 'Rights at Work' where he makes the case for the significance of legal mobilisation, especially as it dually encapsulates the assertion of rights and dispute resolution processes. According to McCann, the culmination of this makes legal mobilisation a central aspect of social structure, organised for the most part by how actors assess themselves through their objectives and strategies.

Subsequent studies however brought forth more nuanced insights, and it soon became apparent that costs and accessibility of legal representation were not the sole causes of the evidenced lop-sided legal mobilisation patterns (Silbey 2005). The portrait was less linear and more systemic. Although economically underprivileged actors made less recourse to law and legal institutions, racial and ethnic minorities groups (Handmaker and Matthews 2019), for instance, were more likely to be underprivileged and thus generally less inclined to mobilise the law (Mayhew 1975; Mayhew and Reiss 1969; Silbey 2005). Thus, generalities such as disadvantaged actors being especially inhibited in their legal mobilisation efforts are largely unhelpful as there are myriad factors at play including objective, psychological and historical dimensions (Sarat and Felstiner 1989; Silbey 2005). This consequently led the scholarship to concede to the possibility that dispute resolution via formal legal structures may not be the overarching ambition of disadvantaged actors faced with potentially justiciable experiences, especially not when the issue can be resolved by alternative mediums, outside of the law (Sarat and Felstiner 1989; Silbey 2005).

This acknowledgement warranted more intimate investigations into structures of power and inequality inherent in society, as they affect the actors' cognition of the law outside of official legal channels (Sarat and Felstiner 1989; Silbey 2005). Per Sarat (1986), 'whether and how people participate and use legal process results is [...] in large measure [derived] from the way law [it] is represented [...] and through cultural systems in which citizens are embedded' (p. 539). In simpler terms, the willingness and decision to engage the law and courts system includes an ideological or normative dimension which may well serve to promote and/or inhibit their legal mobilisation prospects. More pertinently, this called for a decentring of formal legal institutions and officials, and instead a prioritising of the actor's engagement with the law on their own behalf, including their individual decision-making patterns and behaviours. In search of a more nuanced understanding of legal mobilisation behavioural patterns, scholars adopting this agenda, just like their legal consciousness counterparts, began to seek out the law as located within the complex fora of indeterminate, pluralistic, contested social substructures and cultural norms entrenched throughout society (McCann 1994; Merry 1994; Silbey 2005).

This agenda turned to the understanding of how everyday events may come to be transformed into disputes and litigation, and the relevant subprocesses that may contour the transformative trajectory (Kritzer 2010). Indeed, Kirk (2020) recently reported on the impact of employment status and legal mobilisation in a challenged to perceived 'bogus' self-employment. It is against this backdrop that the transformation of disputes and the dispute processing pyramid framework was developed so to tease out the antecedents of legal (in) action (Felstiner et al. 1980; Kritzer 2010).

The Dispute Transformation Pyramid: Naming, Blaming and Claiming

It is acknowledged that only a finite proportion of legal claims proceed to trial, and more so, even fewer potentially justiciable encounters progress to formal legal claims (Engel and Steele 1979). Felstiner et al. (1980) developed a dispute processing pyramid of transformations, called 'naming, blaming, and claiming', to discover the reasons why perceived injurious experiences (PIEs) mature into legal actions, and particularly why others fail to. The metaphor of the pyramid thus encapsulates the notion that fewer and fewer cases endure as matters progress up the pyramid – from grievances to claims to disputes and finally legal action (Kritzer 2010). The base of the pyramid houses all PIEs the subjects have encountered (Felstiner et al. 1980). A PIE is described as any experience that is disvalued by the individual to whom it occurs. While there may be some vague consensus on experiences generally deemed as of disvalue, these sentiments are never always unanimous. Thus, the first task set in this pyramid is towards understanding the distinctions that underpin why individuals perceive similarly valued experience differently (Felstiner et al. 1980). This aptly segues into the first transformation which is identified as 'naming' which occurs when an individual admits that a particular experience has been injurious. When actors 'name' a grievance, they redefine 'as unjust or unfair, those conditions or practices previously seen as acceptable or tolerable' (Levitsky 2008, 557). This transformation does not require actors to translate their experience as unequivocally unlawful but rather may also involve moral consciousness or the application of an 'injustice frame' in acknowledgement that a specific experience or circumstance contravenes some moral or legal value system (Hirsh and Lyons 2010). The next transformation, 'blaming', is triggered when the PIE is transmuted into a grievance. This occurs when the individual attributes the injury suffered as due to the fault of another person or social entity. These targets must be specific individuals or groups, rather than abstract and impersonal entities such as 'society' (Felstiner et al. 1980). Following the externalisation of blame to a potentially responsible party, the grievant may either choose to 'accept it' (i.e. choose to do nothing) or approach the other party (directly or through an agent) to initiate a claim (Felstiner et al. 1980; Levitsky 2008). When they do take action by communicating their grievance, this process is termed as 'claiming' which concludes the transformation in the pyramid. Individuals 'claim' when they specify 'some course of action to ameliorate the perceived harm' (Levitsky 2008, 558). A claim may in turn be transformed into a dispute when it is contested or rejected by the other party. This rejection need not always be expressed but can be implicit in subtler acts such as a compromised offer or delay in response, which the claimant may well construe as a rejection in some sense (Felstiner et al. 1980).

Thus, the socio-legal researcher's task here is to discern the intermediating variables that influence the actor's progression through naming, blaming and claiming. This agenda is justifiable for the fact that it is apparent that the bulk of the encumbrances to legal mobilisation occur mostly at the initial stages. More so in terrains where apparently problematic experiences are not perceived as injurious, perceptions are not actioned and thus do not ripen into grievances, and grievances are voiced to associates as opposed to the person deemed responsible (Felstiner et al. 1980). This makes it so that a substantial proportion of disputes exist outside of legal institutions, residing only in the minds of disputants. In this way, attention to the early stages of disputes (the 'naming, blaming and claiming') is particularly pertinent as they reflect the broader range of behaviours that are limited in the later stages of disputes where institutional factors may very well restrict the options available to disputants. As these transformations reflect social structural variables as well as personality traits, this agenda enables the unravelling of the intricate social arrangement of disputing (Felstiner et al. 1980).

Between social inequities and claims-making

The theme of existing social inequalities has often been implicated as an underlying factor that may impede the actor's journey through the dispute pyramid. Scholars appropriating this agenda have advanced an array of explanations for why disadvantaged actors fail to progress to claims-making. Examples range from behavioural factors (Fiske et al. 2002; Kaiser and Miller 2001, 2003; Major et al. 2003) and organisational complications (Edelman et al. 1993; Edelman et al. 2001) to the lack of financial resources (Berrey and Nielsen 2007) and a cynicism of legal processes and institutions (Nielsen 2000).

Scholars including Calhoun and Smith (1999), Fletcher (1999), Hoffmann (2005) and Marshall (2005) have provided feminist theories towards dissecting the intersections of gender and power dynamics in workplace disputes. These authors report that in contrast to their male counterparts, women often bear the brunt of gender-based inequalities which consequently inhibit their claims-making prospects. Studies have similarly documented the cultural nuances present in actors' disputing behaviour. Felstiner et al. (1980, 652), for instance, reports that disadvantaged Americans are lethargic in identifying an experience as injurious due to what the authors term a 'cult of competence' which effectively dissuades these actors from perceiving themselves as victims of maltreatment. This impression is reified by the social stigmatisation of victimhood, on the one hand, and appreciation of resilience on the other (Felstiner et al. 1980). Bumiller (1987) in a study centred on African American subjects in the workspace reports how an ethos of survival often led actors to refuse to acknowledge the occurrence of an adverse experience so to preserve self-worth and contentment in the ability to 'make it through the rain' and 'weather the storm' (Bumiller 1987, 431–32). Inherently subjective impediments may also include self-blame, fear of retaliation and a belief in the futility of complaining (Bumiller 1987; Merry 1990) and an 'ethic of survival' (Bumiller 1987).

Meanwhile, the theory of attribution asserts that an individual's perception of causation following an injurious experience is often a critical indicator to the responses that may ensue (Groth et al. 2002; Miller et al. 2007). Self-blame has been identified as an impediment to actors' claiming prospects wherein those who blame themselves for an incident are less likely to identify the situation as injurious, let alone to pursue a remedy. And conversely, they are more prone to continue when responsibility for blame can be passed on to another (Kritzer 2010). It is also reflected in the literature that attribution patterns may be structurally correlated with socioeconomic status, and members of disadvantaged groups are more disposed to self-blame (Felstiner et al. 1980). Gillom (2001) sums up the empirical association between social status and dispute behaviour when asserting that 'institutional, structural, and social pressures push against the assertion of rights' (p. 91). Although these are all factors that may cause actors across the spectrum to increasingly reject victimhood and prevent their actioning troublesome encounters, marginalised people, it is hypothesised at least, are more prone to these experiences than *ordinary citizens* (Nielsen 2004, 98).

Notwithstanding, these insights do not establish a generalisable template. Felstiner et al. (1980) succinctly identifies the prominent features of dispute transformations as being subjective, unstable, reactive, complicated and incomplete processes. They are subjective in the sense that they are an individualised progression of perception and need not be accompanied by any ostensibly identifiable behaviour (Felstiner et al. 1980). However, as feelings are erratic and prone to change continually, these transformations are inherently reactive. Disputes even in mundane contexts are essentially complicated occasions often involving ambiguous behaviour, faulty recall, uncertain norms, conflicting objectives, inconsistent values and complex institutions (Felstiner et al. 1980). These complications are exacerbated by the fact that the disputant's feelings and objectives may well change as time progresses. Even then, actors rarely fully relegate encounters to the past, there exists a residuum of attitudes, tactful lessons and sentiments that may eventually come to contour actors' behaviour and meaning-making processes for subsequent encounters (Felstiner et al.

1980). These insights result in transformations that are inherently incomplete.[8] Thus, due to the indeterminacy and intermittence of the transformation process, to identify the underpinnings of a dispute situation, including the meaning and effect generated for the actors thereof, necessitates circumstantial insights that can only be assembled through a methodology which centres on the subjective narratives provided by participants. It is here that notions of legal consciousness can be interjected into the dispute processing studies in search of a more immersive understanding of how actors may appropriate social constructs, especially law as a schema to reconceptualise dispute situations and to generate idiosyncratic meaning.

Between the dispute pyramid and legal consciousness

The dispute transformation agenda and the framework of legal consciousness are somewhat analogous (Calavita and Jenness 2015). While they may distinctly set out to explore the social emergence and transformation of disputes, on the one hand, and the actors' participation in the (re)construction of legality,[9] on the other, these implicate one another. The nexus between both concepts has long been alluded to by classical scholars including Weber (1978) who thought it useful to distinguish between the forms and substances of law (Liu 2015). According to Weber (1978) the substance of law refers to the individual actions and institutional structures related to the normative egalitarian standards frequently associated with law, including notions of liberty, justice and equality. Empirical agendas that appropriate from the substance of law in this sense will include the social construction of legal consciousness (Ewick and Silbey 1998) and legal mobilisation in the workspace (McCann 1994). The forms of law on the other hand allude to the social structures and processes that underpin perceptions of the legal system. Examples include the recurrence of legal change (Halliday and Carruthers 2007), spatial mobility of legal practitioners (Liu et al. 2014) and more notably in this regard, the transformation of disputes (Felstiner et al. 1980; and Miller and Sarat 1980). Succinctly, forms constitute the spatial and temporal shape of the legal system, whereas substances flesh it out with power relations and ideology, and thus

---

8. For instance, in a study primed on debt situations, Jacob (1969) finds that the most apt indicator that a subject may pursue the route of bankruptcy was having had contact with someone who had previously been through bankruptcy and was therefore acquainted with the legal process.
9. Legality has been explained as 'the meanings, sources or authority and cultural practices that are commonly recognized as legal, regardless of who employs them or for what ends' (see Ewick and Silbey 1998, 22).

complementing each other towards a more profound understanding of the 'socio-legal' (Liu 2015).

Further expounding on the relationships between both schemas, Emerson and Messinger (1977) insist that disputes are an almost inevitable facet of *lived* social structure, individuals being entangled in problematic situations are not rare occasions as the social landscape is riddled with ambiguous complications. Legal consciousness develops this assumption further in trying to identify of the ways through which legal constructs may come to influence the objectives, options, and problems and decision-making of ordinary actors, for which dispute situations and the meaning-making therefrom feature (Merry 1995). The amenability of both concepts can be further illustrated by a common understanding of the law as more localised and dependent on the values, beliefs and behaviours of individuals. In this sense, the law is subject to the perception and practices of actors who seek to engage it, for instance by violating, invoking or even avoiding it. The behavioural implications of law only become possible when individuals are aware of its existence and come to have expectations of it (Ewick and Silbey 1998; Merry 1995; Silbey 2005). These expectations are conversely moulded by variables including past social interactions and experiences, and individuals may well choose to act on these expectations in a myriad ways. These include instigating formal legal action, engaging the services of lawyers, placing markers on personal property to signify ownership, and even when they choose to do nothing. It is through these mundane social interactions that ordinary people reproduce law in the everyday (Ewick and Silbey 1998; Merry 1995; Silbey 2005).

A further synonymy between both concepts is discernible from their deviation from the positivist portrayal of the law as determinately chartered and value-free. On the one hand, law as constituted by the state maintains the moral authority to regulate social behaviour due to its perceived legitimacy which furnishes it with an absolute monopoly on the use of force (Ewick and Silbey 1998; Merry 1995; Silbey 2005). While on the other hand, law also brings forth an arena ripe with possibility for liberation and empowerment, as it creates novel possibilities for choice and action towards social betterment (McCann 1994; Merry 1990, 1995). Last, while both concepts acknowledge law's pervasion as inherent in its ability to permeate all strata of social structure, there is not an absolute deference to it. In this sense, while the law contours our choices and actions, it does not wholly nor directly determine them. There is always latitude for resistance and deviance as actors possess the agency to determine their position in relation to existing law or legal norms. It is at this juncture between the law and preferred action where lies the arena for individuals to exercise agency in determining how law will influence their behaviour (Marshall and Barclay 2003).

An early illustration of this intersectional agenda can be found even in the work of Felstiner et al. (1980) regarding the emergence and transformation of disputes. In the first section, they chart the transformative process from 'naming, blaming to claiming', while in the second part, they explore the intricacies of the transformation, as inherent in the parties' choice of mechanisms, ideology and reference groups, each of which may potentially serve to shape the trajectory of the dispute as it progresses (or fails to) through the pyramid (Felstiner et al. 1980). Hoffmann (2003) similarly deploys the framework of legal consciousness in a study of disputing behaviour at two similar cab-hire firms as she analyses employees' claims-making behaviour within both companies. Though located within the same industry, Hoffman observes that both firms were distinct in their internal organisation; one firm adopted a flexible structure and increased levels of employee-management cooperation, whereas the other had a more rigid, formalistic hierarchy. Hoffmann demonstrates how these divergent arrangements in effect generate distinct grievance cultures that consequently inspire variant understandings of available choices and appropriate means for resolving disputes (Hoffmann 2003). A further example is provided in Boittin's (2013) work on the legal consciousness of sex workers in China. As centred on the subjects' renditions of abusive experiences while partaking in an illegal activity, Boittin demonstrates that sex workers, with relative ease, were able to name an experience as abusive and/or injurious, and apportion blame to those deemed responsible for it, but only rarely did they ever make claims as they typically presented with an 'against the law' strand of legal consciousness – individuals who know better than to make a legal claim in response to an individual act of abuse. As illegal actors, they assume that a most likely outcome will be that the authorities will disregard their claims (Boittin 2013, 269). Last, this approach has also been deployed within organisational contexts by Marshall (2005) in a study primed on analysing women's legal consciousness in responding to unsolicited sexual attention in the workspace. Here she reports that the structural implementation of grievance procedures often serves to impede subjects' efforts at claims-making and the assertion of workplace rights. Marshall further reports how the execution of policies may come to transform the very definition of sexual harassment and as such fall short of protecting women's rights in the workspace (Marshall 2005).

Thus, informed by the literature, our agenda is to isolate legal consciousness as an interceding variable that may contour the dispute transformation process as individuals progress towards an understanding of experiences as detrimental and deserving of redress, and where they do not. Further, and conversely, how these dispute situations may in turn impact actors' perception of law and legality (Hirsh and Lyons 2010, 271). This scholarship deviates from a limited view of law as simply a tool for normative ordering and conflict resolution in favour of a more constitutive rendering wherein legal consciousness is mirrored in the stories people tell about their everyday lives, including their problems, engaging in disputes and avoiding conflict (see Ewick and Silbey 1998; Merry 1990).

Part Three: Of the State, the Migrant and Semi-Legality

Deconstructing 'legal status'

Although migration has been intrinsic to humanity's subsistence, a relatively novel emergence is its bureaucratic administration. The subject of legal status via the law is specifically attested to be integral to the migrants' residence in the host state. It pre-sets the terms of migrants' engagement with the state's social institutions including employment, education and social benefits, including what civil protections and resources they may access (Abrego 2011; Calavita 1998; Guild 2004; Kubal 2013). Legal status is dually constructed by 'the law' on the one hand, enacted through the institution of the state, within its remit as the overarching bureaucratic administrator which brings forth with the political and moral authority to control mobility across and within its borders (Calavita 1998; Kubal 2013), and the machinations of individual agency.

The state

The laws that define migrants are multiple, intersecting and indeterminate (Coutin 2011), and their meaning therefore depends on the actions of the state institutions and agents tasked with implementing the law (Chauvin and Garces-Mascarenas 2012). The state in this construction is far from a monolithic figure whose political objectives are always easily apparent or coherent, neither are its enforcement strategies wholly determinate. Instead, the 'state' herein is symbolic of the sum of its administrative functions, which is literally constituted of the various departments, each with different remits, interests and scope of authority, that nonetheless contribute in executing migration policies, albeit acting in tandem or in isolation from one another (Calavita 1998; Kubal 2013). Schuck's (2000) study, for instance, finds that the bulk of immigration decisions on legal statuses are performed closer to the frontline, in arenas far removed from the symbolic locations of state authority. This insight may well be appropriated to account for the interactions with the UK visa application system (including for potential international students) which is heavily reliant on the outsourced services of third-party logistics providers.

These commercial agents effectively act as the bureaucratic gatekeepers between the visa applicant and the UK state.[10]

This portrait illustrates how the state's complex bureaucratic structure will often mean that the de facto implementation of immigration policies may come to be influenced by negotiations, power struggles and trade-offs involving a range of state and third-party actors. This can prompt a significant rift between substance and implementation. For instance, a Law Society study found that almost 50 per cent of UK immigration and asylum appeals are upheld, which it said was 'clear evidence of serious flaws in the way visa and asylum applications are being dealt with' (Law Society 2018). Yet on the other part, these structures may well be enforced just as intended even when the results are seemingly unpleasant or unfair. More so, it is documented in the scholarship how duly constituted institutions weaponise the exclusivity of citizenship in the promulgation and enforcement of immigration laws and policies. The widely publicised Windrush generation scandal in 2018 in the UK is an apt illustration. This incident involved thousands of immigrants from the Caribbean who had arrived in the UK between 1948 and 1971 to mitigate labour shortfalls and rebuild the UK economy following the Second World War.[11] Most had been living in the UK for decades and found themselves unfairly classified as illegal immigrants, following which many had lost their jobs, were made homeless, were denied healthcare, and faced detention in immigration holding facilities and deportation to countries they had long left as children and with which had maintained minimal ties. This unfair treatment had been due to lapses in the British immigration system (BBC 2018) and was politically underpinned by the 'hostile environment policy' initiated by former prime minister Theresa May during her time as the Home Secretary (2010–016) to tackle illegal immigration.[12] A Commons Select Committee Report on the matter concluded that

---

10. While the Home Office remains responsible for reaching decisions on visa applications, potential applicants will rarely interact directly with the Home Office for the administrative requirements of applying for a visa as third-party commercial intermediaries usually assume the role as the primary point of contact.
11. The Home Office, however, failed to maintain records or issue relevant paperwork to those granted leave to remain within this cohort, more so, the landing cards that may have otherwise provided evidence that they had emigrated to the UK legally had been destroyed by the Home Office in 2010. This cumulatively made it especially tenuous for the Windrush generation to prove that they had legal rights of residence in the UK.
12. This environment brought with it changes to immigration policy beginning in 2012, which require non-citizens to present documentation that proves their legal immigration status prior to seeking employment, renting property or accessing benefits, including healthcare (Gayle 2018).

the Windrush scandal demonstrates a combination of a lack of concern about the real-world impact of the Home Office's immigration policies compounded by a systemic failure to keep accurate records, meaning many people who are British Citizens or have leave to remain in the UK do not have the paperwork to prove it.[13]

Meanwhile, commentators have been equally damning in their critique of the institution (Perkins and Quinn 2018) as these and likeminded occurrences, albeit decried, form part of the state's remit in so far as it is a consequence of its bureaucratic provisions in respect of the weaponisation of migration control.[14]

The migrant

For the migrant, it is well noted that the subject of legal status exceeds a rudimentary label that distinguishes non-citizens with regards the substance of their legal relationship with the state. It presents far-reaching implications for the individual and is undoubtedly fundamental to their paths to incorporation and overall subsistence, just as it intends for them to act in subservience to the terms prescribed by it (Abrego 2011; Calavita 1998; Kubal 2013). In the growing literature, it is noted how immigration regimes are often implemented in ways that engender apprehension and precarity in the lives of all classes of migrants, but especially for the legally tenuous, undocumented or irregular migrant (Abrego 2011; Calavita 1998; Kubal 2013). For the *irregular*, this is renowned to markedly predispose them to a range of detriments, from stigmatisation and fugitivity, to disruption and uncertainty (Bacon 2008; Hagan et al. 2010; Kubal 2013; Yngvesson 2006).

The present socio-legal scholarship has also accounted for the various mediums and avenues through which migrant legal status and bureaucratic structures may interfere with the lives of migrants in distinct spheres. Studies from this scholarship have since documented the debilitating implications of immigration law and policies especially as they perpetuate and reinforce systemic violence by way of social marginalisation and exclusion, and condemnation to life in the underground socio-economy due to their preclusion from accessing resources only accruable to 'citizens' with full membership or indeed more regular non-citizens (Abrego 2011; Calavita 1998; Kubal 2013). Calavita

---

13. 'Windrush Generation and the Home Office'. Available at https://publications.parliament.uk/pa/cm201719/cmselect/cmpubacc/1518/151803.htm.
14. For further commentary on the Windrush scandal, see Hewitt (2020) and Tuckett (2019).

(1998), in a case study of migrants caught within the Spanish immigration regime, asserts that their ensuing experiences of exclusion and marginalisation are a direct consequence of ambiguous Spanish immigration laws. Their circumstance is the result of persistent interjections from the state bureaucracy regarding legal status which is structured in a way that in reality guarantees them impermanence and irregularity. According to Calavita (1998), the law and the state are complicit in perpetuating 'irregularity' in subtle ways, effected through unavoidable lapses built into the immigration system, and the construction of 'illegality' more or less thrives off a variety of intersecting factors, including the contingency of legal status and a range of bureaucratic catch–22s.

Meanwhile Abrego (2008) in a study primed on revealing the effects of a California State Assembly Bill granting undocumented migrant students an exemption from non-resident tuition rates in higher educational institutions, reports of the malleability of legal consciousness in more collective contexts as migrant students used the language of 'justice' to claim legitimate spaces for themselves in higher education, notwithstanding their tenuous legal status. Abrego continues that in contrast to their adult counterparts who were socialised in their home countries, the undocumented youths' interpretations of law were largely informed by American socio-capitalist values that venerate meritocracy. She concludes that the role of life-stage at migration and work-versus-school contexts importantly inform immigrants' legal consciousness, while fear dominates in the legal consciousness of first-generation undocumented immigrants, the legal consciousness of the younger generation veered towards stigma (Abrego 2008, 730). Subsequently, Abrego (2018) demonstrates how the legal consciousness of the erstwhile undocumented beneficiaries of the Obama administration's Deferred Action for Childhood Arrivals[15] shifted towards a greater sense of nationalistic pride and belonging in the United States. Especially as it concerns migrant labour and legal status, Gleeson (2010) in a legal consciousness and mobilisation study of undocumented immigrant-workers in the United States, finds that being undocumented, in particular, leaves immigrants with an exceptionally pragmatic and short-term understanding of their working life in the United States, rendering their working conditions temporary and endurable to them (see also Abrego 2018).

However, these works are somewhat indicative of the broader socio-legal literature on migration and legalities where there is laden a focus on irregular,

---

15. An executive action that provided deportation relief, a temporary work permit and driver licenses for almost 800,000 undocumented immigrants who grew up in the United States.

undocumented or indeed 'illegal' migrant groups. This apparent slant towards legally tenuous migrants is understandable, if for no other reason than the sheer emotiveness of notions that an individual may be *illegal* or *flawed* solely due to some policy-oriented designation, and transnational mobility. As a negative, however, this approach is inherently problematic for reasons which we discuss in the following section.

The Concept of Semi-Legality and the Student-Migrant-Worker

The centring of a migrants' legal status according to state rules in the bulk of the literature, although poignant, is somewhat dated. For one, this goes against the spirit of classical jurisprudence readings, only acts are criminal or illegal, not the individual that perpetuates them (Edwards 2019; Kubal 2013). Then its prevalent deployment sees the risk of illegality being an umbrella term, a *go-to designation* for all migrant conduct that strays from the confines prescribed by the state regardless of gravity, from illegal entry to the country, overstaying, to illegal employment, leaving little flexibility for a more nuanced understanding of the gradations therein. Furthermore, the construct of illegality through migration also denotes elements of criminality, even in instances where none exist. For instance, 'illegal' or 'irregular' migration is often stretched to include individuals who intend but are yet to make an asylum claim, especially as international law edicts provide that refugees should not be punished or deemed criminal for extra-legal entry into the state (Kubal 2013).

> Bogus asylum-seekers, economic refugees or transit migration, became codes for illegal migration [...] the concept often overlaps with other controversial forms and practices of migration such as human smuggling, human trafficking, but also with the flow of refugees. (Düvell 2008, 484)

Succinctly, there is a looming intellectual dissonance if we are to capture every aberrant context of migrant's agency as outrightly within the spheres of illegality, as 'these sorts of binary, black and white oppositions have little reference to real-life, empirical phenomena' (Kubal 2013, 562). These concerns inter alia have consequently caused a number of immigration scholars and international institutions to advocate for replacing the term illegal migrant/migration for a more euphemistic, or morally neutral, construct. Düvell (2008) adopts the phrase 'clandestine migration' as 'clandestine exit, journey and entry, clandestine residence and clandestine employment' (p. 486). Meanwhile international bodies including the United Nations opt for 'irregular migrants' as allusion to persons who do not fulfil the requirements established by the country of destination to enter, stay or exercise economic activity.[16] De Genova (2002), somewhat amusingly proffers the term 'formal illegality' deemed to exist within the structures of immigration bureaucracy.

Although these efforts to move away from the concept of illegality can be applauded, these propositions are mere euphemisms and empirically fall short of accounting for the full range of intricacies regarding migrant behaviour and the conditions that we already know to exist (De Genova 2002; Duvell 2008; Kubal 2013). Further, these formulations do not quite function in respect of student-migrants who retain legal rights to remain, but engage in paid employment beyond the extents permitted by their visas, say for example by working in excess of the allotted 20 hours per week limits. It would seem that 'for 20 hours a day [*sic*] they are perfectly legal immigrants, but for the remaining three hours they are covert/illegal immigrant workers' (Düvell 2008, 48). Or indeed where the student's de facto employment relationship potentially broaches into proscribed designations of independent contractor or genuine self-employment, but indeterminately so pending formal legal determination.[17] Both these instances give way to a *Schrodinger-esque* state where the individual can be both legal and illegal, regular and irregular, or indeed fluctuate between both ends dependent on the context of employment.

The literature reveals a number of theoretical propositions in service of capturing irregular migrant activity that effectively straddles the monotonous divide between legal and illegal. These include the 'in-betweens' proposed by Schuck (1998), 'liminal migrants' as understood by Menjiver (2006), 'quasi-legal' per Düvell (2008), 'a-legal' per Lindahl (2010), 'semi-legal' (He 2005; Kubal 2009; Rytter 2012), and 'semi-compliant' (Ruhs and Anderson 2010). Further, it should be noted that this list is not intended to be exhaustive. These conceptions all allude in some way to the grey areas that exist between legal and illegal conduct surrounding migration bureaucracy and are all innovative and thoughtful in some way. However, perhaps the most elaborate construct, and one that is especially relevant here, is Kubal's vision of 'semi-legality' which she so eloquently deploys as a multidimensional heuristic and analytical schema to capture the range of behaviours that implicate not entirely compliant responses to immigration regulations. According to Kubal (2013), semi-legality can be deployed to account for the avenues wherein migrants' formal relationship with the state defined as legal status may interact with various structures of agency and result in circumstances that blur the confines between acceptable and unacceptable conduct relating to migration and migrants.

---

16. Programme of Action of the International Conference on Population and Development (ICPD 1994).
17. See Chapter 5 'The Student-Migrant + Temporary Agency Worker = Precarity?'

Although state bureaucracy administers the legal frameworks that determine the legality of migrants' entry, residence and employment (Ghosh 1998; Ruhs and Anderson 2010; Tapinos 1999), it would be a disservice to assume that the interactions brought on by structures of migration and employment are exclusively the responsibility of state bureaucracy. Migrants as complex social actors can choose to act in ways that blur the definitions of legally sanctioned behaviour of immigration precepts. Semi-legality is cognisant of this and accords migrants' agency as co-participants in the co-production of meaning and consequence (Kubal 2013):

> Semi-legality can therefore range from migrants' interactions with law, demonstrating a divide between legal and 'illegal' is not a strict dichotomy, rather a tiered and multifaceted relationship with degrees of membership that distinguish beyond citizens, permanent legal temporary legal residents, and 'other' migrants. (p. 567)

Kubal then proceeds to identify three broad conditions that can give rise to semi-legality for future research, the first of which is brought on by incomplete responses to immigration regularisation programs. The second is driven by migrants' mobility in efforts to equalise the temporality of residence in the host state; with *under-staying* at one end, and overstaying on the other. The final condition, and especially relevant for this study, is semi-legality engendered by the intersection where employment privileges meet immigration control (Gonzales 2011; Kubal 2009, 2012b; Ruhs 2010).

Semi-legality aptly captures the circumstance of student-workers who may be engaging in employment beyond the terms of their visa. They are acting in a legal sense in that they maintain their 'leave to remain' and indeed work, but only so far because they work in excess of the employment restrictions attached to their immigration status. Insights provided by Ruhs and Anderson (2010), whose frame of 'semi-compliance' closely parallels semi-legality in its representation of a contested terrain of legality, is especially relevant here (Kubal 2013; Ruhs and Anderson 2010). Per Ruhs and Anderson (2010), semi-compliance alludes to 'a situation where a migrant is legally resident but working in violation of some or all of the employment restrictions attached to his/her immigration status' (p. 1).

Furthermore, stepping outside the confines of immigration control in this way is not without its implications, this much being illustrated in Ruhs and Anderson's (2010) study on Eastern European workers undertaking employment in the UK albeit in breach of their residence permits. The authors demonstrate how semi-compliance pushes migrant-workers into low-pay, low-skilled employment located in niche industries infamous for erratic law enforcement and employers with questionable intentions who are equally culpable, especially as it provides them with cheap, disposable labour. Focusing on a similar cohort, Kubal (2009, 2012a) demonstrates how Eastern European (post-EU enlargement) migrants as newly recognised EU citizens likewise sought employment in the UK in violation of immigration policies (Accession 2004 Regulations) and employment regulations.[18] Here, Kubal reports of an array of implications brought on by semi-legality within the context of migrant labour, reflecting both regularity at one end, detraction and uncertainty at the other (Kubal 2013).

Yet, semi-legality, as understood by Kubal (2013) or semi-compliance per Ruhs and Anderson (2010) as analytical frames do more than account for a middle ground between legal-illegal migrant behaviour and merely noting how migrants may be worse off for it. Semi-legality marks out a terrain of opportunity and defiance just as it does for despair. While engaging migrant-workers under semi-legal conditions may provide complicit employers and employment brokers access to a malleable workforce ripe for deployment as cost-cutting instruments, it equally provides a path for migrants to earning possibilities that would be otherwise unobtainable with complete compliance with work restrictions attached to their terms of entry. In this way, semi-legality effectively poses an existential critique of the stereotypical depiction of migrant-workers as a victimised collective prone to abuse due to their socio-economic situatedness, and more so presents a forum for enacting resistance (Anderson 2010; Kubal 2013).

We now turn our discussion to how our study intends to further develop the understanding of semi-legality, using student-migrant employment as a demographic, and how this informs our socio-legal objectives.

Semi-Legality as a Dynamic, Varied and Intricate Process

Although the scholarly contributions from Ruhs and Anderson (2010) and Kubal (2013) have ably highlighted the existence of grey areas that exist in breaching the monotonous demarcations between legal and illegal, they also treat the subject as if it were an end-state, as opposed to a processual phenomenon that requires wilful agency and intentionality on the part of the actor. Specifically, in respect of the subjects of our study, these works have stopped

---

18. Kubal highlights how these subjects were, on the one hand, at times compliant with UK workplace regulations, such as with regards to National Insurance provisions and taxation, meanwhile they were working in violation of immigration regulations and especially the Workers' Registration Scheme, a prerequisite attached to their status as 'accession nationals', on the other hand.

short of questioning the specific nuances presented by student migration and employment structures. Although reprieve is due because these scholars do not explicitly set out to capture student-migrants, the extant corpus of knowledge on the topic remains sporadic. For example, while both Ruhs and Anderson (2010) and Kubal (2013) note that the employment of student-migrants may broach into semi-legality/compliance where they work for more than the legally prescribed 20 hours per week, for which there will be graded receptiveness depending on the extent of violation (i.e. a student working 21 hours a week is likely to be more tolerated than another who works for 40 hours, (Ruhs and Anderson 2010)), they pay little attention to other visa restrictions that exist beyond this. This is especially so those that proscribe student-workers from undertaking business activities as independent contractors or self-employed agents, and how the specific context of semi-legality may differentially affect the actor's experiences and meaning-making process, especially in everyday, socio-legal contexts.

More so, these attempts to subsume students within broader migrant-labour populations renders only a superficial portrait that does little to account for their exceptional circumstance. Student-migrants, unlike other categories of migrant-workers, are not formally recognised as labourers because this betrays the stated intents of their admission into the country, which is for academic endeavours. On the contrary, it is expected that an overseas education will entail the individual expending substantial resources. A further novel contemplation is thus the contextualisation of semi-legal economic activity in spite of the state's concerted stance against all forms of unauthorised migrant-labour efforts to keep *students as students*. Semi-legality appropriated to the context of student-migrant-workers must be framed in light of the bureaucratic measures and approaches put in place to pre-empt migrants' *illicit* labour market participation, more specifically the 'whole government approach' and 'degrees of harm' highlighted previously.[19] A reading of semi-legality is fragmented in as much as it excludes an examination of the migrant's agency as they try to evade or resist the detriments associated with these structures, including whatever forms these efforts may assume, acting individually or in tandem with accomplices, and the implications of this.

The corpus of literature deals with this matter in a fleeting manner. Ruhs and Anderson (2010) have intimated that semi-legality and migrant-labour often involve the connivance of both the worker and employer, especially as their socioeconomic interests become aligned – migrant-workers as target wage earners on the one part and the employers' desire for cheap, disposable

---

19. See Chapter 3 'The student-migrant-worker and the state: Keeping students as students'.

labour on the other. Meanwhile, the likes of Nyland et al. (2009) report of students engaging in employment for periods longer than permitted per their visas having to work hours spread over two jobs, especially without the employer's knowledge due to trust issues. It thus becomes apparent that the process of semi-legality may consequently implicate and subsume an assortment of arrangements and patterns that may potentially present with varying implications, with legal vulnerabilities for the actor involved. Succinctly, we know less of how factors such as these may affect the students' engagement in semi-legal work, or indeed how these motions may serve to reify or counteract precarity associated with the transience of their residence in the host state.

Another aspect of the literature on semi-legality in need of examination has to do with the ways in which engaging in semi-legal work may extend to other facets of the individual's lived reality as a multidimensional entity. Menjivar (2000) has alluded to the pertinence of legal status as a dominant feature in the lived reality of migrants, with potentially far–reaching implications for their interactions with other social structures in the host state (Kubal 2013; Menjivar 2000, 2006). Menjivar (2006) illustrates this while appropriating from the legal pluralist conception of society as being composed of several distinct semi-autonomous spheres that represent aspects of social life including social networks, family, employment, relationships and so on. In this understanding, an individual's legal relationship with the state as delineated by immigration status potentially seeps into their relationship with other social institutions. Menjivar (2000) concludes that there is in effect a hierarchal structure to these semi-autonomous spheres for which immigration status through the law assumes a principal position. Meanwhile scholars including Cvajner and Sciortino (2010) have instead contended that while it may be conceded that notions of legality may be transmitted into the other facets of the individual's life, it may not always assume dominance. These scholars assert that the individual's immigration status may bear pertinent implications for their broader social situatedness, but this is only relevant in situations where the migrant's legal designation directly impedes their agency in these other social realms in very specific dimensions (Cvajner and Sciortino 2010, 397). In this understanding, legality within the context of immigration control does not define the entirety of 'self,' but rather an aspect thereof and only where relevant (see Coutin 2000; Cvajner and Sciortino 2010; Kubal 2016).

Nonetheless, the prevalent readings on the experiences engendered by irregular migration informs us of how their tenuous legal status brings with it far-reaching potential for the individual's life in terms of finding employment, accommodation, raising a family and so on. But these can be perceived as worse circumstances with a direness that cannot be effectively appropriated to account for semi-legality as a mitigated state of legality. While it is plausible to assume that the context of semi-legality in terms of student-migrant-workers may not elicit such dire consequences, there is an implicit concession for the potential of semi-compliance/legality as neither entirely isolated nor closed off from other facets of the individual's affairs, to what extent remains to be accounted for in the extant corpus of knowledge. Thus, we consider it crucial to account for the ways students' *semi-legal* relations may be implicated in other aspects of their lived realities. And it is at this juncture the concepts of precarity, legal consciousness and mobilisation identified prior all become relevant.

Socio-Legal Study Objectives

At its most fundamental, our study sets out to account for the employment experiences of student-migrants especially nuanced by the socio-legal distinctions of migration, whilst appropriating from the schematic frames of semi-legality, precarity, legal consciousness and legal mobilisation.

First, as previously noted,[20] a review of the existing scholarship reveals a dearth in knowledge as it relates to the various means and strategies through which semi-legality is enacted de facto within the contexts of student-migrant employment, and how these divergent strategies may impact the individual's legal consciousness and mobilisation efforts. The literature identifies that undocumented migrants as marginalised subjects are mostly given to an 'against the law' strand of legal consciousness marked by a resistance to legality, just as their precarious legal status deems them unwilling to access legal resources as a medium for dispute resolution and claims-making (see Abrego 2011, 2018; Gleeson 2010; Kubal 2013). However, whether or not this insight holds true for semi-legality, a tempered form of legality remains to be seen. Likewise, it can be assumed that engaging in semi-legality can bring with it distinct implications for the individual's legal mobilisation prospects and disputing behaviour in the workplace; this reading is informed by the well-documented portrayal of migrant-workers' especially precarious legal status and employment relationships as perhaps the most vulnerable yet unlikeliest group of workers to contest labour abuse and exploitation (Bernhardt et al. 2009). How and to what extent this applies to student-migrants engaging in semi-legal employment is yet to be concluded. For instance, while undocumented and irregular migrants may be fated to life in the underground economy, outside of formal institutions ab initio (Abrego 2011, 2018; Bernhardt et al. 2009; Bosniak 2008; Gleeson 2010; Kubal 2013), a student working in breach of immigration conditions attached to their status may

---

20. As noted in 'The Concept of Semi-legality and the Student-Migrant-Worker' above.

encounter minimal hindrances accessing public services including healthcare and education. However, they may encounter vulnerabilities in asserting their employment rights or pursuing recourse in the event of workplace grievances (Bosniak 2008).

Thus, given its underlying and recurrent manifestations in the lived reality of subjects, the process of semi-legality and the potential for insecurity engenders may assume a normative dimension that can serve to shape the way workers come to perceive the law, and react to indiscretions in the workplace. However, there been little empirical evidence to confirm this.

These insights inform this study's overarching socio-legal objective that seeks out the ways through which the various devises of semi-legality may impact the student-migrants' disposition towards law. That is, how semi-legality impacts actors' participation in the reproduction of legality according to their legal consciousness, and their claims-making behaviour as regards grievances emanating from the workplace, in the manner of legal mobilisation.

Second, building from the previously stated theorisations, this study frames discernible semi-legal behaviour largely as a strategic response to notions of socioeconomic inequity and precarity. Subsequently, we present a nuanced vision of semi-legality as an empirical schema which is reflected in the various strategies these students may undertake in their attempts to navigate and often times, resist, the contours on what makes for acceptable and unacceptable conduct in respect of student migration precepts and employment. In particular we note how this process implicates notions of precarity and inequities in their lived experiences as subjects of immigration control. This is in acknowledgement of its potential as a forum of resistance against the convergent mediums of precarity and socioeconomic disadvantage engendered by the socio-legal, political and economic structures that mediate their employment contexts and residence in the UK. In this framing, semi-legality is enabled by the complex interactions and associated trade-offs that ensue involving students adopting the role of migrant-workers as they travail through a novel terrain especially rife with the potential for exploitation, just as it does for opportunity. More so, we undertake to unravel the forms of participation and interpretation through which the student-migrant-workers sustain, reproduce or amend the circulating structures of meanings concerning law, as it serves to constrain or amplify their agency in their attempts to manoeuvre and resist the 'they say(s)' and 'supposed to(s)' presented by the intersection of migration, study and employment (Sarat 2004). This is the exchange which this study sets out to capture towards a more critical rendition of the constitutive theory of law in society.

Chapter 5

THE 'STUDENT-MIGRANT-WORKER' MEETS 'PRECARITY'

Introduction

In this chapter we begin by exploring the literature surrounding the employment experiences of student-migrant-workers in respect of migrant labour, their position within the broader labour market and how this interaction potentially engenders notions of insecurity for the individual. This approach provides the context on which the empirical evidence presented in this study is assessed. First, we situate student-migrant-workers within the broader literature surrounding migrant labour, noting the distinctions that set them apart from other cadres of migrant-workers. This segues to a discussion of the analytical framework of precarity, highlighting its relevance to the study population. We contextualise this conversation through a discussion of atypical forms of work that fall under the auspices of 'precarious' employment. The focus then progresses to one example of atypical employment relationships, TAW, illustrating its allure to the student-migrant-worker population and its detrimental features that are present in precarious employment. The socioeconomic profile and legal indeterminacies surrounding the employment status of workers engaged in this work form are also considered. We close the chapter with an explanation of how the empirical objectives on which this book is based are informed by the relative dearth of literature surrounding the student-migrant-worker population with regard to the analytical frame of precarity.

Unravelling the Employment Experiences of Student-Migrants

In the UK, much of the existing scholarship on migrant work has focused not on international students, but rather individuals engaged in various forms of atypical forms of employment (including both national workers and non-nationals) and their lived experiences,[1] the lived experiences of irregular

---

1. See, for instance, McBride and Smith (2018) on atypical employment and the experiences of UK-based workers as it applies to their pay, working contracts and

migrants, and migrants from the European Union (EU) and their experiences before and after the UK's withdrawal from the EU.[2] A limited number of studies have considered the position of international students as migrant-workers. First, the student-migrant-worker population and their labour market participation has been explored from the perspective of sending countries (e.g. Gribble 2008). In respect of specific jurisdictional studies, in an Australian context, Robertson (2011) has assessed the notion of international students and the social and political consequences of the education-migration nexus in Australia. Specifically focusing on employment laws and policies, Howe (2019), while noting the limitation of international students, as a cohort, as a focus of labour law scholarship, provides an insight into the vulnerability of international students in domestic labour markets in a comparative study of Australia and the UK.

As outlined in earlier chapters,[3] the literature on student-migrants and their mobilities, generally, and certainly within a UK context, is limited, and this paucity of material extends to the subject of the migrant-workers' experiences of temporary employment while enrolled as a student. Notwithstanding the apparent scarcity of concise, up-to-date data on the extent and context of this migrant group's involvement in temporary employment, it is possible to draw upon the broader scholarship on migrant labour in the UK, with reference to studies concerning the experiences of international student-workers from other national contexts with bureaucratic structures akin to that in the UK.[4] This provides, at the very least, an indicative understanding of what can come of this interaction.

Migrant-workers, irrespective of legal status, are documented as constituting a vulnerable group in workspaces across most industrial states, not just in the UK. Their labour market profile has been consistently associated with positions of disadvantage; they tend to populate low-skilled and low-pay roles, with little prospect of career development; they are reportedly prone to encounter inhumane work conditions including little to no work benefits, breaks or requisite safety equipment; and there are systematic ill-practices including pay below statutory minimums, wage theft, unlawful pay deductions and so

---

multiple employer relationships; and Alberti (2020) and Alberti et al. (2018) on similar themes as they apply to migrant-workers.
2. On the matter of the change in the law affecting EU citizens following the UK's withdrawal from the EU, and in particular the legal and economic consequences on the immigration systems, see Portes (2016) and in respect of residence rights of EU citizens in the UK see O'Brien (2021).
3. See Chapter 3 'Moving on from trends' and 'Towards centring the student-migrant-worker'.
4. This includes countries and bodies such as Australia, the EU and the United States.

on to report of (see Benach et al. 2011; Fernández-Reino and Rienzo 2020; Milkman et al. 2010). Then there are temporalities associated with migratory processes and difficulties associated with the job search process that reify their overdependence on specific jobs and employers (Dean 2018; Williams 2009). Finally and furthermore, their inherent racial distinctiveness often leaves them as being subject to discriminatory and xenophobic attacks in and outside of the workplace (Gayle 2018; the International Labour Office 2010).

It is apparent that the student-migrant workforce represents only a peripheral proportion of the entire migrant labour population in the UK. The most recent statistics available demonstrate that there are in total 3.65 million migrant-workers in the UK, who share a range of attributes that likely contour their employment experience (Office of National Statistics (ONS 2020)). These features may include financial difficulty following the costs of migration, the naïveté that comes with being placed in novel terrain without a social and family support network, an absence of cultural awareness of their new surroundings and a lack of knowledge of the local labour market. Similarly, they often have a poor knowledge of rights at work lack and are unable to access forms of social security that underpin the position of domestic workers, this includes exclusion from access to welfare benefits (Kubal 2012b; Nyland et al. 2009). The situation is compounded by parochial and predatory behaviour on the part of many employers and employment brokers who have been found to prey on recent migrants, including students (Nyland et al. 2009).

The handful of published studies that have contributed to the body of literature all seem to replicate such a dismal portrait. Ruhs and Anderson's (2010) report of EU student-migrants in the UK and found evidence of this group being driven to low-pay, low-skilled employment located in niche industries infamous for light regulations and employers with 'questionable' intentions. In respect of the same demographic, Kubal (2009, 2012b) documents the range of experiences encountered by East-European (post-EU enlargement) student-migrant-workers in the UK. Kubal observed how the student-migrant-workers often underwent both steady engagement (with a contract of employment) and precarious employment. From having taxes deducted for some, with some or none being deducted for others. From engagement in a workplace that respects labour laws, to those that blatantly abuse them. Kubal, however, found that even when attaining EU citizenship, such a status did little to shield the workers from falling prey to unscrupulous employers and discriminatory practices in UK labour spaces (Kubal 2012b). Further, the psychological impacts of balancing academic interests with extensive work hours have also been identified in the literature. Findings have portrayed international students as being prone to experience anxiety and stress-related ailments, and other reports suggest student-workers tend to present with increased rates of work-related injuries and commonly experience inadequate sleep and exercise (Neill et al. 2004; Nyland et al. 2009). Nyland et al. (2009) allude to similar findings in a study primed on the employment experiences of 200 international students studying in Australian universities. Evidently, each of these characteristics are likely to impede classroom performance and the overall well-being of the student.

Following from their study in 2009, Nyland et al. (2009) proceed to argue for the inclusion of student-migrants in policy and academic discourses centred around vulnerable workers. This was based on their findings that this group of workers are often compelled to undertake employment in very poor and exploitative conditions. While a similar agenda is yet to be replicated within UK contexts, it is pertinent to note that these studies stop short of detailing the holistic experiences of student-migrant-workers in a way that accounts for their location within the broader labour market structure and its socio-legal underpinnings. This insight is critical because acknowledging student-migrants as vulnerable and in need of support is one thing, but as far as actionable agendas go, this works less with a fragmented depiction, absent of the structural contexts of the labour market within which they participate in the first place, and more so how migration precepts interact with this.

Our study takes on this task, albeit with a novel twist. In documenting the experiences of these student-migrants we opt for the empirical schema of 'precarity' with its roots in the industrial relations scholarship, as this frame, we feel, more aptly reflects the experiences of the student-migrant-workers, for reasons discussed in the following section.

Analysing Precarity and the Migration Scholarship

'Precarity' is far from a novel concept in readings centred on industrial relations. This theory has been alluded to by classical sociological scholars including Durkheim in his 'Division of Labour' (1933), Marx (1887) in his theorisations of the labour process and alienation and Weber (1978) in respect of bureaucracy and social closure. While in synonymy with other sociological constructs, it is perhaps impossible to present a unanimous definition of 'precarity' as an analytical schema. The concept, in its most prevalent deployment, has been linked with contingent labourers' experiences of the intersecting socioeconomic insecurities that plague their employment (Beck 1992; Sennet 1998). The term, however, achieved peak popularity in academia following Guy Standing's (2011) work *The Precariat: The New Dangerous Class* where he portrayed the 'precariat' as a new, global, 'class in the making'. This work catalysed its recognition as an analytic framework of empirical value.

A review of the literature reveals two distinct albeit related readings of precarity. Scholars including Standing (2011) advocate for a segmented approach based entirely on employment structures. Standing (2011) develops the concept of 'the precariat' in allusion to a worker given to forms of insecure employment. Employment that often features erratic labour demands, indeterminate contractual obligations, minimal opportunities for training and career progression, income insecurity, and work contexts where labour standards including unfair dismissal protection, redundancy and union representation have minimal penetration (Kalleberg and Sørensen 1979). Alternatively, scholars including Butler (2006) and Ettlinger (2007) opt for a broader reading, premised on notions that insecurity is an intrinsic feature of social existence, and thus look to account for the ways precarious employment can serve to potentially exacerbate workers' lived experiences of involuntary insecurity and unpredictability.

Albeit noting the reasonable connection between both concepts, it is apparent that the broader theorisation has a greater holistic resonance here as it simultaneously subsumes and expands on the narrower agenda primed exclusively on employment structures. This is more so nuanced by an understanding that the uncertainties engendered by insecure work cannot be considered in abstract to the individual's broader socioeconomic and legal situatedness. According to Paret and Gleeson (2016), 'an analysis of precarity [...] calls for the study of broader political and economic shifts, and how they reshape the relationships between individuals and groups on the one hand, and capital and the state on the other' (p. 280). Consequently, what sets precarity apart from other likeminded empirical constructs, for example 'vulnerability', is that it locates the individual spatio-temporally within the convergence of intersecting institutional precepts (albeit historical, political, socio-legal and economic), while accounting for their agency as multidimensional actors (Beck 1992; Paret and Gleeson 2016; Sennet 1998). It is in this milieu that scholars, especially within the British and Canadian literature, have recently begun to appropriate the framework of 'precarity' to analytically account for the insecurities encountered by migrant-labourers (Paret and Gleeson 2016). This approach is fit for the purposes of our study as it brings together convergent renderings of insecurity brought forth by the contemporary labour market landscape on the one hand, and by the inherent temporalities associated with processes of migration and migrants on the other. This schema more so assumes a critical front, centred on the state as it exercises its moral authority to regulate the residence and behaviour of migrants as new entrants into its territory, and those prompted by a neo-liberal labour market deeply pervaded by the constant need for non-committal workers and contingent employment relationships (Kalleberg and Sørensen 1979; Paret and Gleeson 2016).

The critical undertaking herein searches for a nuanced understanding of the implications of these intersecting features, that is, whether they are contradictory, reinforcing or entirely isolated from each other. More so, it examines the ways through which actors come to interact with these structures, the manifested spaces and the patterns of resistance to the trappings of uncertainty that can permeate their everyday mobilities (Paret and Gleeson 2016).

Typifying precarious employment

'Precarious work' is a euphemism for employment that is uncertain, unpredictable, transient and risky, especially from the workers' point of view (Kalleberg 2008). This idea made its way into the industrial lexicon following French anthropologist Pierre Bourdieu's study differentiating the experiences of casual workers from their permanent counterparts in Algeria (see Waite 2009, 414). Rodgers and Rodgers (1989) describes four principal dimensions that make for precarious employment: (i) the degree of certainty of continuing employment; (ii) control over the labour process, which is linked to the presence or absence of trade unions and professional associations, and relates to control over working conditions, wages, and the pace of work; (iii) the degree of regulatory protection; and (iv) income level (p. 1). Per dual labour market theories, precariousness is hypothesised to fester within the secondary/informal divide, and is typified by low pay, disposable labour, entry-level/frontline job roles, minimal progression prospects, and is clustered within specific industries (Jayaweera and Anderson 2008; van Riemsdijk 2014; Zou 2016).[5]

It is, however, impossible to discuss precarious work without contextualising it as a representation of employment arrangements that do not present with the securities and/or continuity associated with typical, more traditional '9–5's with its guarantees of definite contractual obligations, work hours, wages and/or location for work performance (Choonara 2019). These divergent employment forms have been referenced in a myriad ways: alternative work arrangements (Polivka 1996; Sherer 1996), market-mediated arrangements (Abraham 1990), non-traditional employment relations (Ferber and Waldfogel 1998), temporary and flexible staffing arrangements (Abraham 1990), non-standard working practices (Brewster et al. 1997), atypical employment (Cordova 1986; De Grip et al. 1997; Delsen 1995), nomadic and/or peripheral employment (Summers 1997), disposable work

---

5. Sectors where migrant-workers are known to be concentrated include agriculture, construction, hospitality, the care sector and in domestic help.

(Gordon 1996), new forms of employment (Bronstein 1991), and contingent work (Belous 1989; Polivka and Nardone 1989) to mention but a few.[6]

The Antecedents and Proliferation of Precarious Work and Atypical Employment Relationships

To understand precarious employment, one must predicate it as a marked deviation from typical or standard employment arrangements, through the proliferation of alternative, flexible working arrangements in the contemporary labour market. Indeed, it is argued that the prevalence of these alternative employment forms calls for the abandoning of labels including atypical or non-standard employment as this betrays the de facto reality that such arrangements may have well become the new typical/standard employment form (Marson 2013; Storrie 2003, 2007).

Although employment contexts that deviate from the norms of assured continuity and security of tenure have always existed in some form, the resurgence and proliferation of alternative, more flexible work arrangements can be vaguely traced back to the mid-1970s (Kallberg 2008). The onset of the 'globalisation era' coupled with the great recession and post-war industrial landscape brought with them steep changes to labour market structures within most developed countries. These changes unequivocally reworked the relationship dynamics and sanctity that had previously existed between relevant stakeholders in the labour production process, including workers, employers, trade unions and the state (Kallberg 2008; Quak and Van de Vijsel 2014). This period coincided with languid economic growth, which saw industries struggle to generate the requisite fiscal resources to retain a dedicated workforce. Indeed, the rigidity of definite employment relationships left little leeway for firms to adequately respond to fast-changing markets, just as the onset of globalisation reified the erosion of market borders and steeper competition amongst firms and workers alike on an international scale (Boulin et al. 2006; Kallberg 2008). The need to operate as efficiently and in as profitable a way as was practicable increasingly called for cost-cutting, especially as technological advancements curtailed the reliance on physical labour (Boulin et al. 2006; Kallberg 2008). A staunch

---

6. Meanwhile in contemporary mainstream discourse, the 'gig economy' is a common phrase of reference coined in allusion to this very feature of the contemporary labour market marked with a pervasion of temporary and freelance employment relationships. The phrase is derived from each piece of work being akin to an individual 'gig', where workers are engaged for a specific task or a series of intermittent one-off jobs.

reconstruction of the industrial landscape soon followed, this brought with it the emergence of more complex substructures; new levels, new players and institutions; and novel forms of horizontal and vertical relationships, integrations and interrelations across virtually all sectors of the economy (Keune and Marginson 2013). As a negative, however, this consequently gave way to higher unemployment rates, volatility in wage determination, decentralisation of collective bargaining and deregulation of labour standards. A decline in workers' attachment to employers, increases in long-term unemployment, job insecurity and risk-shifting from employers to employees were further consequences of this movement (Kalleberg and Vallas 2017).

Casey (1988), for instance, in documenting the growth of atypical employment within the UK labour market from 1980 to 1984, reported that approximately 20 per cent of organisations engaged the services of contingent staff. Notably by 1987, this proportion had grown to about 50 percent (McGregor and Sproull 1992), and fast-forward to 1998 where more than 61 per cent of firms in the UK workspace utilised the services of temporary workers (Cully et al. 1998). Presently, there are eleven or more identifiable employment arrangements referred to as atypical or non-standard that may be considered types of precarious work, including consultants, casual workers, seasonal workers, fixed-term workers, agency workers and so on, with some categories overlapping each other (per Casey 1988). In the UK, it is estimated that approximately five million people are engaged in these capacities and thus may invoke notions of 'precariousness' (see Biggs 2006; Casey 1988; Office of National Statistics 2018).[7]

However, given the vast array of the employment forms and relationships that can be deemed as precarious work, it is useful to narrow our focus. Thus, for this study we opt for a more sentient approach by focusing on one such example of an 'atypical employment relationship' that frequently appears in discourses of precarious work, TAW. This is particularly apt for this study given that as many as 90 per cent of the 37 participants for this study indicated they had or were presently undertaking work through intermediaries (employment agencies), and therefore we considered that this propensity warranted special consideration.

---

7. While the terms 'agency worker', and 'temporary worker' or 'temp' are terms used interchangeably in reference to non-permanent workers in the contemporary lexicon, they are, however, different, with the former being a type of the latter (Biggs 2003), and both ultimately fall within the ambits of 'atypical work'.

Temporary Agency Work and Its Benefits

TAW is one form of atypical employment that has become a fixture of the contemporary labour market structure throughout the industrial world (Casey 1988). The heterogeneity of this workforce presents difficulties when attempting to form a singular explanation of its features. However, what establishes TAW as unique is the tripartite employment relationship at its core. Although the minutia of each set-up may differ, it typically involves employment agencies who act as intermediaries between job seekers and third-party hiring firms. In its simplest form, the worker is engaged by the employment agency, for supply, to a third-party organisation (Casey 1988; Casey and Alach 2004; Storrie 2003). Davidov (2004) distinguishes these practices into two broad groups depending on the dynamics of the employment relationship between the three parties; in the first group, there is the traditional trilateral relationship where the agency assumes responsibility for the worker,[8] whose services are subcontracted to client-firms on an ad hoc basis. In the second group, there exists a 'payroll' arrangement where the worker is subcontracted to the user firm for a medium to long term, sometimes even indefinitely, and this worker generally performs work in a manner akin to other employees of the firm, albeit the worker is paid by the agency[9] (Davidoff 2004; Mangum et al. 1985). For the student-migrant-workers in our study, the former scenario was the most prevalent form of employment relationship encountered.

Although estimates of the precise extent of this workforce may differ depending on the methodology adopted, the UK temporary agency workforce is thought to be the largest in Europe (ONS 2018). Data from the Labour Force Survey identifies the current figure at approximately 900,000 workers, a 30 per cent rise from 2011, and this figure was set to reach one million before the end of the decade.[10] Agency workers tend also to cluster within certain industries, most notably manufacturing, logistics, communications, health and social work (Judge and Tomlinson 2016).

The literature identifies benefits of TAW for both workers and the user firms. Golden and Appelbaum (1992) assert that the evidenced surge in the agency work industry was less the doing of an all too eager pool of workers keen on this employment form, rather it was the firms' heightened demand for

---

8. Including training, wage determination and reviewing the individual's performance.
9. Outside of rendering 'pay-roll services', the work agency assumes only a peripheral role in this relationship as the core administrative responsibilities, including decisions on hiring, wage-setting, terminations and the allocation and supervision of tasks are dealt with by the user firm.
10. Significant given the subsequent withdrawal by the UK from the European Union and the forecasted slowdown in employment growth post-Brexit.

temporary workers and the concerted entrepreneurial efforts of temporary-employment agencies (Grimshaw et al. 2001). For firms, the most renowned benefit of this work form is the flexibility it enables; TAWs provide a flexible buffer of labour that can be deployed or withdrawn expeditiously in the face of fluctuating employment requirements and market uncertainty (Abraham 1990; Atkinson 1985). Then of course there are financial benefits of engaging the services of agency workers. Temporary agency workers are often utilised by firms as a cost-cutting measure since they frequently are paid at a lower hourly average and require less commitment when compared to permanent employees (Autor and Houseman 2005; Forde and Slater 2005). This means that agency staff may be taken on as new workers without disturbing internal wage structures. More so, employers are not legally mandated to extend non-wage benefits such as National Insurance coverage to agency workers, and these workers may have their employment contracts terminated with lesser costs as they do not qualify for various statutory rights including the dominant claims for redundancy or unfairly dismissal (see Marson 2013). A further benefit for firms is that the engagement of agency workers can pre-empt the troubles associated with recruitment, as the agency assumes these responsibilities. More so, the literature also alludes to agency workers' presence in the workspace as having a positive effect, albeit indirectly, on overall productivity, especially as the engagement of these workers enables the optimal mix of skills and qualities in ways that may complement and/or provide competition for existing staff (Bryson 2013).

For workers, flexibility is often cited as the principal underlining motivation for undertaking agency work (Stabile and Apouey 2019; Hünefeld et al. 2020). Flexibility can manifest itself in this type of employment relationship in a variety of ways, from the agency's ability to match employment arrangements to individual circumstances, to the increase in the individual's control over the hours worked. Flexible working hours – 'flexitime' – is described as an arrangement where workers can decide, within limits, when to begin and end their work each day (Olofsdotter 2012). This can be crucial for individuals who have commitments that run concomitantly with their employment interests, for example, child-care or academic study. An equally important draw is that agency work can serve towards labour market integration by breaking in and providing a speedy route into gainful employment for new entrants (especially recent migrants, young persons, etc. – see Feldman 1994). In this sense, it allows prospective workers to delegate the job search process to recruitment consultants of the agency firm (Casey 1988). A final, and often-cited peripheral benefit is that it enables workers to develop a range of skills that may prove transferrable (Casey 1988; Casey and Alach 2004; Storrie 2003).

Temporary Agency Work as Precarious Employment

Notwithstanding evidence of its reported appeal, agency work has for a long time been associated with precarious employment, even so far as a posterchild for 'bad, undesirable jobs' (Kallberg 2008; McGovern et al. 2004). Disparaging factors associated with this work form range from unfavourable and exploitative work conditions (Judge and Tomlinson 2016; Kallberg 2011; Mitlacher 2008) to low pay[11] and lack of access to statutory benefits including sick pay, occupational pensions (McGovern et al. 2004), underemployment and the proliferation of zero-hour contracts (Judge and Tomlinson 2016), limited opportunities for progression, and training and professional development (Bonet et al. 2013; Booth et al. 2002; Knox 2014; Underhill and Quinlan 2011).

Studies have since documented such transience as affecting the socio-economic and psychological state of the worker. Although employment contracts of limited duration are not exclusive to agency work, and indeed some agency workers are engaged on open-ended contracts, there is nonetheless a proliferation of zero-hour contract terms in this work arrangement (Storrie 2007). Zero-hour contracts, for all the flexibility they facilitate, can have detrimental effects for the worker who is often left socioeconomically insecure, and unable to budget effectively for the future (Ball et al. 2017). Storrie argues that this is because agency work is located in the secondary labour market, that happens to be highly dependent on market forces of demand and supply (Storrie 2007). More so, this lack of continuity leaves no guarantees of the availability of suitable work assignments, and studies have documented workers' complaints of shorter-than-expected hours per week and conversely, hours that are too lengthy. Some sectors report of high levels of underemployment, while in others, 'worker satiety' is identified (Ball et al. 2017; Biggs 2003; and Corlett and Gardiner 2015). The unpredictability of work locations is a further avenue for precariousness creep, especially in those TAW arrangements.

When considering its psychological implications, it is noted how being an agency worker may engender social isolation and make it arduous for the individual to cultivate meaningful workplace relationships (Biggs 2003). It is similarly documented how agency workers are more susceptible to sustaining workplace injuries, experiencing harassment and work-related psychological strains, and they are prone to feeling undervalued due to the dispensable

---

11. The Resolution Foundation, for instance, demonstrates that not only do agency workers on average earn up to £2.57 an hour less their non-agency counterparts, there is also in effect a pay penalty of around 22 pence per hour associated with agency staff, which equals to an annual loss of approximately £430 per worker (Judge 2017).

nature of their employment (Connelly and Gallagher 2004; Knox 2014; Mitlacher 2008; Oxenbridge and Moensted 2011; Rogers 2000; Underhill and Quinlan 2011). A survey on working conditions across the EU found that agency workers are the least satisfied with working conditions when compared against other forms of employment relationships (Paoli and Merllié 2001).

Precarious employment status

Another apparent avenue for insecurity stems from the indeterminacies embedded in the legal framework which regulates employment relationships in the UK. This is ably demonstrated in the long-standing struggle as to the conclusive and predictable determination of employment status of individuals at work, that is, is the individual at work an 'employee', a 'worker' or do they operate independently as an 'independent contractor'. This subject presents pertinent issues that potentially affect the entire employment relationship and the respective statutory responsibilities that may flow therefrom (Marson 2013; Practical Law 2019).

The legal framework through which workers and even employers may come to understand their rights and obligations that flow from the employment relationship in the UK is inherently problematic. As noted, there exist three broad categories of employment status: employees, workers and independent contractors, and where one falls within this scale has determinative implications for the legal entitlements and responsibilities due in the employment relationship, including the applicable taxation provisions (Emir 2020; Jefferson 2018; Kidner 2019; Marson 2013; Practical Law 2019). These operate on a spectrum. At the topmost tier there is the employee who is afforded the most robust legal rights and protections such as rights to claim redundancy payments[12] and seek compensation where they feel they have been unfairly dismissed.[13] With this status, the employer is also under various obligations such as deducting from the employee's pay various contributions (pension and National Insurance) while also making their own National Insurance payment through making a profit from the employee's labour. Next is the status of 'worker', an EU-construct which offers protections not afforded to independent contractors but not as comprehensively protective as those provided to employees.[14] During

---

12. Employment Rights Act 1996 s. 135.
13. Employment Rights Act 1996 s. 94.
14. Individuals holding this status are not entitled to claim unfair dismissal or redundancy payments but do enjoy protection against discrimination and access to equal pay measures through the Equality Act 2010. They may also access statutory sick pay, holiday pay and rest break provisions.

the UK's membership of the EU, there subsisted a disposition to award rights to 'workers' rather than 'employees' due to the restrictions and exclusivity witnessed in previous doctrines and to broaden the legal coverage of employment protections given the intricacies in accurately determining employment status.[15] At the end of the employment status spectrum exist the 'genuinely self-employed' independent contractors. They too enjoy protection against various forms of discrimination[16] in employment, access to some statutory rights and protection of their health and safety. Naturally, based on their definition and the nature of their contracting with employers (not being on the relational contracting of employer-employee but rather a commercial contract of employer-business) they enjoy the fewest employment rights and, fundamentally, the employer is not, for instance, responsible vicariously for torts committed by the contractor and typically makes no deductions from their pay (Emir 2020; Jefferson 2018; Kidner 2019; Marson 2013; Practical Law 2019).

In terms of the statutory definition, the Employment Rights Act 1996 (ERA 1996), s. 230 provides the following:

> An 'employee' is an individual who has entered or works under [...] a contract of employment. Contract of employment is a contract of service or apprenticeship, express or implied.

While there is no similarly overarching statutory definition for a worker, s. 230 of the ERA 1996 specifies

> A 'worker' is an individual who has entered or works under a contract of employment or any other contract, express or implied, where the individual undertakes to personally perform any work or services for another party to the contract, whose status is not by virtue of the contract that of a client or customer of any profession or business undertaking carried on by the individual.[17]

---

15. For example, agency workers in the UK are typically covered by the National Minimum Wage Act, and by several elements of UK implementation of the EU Working Time Directive, in particular the entitlement to 20 days paid annual leave.
16. As way of a couple of examples, these individuals have protection against discrimination on the basis of their trade union membership or non-membership (The Trade Union and Labour Relations (Consolidation) Act 1992 s. 296) – a protected characteristic (Equality Act 2010 s. 13) or if they pursue equal pay (Equality Act 2010 s. 66).
17. This definition is also contained in the Working Time Regulations 1998, National Minimum Wage Regulations 1998 (SI 1998/2574) and Part-time Workers (Prevention of Less Favourable Treatment) Regulations 2000 (SI 2000/1551), and there is an extended definition under the Public Interest Disclosure Act 1998.

Conversely, the position of 'independent contractor' is not subject to such guidance and consequently the term is often used interchangeably with, for example, the 'genuinely self-employed' to represent those undertaking work as part of their own business, on their own account and who assume individual legal responsibility for their employment conduct as theirs is a 'contract for services' (Emir 2020; Jefferson 2018; Kidner 2019; Marson 2013; Practical Law 2019).

However, the demarcations between employees and workers in particular are not clear, especially as the statutes offer meagre guidance as to what constitutes 'a contract of service' (Marson 2013; Practical Law 2019). This legislative lapse is, argues Marson (2013), deliberate as it allows an implicit deference to the system of courts and tribunals to administer these matters on a case-by-case basis[18] (Emir 2020; Kidner 2019; Marson 2013), through the application of a 'mix of law and fact' approach where adjudicators take into consideration the intricacies of the employment relationship present in each matter before coming to a decision on the question of employment status (Practical Law 2019). This is perhaps a necessary, albeit wholly unsatisfactory, method given the power imbalance between the employer and individual and the negative consequences for individuals who are not assigned an accurate employment status. Indeed, the point was noted succinctly by the Supreme Court of Canada where it remarked

> The relationship between an employer and an isolated employee is typically a relationship between a bearer of power and one who is not a bearer of power. [...] The main object of labour law has always been, and we venture to say always will be, to be a countervailing force to counteract the inequality of bargaining power which is inherent and must be inherent in the employment relationship.[19]

It should not be forgotten, in the examination of the lived experiences of student-migrants as workers, that the very precarity established through their immigration and employment status, coupled with their consciousness of this and the tactics adopted to mitigate against these, often have negative implications for their mental health and general well-being. We have seen in Chapter Five how the community has reacted to the antitherapeutic effects of immigration policies and forms of discrimination and abuse experienced. Fundamentally, those tactics were used in contradiction to established laws and processes because of the lack of use of other interventions. However, it

---

18. See *Brook Street Bureau (UK) Limited v Dacas*) EWCA Civ 217 [5].
19. *Slaight Communications v. Davidson* [1989] 1 SCR 1038, per Dickson CJC at pp. 1051–52.

is also clear that many of the problems affecting the student-migrant-workers stem from national employment laws and what is needed is a comprehensive and structural reform of the current laws on immigration, working conditions and employment status (a gateway/roadblock to many protective employment rights), as they apply to this group of student-migrants, and more generally to employment provisions which enable recalcitrant employers to evade their responsibilities and exploit vulnerable groups of workers.

Thus, given that employers have the power to issue contracts on terms set by them, and individuals, especially those at the lower end of the skill sets spectrum, are in a take-it or leave-it situation when deciding whether to enter the employment relationship, it would be unwise to establish a statutory test which would leave open to employers the ability to draft contracts which exclude many individuals (who are often unaware of the distinction between these designations) from fundamental and protective rights. 'Since it is ultimately for the employer to determine how binding workers' obligations are towards it, this leaves the question of the rights that the working relationship can attract largely in the hands of the employer' (Fredmand and Fudge 2013, 118). Therefore, this definitional gap led to the development of a series of common-law tests, albeit with not one single overarching or determinative criterion. These tests and criteria outlined briefly below can be identified as the 'irreducible minimum requirement' developed by the courts that indicate the existence of a contract of service.

The Common Law Tests and Resultant Uncertainties

The first substantive test, the 'control test', was established by Bramwell LJ[20] in a matter concerning the taxation applicable to premises. Beyond that broader matter, it concerned an individual engaged by the employer, and the determination for the courts was whether the individual was sufficiently controlled by the employer to make the employer his 'master'. This test harked back to the historic master-servant relationships where the master controlled everything at work undertaken by the servant. While such relationships had been superseded by the employment relationships being established, it gave the courts an ability to ascertain which individuals were controlled by the employer and which were engaged by them on an equal footing. At its essence, the test operates on the basis that the greater the degree of control available to the employer over the individual, the more likely the individual would be considered an employee. When first introduced, this test was used in isolation and could work well given that many individuals, largely unskilled workers who could

---

20. *Yewens v Noakes* (1880) 6 QBD 530.

only sell their labour, were easily identifiable. They would attend employment at, for example, a factory and do exactly what the employer directed them to. Of course, as demonstrated through numerous cases following *Yewens v Noakes* (1880), the increase in skilled workers who did not require direction as to the nature of how to complete their tasks at work made this test, in isolation at least, untenable. Indeed, skilled individuals experiencing a reduced level of direct control by the employer yet still being held as employees was demonstrated in *Morren v Swinton and Pendlebury Borough Council* [1965] 1 WLR 576; and *Lee Ting Sang v Chung Chi-Keung* [1990] 2 AC 374, among others. The test soon developed to one of a 'right to control' where the employer could stipulate when and where the employee would perform their working duties, but not how to complete them (see *Cassidy v Ministry of Health* [1951] 2 KB 343 CA, and *Walker v Crystal Palace FC* [1910] 1 KB 87).

Subsequently, and in pursuit of the holy grail of an inclusive yet encompassing test of employment status, Denning L.J.[21] offered the 'organisation' or 'integration' test. Here, an individual acts as an employee where they are 'part and parcel' of an organisation, whereas a contractor conversely operates on its fringes (Burchell et al. 1999). The advancement of the test had merits, given it was often easier to look at an employment relationship and 'see' who is an employee than to try and define such a relationship in the abstract. Yet, and fundamentally, Denning failed to define what 'integration' meant and criticism soon followed. In *Ready Mixed Concrete (South East) Ltd v Minister of Pensions & National Insurance* [1968] Mackenna J remarked 'This raises more questions than I know how to answer. What is meant by being "part and parcel of an organization"?'

The judiciary were not content with giving up on establishing a meaningful test despite the existing case law 'leading to a maze of casuistry without much principle'.[22] The economic reality/entrepreneurial test set out by Cooke J[23] sought determination based on whether the individual was in business on their own account. If the answer is in the affirmative then the contract is one for services (they are an independent contractor); however, if they work for another who bears the ultimate risk of loss or chance for profit, then the contract is one of service[24] and the individual is more inclined to be an employee (see Taylor and Emir 2019). This test appeared a first sight to give the direction

---

21. See *Cassidy v Ministry of Health [1951] 2 KB 343*, and *Stevenson Jordan and Harrison v Macdonald and Evans* [1952] 1 TLR 101.
22. Otto Kahn-Freund, 'Servants and Independent Contractors' (1951), *Modern Law Review*, 14, no. 4: 504, 507.
23. See *Market Investigations ltd v Minister of Social Security* [1969] 2 QB 173.
24. Per Lord Griffiths in *Lee Ting Sang v Chung Chi-Keung* [1990] UKPC 9.

to employment status given that many employees are not subject to financial risk or investment in the business to which they are engaged, nor do they have rights of management to direct/control their work. Yet, individuals who work in the financial services industry, consultants and agents, for example, may have such features present in their employment but are still considered employees (see Leighton and Wynn (2011) for a thorough discussion of this topic).

The contemporary approach is the multiple test adopted in *Ready Mixed Concrete*. Here the courts and tribunals perform a balancing act by weighing up all the factors that lean towards a contract of employment, and all those that allude to a contract of service, the outcome of which may be almost impossible to predict in advance as no one factor is decisive[25] (Deakin and Morris 2009; Freedland 2003; Marson 2013). Nolan LJ perhaps sums up the position best

> to decide whether a person carries on business on his own account it is necessary to consider many different aspects of that person's work activity… The object of the exercise is to paint a picture from the accumulation of detail. The overall effect can only be appreciated by standing back from the detailed picture which has been painted, by viewing it from a distance and by making an informed, considered, qualitative appreciation of the whole. […] Not all details are of equal weight or importance in any given situation. The details may also vary in importance from one situation to another. The process involves painting a picture in each individual case.[26]

However, two features are fundamental to employee status. The first is that control by the employer over the individual must be exercisable. Once the employer's right to control is established, the court/tribunal will have to be satisfied that there exists a mutuality of obligations between the parties (a test created by Mackenna J).[27] It provides that there ought to exist a mutual exchange of commitments that amounts 'to a fixed and definite obligation, identifiable at any given moment, upon the employing entity to offer work in future, and, symmetrically, upon the worker to accept work as offered' (Freedland 2003, 104).[28] Thus, if per the terms of the employment relationship an employer

---

25. See *Hitchcock v Post Office* [1980] CLY 1045.
26. *Hall v Lorimer* [1994] 1 WLR 209 (at p. 217).
27. *Ready Mixed Concrete (South East) Ltd v Minister of Pensions and National Insurance* [1968] 2 QB 497.
28. See *Bebbington v Palmer T/A Sturry News* UKEAT/0371/09/DM.

may decline to offer work and/or the worker can decline to accept the job once offered, then there is no mutuality of obligations and it is likely that no contract of employment exists (Deakin and Morris 2009). This test, crucial as it is, is not without its own flaws and inconsistencies, having been seen in the approaches where the mutuality can be interpreted broadly (using the term 'an umbrella contract' to cover the entirety of the employment relation) to a much narrower view of mutuality of obligations and the consequences for the ability to decline work (see Marson 2013). Furthermore, this test also requires the existence of an element of personal service which effectively means that if an individual is permitted an unfettered right of substitution at work, no contract of employment can exist[29] (Deakin and Morris 2009), scholars including Marson (2014) have since argued more optimistically that the unavailability of a generic statutory definition for the various forms of employment status is not necessarily a negative feature of English law. It affords to tribunals sufficient flexibility to not only adequately absorb the relevant facts so to fairly decide each case on its merits, but also to best ascertain the true intentions of parties and offer protection to vulnerable individuals where necessary. This position is also predicated on the hypothesis that the introduction of proscriptive statutory definitions may forearm employers with measures to circumvent the imposition of employment rights and obligations accruable to a more protected employment class for all its pecuniary implications. There is a downside to this situation given the uncertainty that this approach breeds. Stakeholders, including employers and workers, must look to complex and often contradictory case authorities as indicators of potential judicial leanings, and even then, these provisions are far from conclusive on the issue as decisions are reached on an ad hoc, case-by-case basis[30] given the factual dimensions present and due to the courts and tribunals not addressing employment in isolation but as the first issue in a broader employment claim. Furthermore, courts have been wary of the mislabelling of individuals as contractors or employees even where the minutiae of the employment relationship suggests otherwise, just to reap specific benefits or to evade statutory

---

29. See *MacFarlane and Skivington v Glasgow City Council* [2000] EAT/1277.
30. The potential inconsistencies that follow can be made apparent through a comparison of the cases of two similar cases: *O'Kelly v Trusthouse Forte plc* [1983] ICR 728 – where following a strict application of mutuality, workers apparently engaged as casuals were deemed as independent contractors due to a lack of 'palpable' evidence of mutuality; and *Nethermere (St Neots) Ltd v Gardiner* [1984] ICR 612 – where following the adoption of a broad interpretation of the mutuality test, home workers were held as employees due to the existence of a degree of mutuality.

responsibilities.³¹ For instance, some employers have been seen to ostensibly label workers engaged as independent contractors in order to escape the financial liabilities associated with the more protected classes of 'employee' or indeed the worker. A study commissioned by an independent think tank reports that small- and medium-sized firms may potentially save up to £2 billion in tax payments just by altering its contractual terms from engaging employees to independent contractors (Marson 2013). Of course, this does not change the legal position. Per Denning LJ,

> the law, as I see it, is this: if the true relationship of the parties is that of master and servant under a contract of service, the parties cannot alter the truth of that relationship by putting a different label upon it.³²

Yet the view of the think tank does present a pragmatic appreciation of the tactics entertained by some employers, and this is more likely to be pursued against a cohort of individuals at work who are not well versed in the legal definitions. Exacerbating these indeterminacies even further is the fact that the determination of employment status will differ according to the specific legal protection sought. For example, agency workers are deemed 'workers', entitled to protection through statutory measures including the Working Time Regulations 1998, the National Minimum Wage (Amendment) Regulations 2016 (incorporating the National Living Wage), the Equality Act 2010, the Health and Safety at Work Act 1974³³ and so on. Meanwhile, they may yet be held as employees for claims per the doctrine of vicarious liability where the user firm as a 'temporary deemed employer' who may be found culpable for tortious acts and omissions of the tortfeasor.³⁴ Whereas for taxation purposes, such individuals are ostensibly deemed employees as provided by

---

31. See *Pimlico Plumbers Ltd and another v Smith* [2018] UKSC 29 and *Uber BV and others v Aslam and others* [2021] UKSC 5.
32. *Massey v Crown Life Insurance Company* [1978] IRLR 31, CA, see also; *Young and Woods Ltd v West* [1980] IRLR 201.
33. This inconsistency was evident in the case *Lane v The Shire Roofing Company* [1995], where a construction worker who was engaged as an independent contractor per the express terms of the contract, was held to be an employee so to prevent the erstwhile negligent employers, who were found to be in violation of health and safety provisions, from relying on the contract label to escape liability thereof. This finding was also made, in spite of the inexistence of evidence, including mutuality of obligations, that may ordinarily allude to employee status. Per Henry LJ, 'when it comes to the question of safety at work, there is a real public interest in recognizing the employer/employee relationship when it exists, because of the responsibilities that the common law and statutes [...] place on the employer' ([1995] PIQR 421).
34. *Cable and Wireless plc v Muscat* [2006] EWCA Civ 220 [27].

the yet-to-be-implemented IR35 Regulation, a measure that explicitly seeks to curtail tax avoidance through the manipulation of employment statuses. This is cognisant of the fact that some individuals may opt to establish their own private limited companies as a conduit to offer their services to employment agencies so to take advantage of competitive corporate tax rates, such workers documented to often identify as independent contractors as opposed to workers or employees (Casey and Alach 2004).

Ultimately, the question regarding employment status can only be decided conclusively following attempts at formal dispute resolution. To this end, it must also be contemplated that insights from the socio-legal scholarship have since demonstrated that the legal case, for all its symbolic essence, is merely the 'tip of the iceberg' of matters that are shaped and interpreted through law (Silbey 2005). For the greater part, many individuals with a contentious employment status never conclusively determine the issue at court or tribunal, and the ones that do, are in essence the outliers, not the norm. Even then, these outliers are fated to a protracted, expensive and unpredictable legal process where their chances for victory are dimmed due to the absence of a concise, coherent methodology. Finally, this conundrum is only exacerbated by the fact that the employment tribunals and other alternative forms of industrial dispute resolution mediums that often hear these matters lack the jurisdiction to establish precedent, and for the most part are not bound by previous decisions (Marson 2013).

The sum of these ambiguities have led the likes of Davies (2009) to protest the lack of a concise methodology that has seen the legal determination of employment status continue as a contentious subject resulting in greater litigation 'as individuals strive to get into a more protected category and employers seek to avoid the legal obligations that would follow from this' (p. 91). Leighton and Wynn (2011) have since vividly described this process as akin to playing the 'legal lottery' due to the proliferation of these tests that are often hard to reconcile with one another and the utter discretion wielded by adjudicators as to which test route to appropriate from towards reaching a conclusion. Meanwhile Davidov (2005) has slated the employment status provisions for being vacuous, and ambiguous.

To conclude this section, it is worth remembering the views of Deakin (2013):

> The concept of the contract of employment has become bound up with an 'epistemic and subject-existential crisis' for labor law. This crisis has arisen because of 'evolutions in labour law systems themselves and in the functionings of labour markets' which have made the employment contract inapt for describing and regulating a growing segment of work relations. (pp. 137–38)

It is arguable that nearly a decade on, we are no closer to conclusively determining employment status and removing the inherent uncertainty and unpredictability this brings for all parties.

The Employment Rights and Status of Temporary Agency Workers in the UK

The prominence of this issue has heightened with the recent rise in more complex, intermittent work arrangements including TAW (Marson 2013). This is especially noticeable by the distinctiveness of the agency work structure, which leaves questions as to the statutory responsibilities that may flow thereunder, and the determination of what party assumes legal responsibility for said worker between the agency or the third-party user firm (Burchell et al. 1999; Practical Law 2019).

It is not uncommon for employers in the care sector to approach employment agencies where they are short-staffed and are unable or unwilling to recruit help directly. Further, albeit a broader issue which is beyond the scope of this study to explore is the correlation between engagement through 'flexible' employment relationships involving a range of intermediaries – and the jeopardising of the safety of care-workers and the employment standards they should expect to enjoy (for commentary on this issue, see the work of Emberson and Trautrims 2019a, 2019b). The use of employment agencies is often the mechanism used by these employers (and certainly by the organisations through which the respondents to our study were engaged) as the individuals are subsequently engaged and paid by the employer (unlike with engagement through employment businesses who simply 'place' the individual but remain their employer). These temporary engagements ensure that the employer is able to obtain the labour needed as it is the agencies' responsibility to provide cover where, for instance, the individual is unable to cover that particular shift. The agency also has the responsibility to provide alternative cover where the employer finds the existing agency worker unsatisfactory, and the employer is not typically responsible for making holiday and sick pay provisions.

Agency workers, albeit not independent contractors, have, since 1 October 2011, and through the Agency Workers Regulations 2010, protections against many forms of discrimination on the basis of a 'protected characteristic' under the Equality Act 2010; have a right to be paid the national minimum wage; have access to trade union membership and associated rights; and have the protections afforded through the Working time Regulations 1998. Importantly and of concern to agency workers generally due to the short-term nature of these engagements is that the access to some employment rights begins on their immediate start, yet others require 12-weeks' employment with the same employer before they become effective.[35] This lack of equality of treatment between workers on different employment contracts may be expedient for employers, yet it causes many individuals engaged on temporary contracts to be excluded, permanently in many instances, from access to protective rights which are deemed appropriate to other workers simply due to the contract under which they operate. Further, given the employer controls the nature of these appointments, and actively chooses to engage temporary workers through an employment agency (admittedly of course, not exclusively for nefarious reasons), and that many parties to these contracts use them because of domestic/visa restrictions on the types of employment available to them, it may lead to a situation where the parties seek to circumvent the most unpalatable aspects of these engagements, justifying such behaviour on the inherent unfair and inequality present.

Since April 2020, the Agency Workers (Amendment) Regulations 2019 have been in force, strengthening many agency workers' rights, particularly with regard to accessing statutory sick pay. Rights to protection on maternity and parental rights grounds have also been brought into effect from day one of employment, rather than following 12-week service. Yet this right is only available to those individuals engaged as employees. Hence, employment status continues to be a significant issue in access to protective employment rights, and is further compounded when viewed from the perspective of agency workers.

Under the tripartite structure, for every assignment there are two establishments who assume de facto responsibility for the worker. More so, the absence of express legal provisions mean that agency workers, at least on paper, may be held as workers, independent contractors or employees of either the agency or user firm as an employment tribunal deems fit (for some historical discussion, see Burchell et al. 1999).[36]

Further, it should be noted that agency workers may not be an employee of either the employment agency *or* the hiring firm after all. Indeed,

---

35. Following the completion of the 12-weeks' continuous service, the agency worker is entitled to access to the same basic employment conditions as if they had been directly engaged by the hiring employer. This refers to salary, commission payments, overtime pay, paid annual leave and automatic pension enrolment (at least where the worker's age and earnings permit).
36. Meanwhile it is often in both firms' strategic interests to deny legal responsibility for all its legal commitments and financial implications, an outcome that especially defeats the express purpose of engaging agency workers, so to provide cheap, non-committal workhands often on an ad hoc basis. More so, the engagement of agency workers is adduced to especially allow user firms to shift the responsibility for, and the risks of, employing labour to other smaller, less organised and regulated agency businesses.

individuals who undertake work via temporary employment agencies are usually not deemed 'employees' or considered as being engaged under a contract of service. The worker's relationship with the employment agency is unlikely to be held as one of a contract of service, and the courts/tribunals are similarly unlikely to imply a contract of employment with the user firm (Practical Law 2019). This lingering ambiguity can be starkly contrasted with the legal position in other industrialised states. For instance, in continental Europe including France, Italy, Spain and Germany, the agency worker is deemed in law an employee with a contract of employment with the employment agency. Meanwhile in the United States, it is often the case that legal responsibility for the agency worker is split between the agency and the user firm. In Canada, this responsibility rests with the user firm (Storrie 2002).

Succinctly, the blurring of organisational boundaries in terms of the multi-employer relationship between agencies, client organisations and agency workers raises concerns about the employment rights and experiences of agency workers in the UK (Davidov 2004; Rubery et al. 2005). This potential for ambiguity can be detrimental for the individual who stands to lose statutory employment rights without legal intervention and may even potentially impair their health and safety at work. For instance, both firms may assume it is the remit of the other to cater to a specific workplace safety issue or training. Meanwhile workers' interests could well suffer at the expense of both firms' commercial interests to maintain an amicable business relationship with one another. Indeed, organisation theorists including Edelman et al. (1993) have reported of the propensity for firms' internal grievance procedures to protect organisational interests as opposed to employee rights.

The employment status attributed to agency workers therefore compounds their precarious position by frequently refusing to them the status of employees (due, in most circumstances, to the lack of mutuality of obligations between the parties). This situation mirrors that commented upon by Fredman and Fudge (2013) when they spoke in the context of women workers.

> Labor law's continuing assumption that the contract of employment signifies the group of workers who should rightly attract employment protection rights has for decades failed the many women who are unable to conform to the stringent pre-conditions for membership of that magic circle. Particularly problematic is the assumption that those workers who are not employed in a bilateral relationship with an employer under a contract of employment are self-employed, independent and therefore undeserving of employment rights. (p. 116)

It is for the aforementioned reasons the frame of precarity aptly captures the insecurity and instability associated with atypical forms of employment and especially TAW, especially when structurally disadvantaged actors like student-migrant-workers are implicated. This insight informs the discussion in the ensuing section.

The Student-Migrant + Temporary Agency Worker = Precarity?

Caught within the intersections of 'migrant-worker' and 'working-student' archetypes, we can speculate that student-migrant-workers must often contend with forms of precarious employment. First, 'student-jobs' are not renowned as being 'vocational' or 'career jobs', just as more recent migrant-workers are known to constitute the bulk of the atypical labour force more given to precarious employment. While it is difficult to know the exact proportion of student-migrant-workers in this employment form, we can make an informed inference from published works. There is an acknowledgement of the disproportional representation of groups already given to structural disadvantage and especially migrants in precarious, TAW (Casey and Alach 2004; Davidov 2005; Storrie 2003). It is estimated that foreign-born workers make up as much as 25 per cent of the agency workforce[37] (Office for National Statistics 2019).

Reasons for the concentration of migrants in this work form vary, from discriminatory practices, to poor language knowledge, illegality, lack of recognition of qualifications and the consequences of global inequalities which means that some migrants are only too prepared to take on jobs at wages and conditions that many domestic nationals will not consider (Anderson 2010). Narrowing our search further, this work form is seen to draw a demographic of migrant-workers that fit the profile of our study subjects – young, students and from ethnic minority groups (Biggs 2003). The Trades Union Congress (2017) has reported that members of the Black community are over twice as likely to be in temporary work than the national average and, further, this group experienced the largest increase in the number of people in temporary jobs between 2011 and 2016 (a 58 per cent increase). Nationally, the increase was only 11 per cent, and 42 per cent of Black workers are in temporary work because they are unable to find permanent employment, rather than it

---

37. These migrant-workers are known to cluster in very specific niches. Geddes (2008), for example, reports that as much as 90 per cent of agency workers employed in second stage food processing were migrants. Workers bearing these demographical features are depicted as the drivers of the growth in agency work.

being an active choice. This compares unfavourably with 31 per cent of the total temporary workforce. Forde and Slater (2005) report that a relatively significant proportion of agency workers are aged between 16 and 24, and as such tend to be from a much younger proportion of workers than those in permanent or typical employment. This propensity may be attributable to reasons including the difficulties experienced in navigating the job market due to structural inequalities and how it affords to younger and more mobile actors including (student-migrants) flexibility in employment as they tend to be new entrants into the labour market.[38] Interestingly, Biggs' study finds that members of the atypical workforce (including agency workers) tend to be the most qualified, while permanent workers are shown to often possess no qualifications at all. Such a finding contradicts the common presumption that agency workers are mostly lower-skilled or less educated than more other types of worker (Biggs 2003).

The sociocultural, legal and economic susceptibility of these students due to their novelty as recent migrants and labour market entrants also has a place in this discussion. Studies including that of Nyland et al. (2009) have demonstrated that it is often the case that overseas students are misinformed or basically unaware of accruable work rights and benefits. More so, Piore (1979) asserts that the seeming transience of a migrant's stay makes it so that work undertaken in the periods proximately following migration may tend to be perceived in purely instrumental contexts – nothing more than as a means to earn. This is closely associated with the propensity for migrants at this early stage to present with lower subjective expectations due to limited sociocultural understanding of the labour market, nonetheless harbouring hopes for moving on to better things as they become more established. It is also asserted that the targeted recruitment efforts may play a role in the concentration of migrants in precarious work forms, with studies including MacKenzie and Forde (2009) documenting how employers often have a preference for more recent migrant-workers as they find them more docile and amenable to work demands than domestic workers, or even long-standing immigrant-workers, 'as migrants stay longer in the UK they become more "British", more demanding and intractable' (Anderson 2013, 85; MacKenzie and Forde 2009).

Further insights from the migration scholarship are offered by Massey (1990) when demonstrating that networks of employment and immigration tend to take on dynamics of their own. As negotiated over time, they may precede the migrants' admittance into the environment, and more so, once

---

38. It has been hypothesized that perhaps TAW attracts workers who are not overtly dedicated to labour force participation in the first place, such as students, this is an impression we would revisit when discussing this study's findings (see Storrie 2003).

networks have become ingrained in specific sectors, they linger even when the legislative framework is altered. This behavioural pattern is historically underpinned by the manifested accessibility of that employment context by preceding actors similarly stationed. These factors further amplify the already superior bargaining strength of employers, including insecurities the employer played no part in creating but on which they may seek to capitalise. This conclusion has been alluded to previously by scholars including Miles (1986) who notably contends that the restraints on migrants' rights to commodify their labour power gives way to a state of precariousness that is desirable by market forces as it provides a means for satisfying the labour needs of specific industries without raising their labour costs. This is continued by Gray (2004) who asserts that migrants' limited bargaining leverage in the workspace predisposes them to the lowlier casual jobs that are disproportionally part-time and temporary, and where wages are either stagnant or increase more slowly when compared with other roles (p. 122).

The interaction between labour markets and immigration has been considerably researched and theorised, but this sub-scholarship tends to focus on 'illegality' on the one hand, and migratory processes on the other, through the lens of precarity (Anderson 2010). However, while we can attempt to subsume student-migrant-workers within these migrant-labour market theories, the nuances associated with their structural location are for the most part lost in this literature. The employment restrictions, that is, international students in UK Higher Education being restricted to a maximum of 20 hours of work per week during term time, prohibited from taking up full-time or permanent job roles and from engaging in economic activity as independent contractors or self-employed workers makes it apparent that they are expected to have only minimal labour market participation while studying, hence the employment restrictions affixed to their visas to keep them from being economic migrants. Such structural impediments essentially predispose these sorts of temporary and insecure forms of employment. Immigration regimes in this sense can be seen to interact with migratory processes and labour market temporality to produce workers with specific features in relation to employers and the broader labour market. This may also mean that student-migrants, just as temporary or more recent migrant-workers, are more amenable to these types of work which offer little or no progression opportunities as they are viewed more opportunistically as temporary fixtures as opposed to 'lifetime gigs' (Curtis and Lucas 2001).[39] These constraints on their labour engagement ostensibly

---

39. Meanwhile, the macro-institutional implications of this contributes to the concentration of migrants in frontline or entry-level roles, especially where substantive career progression is realistically not to be expected or is impracticable, and even in some

predisposes them to industries within the 'grey economy' associated with more atypical and precarious employment relationships where labour standards are ambiguous and have limited permeability, and industries frequently decried for labour code infractions, exploitative and abusive work conditions.

Meanwhile, centring student-migrant-workers in the legal uncertainties surrounding the determination of employment status, it must also be contemplated that their visa restrictions expressly precludes them from undertaking work with any real autonomy as independent contractors. Given that this subject may only be an issue where some legal issue requires classification of the individual's employment status, it is not out of place to assume that some of these student-migrants may mundanely engage in work contexts that breach this divide, wilfully or otherwise.

These reviewed insights ground our inclination that the student-migrant-workers' reality in the host state is, possibly at least, underscored by insecurities sourced from several distinct yet interwoven and reinforcing mediums. Yet, through the available literature we knew less of how these restrictions might impact their everyday experiences, not just of the labour market but more so in general as these student-migrant-workers navigated the dynamics of their inherent subjectivities. The experiences engendered by and in spite of these constraints have lacked critical examination in the literature, and our study sought to rectify that omission. As such, in the following two chapters, the empirical data and a critical assessment of their implications for this discourse are presented.

---

    instances gives way to the subjects' apathy in seeking advancement within that job role or industry.

Chapter 6

THE 'UTTERLY TRANSACTIONAL WORKER'

Introduction

> There are two different types of overseas students, if you look closely ... you have the ones that look like ... like they come from money, you know, come to class with all them expensive designers... And you find that most likely don't even have NI numbers, never applied, haven't done a minute of work since coming here because they don't need to... then there's us, that's the first thing we did ... But we all pay the same school fees. (Abeo)

In this chapter we present a detailed account of the lived employment experiences encountered by a cohort of international student-migrant-workers. In so doing we provide a discussion of the findings gathered from interviews with (predominantly) postgraduate international students of sub-Saharan African descent, all aged between 25 and 35 years. This chapter is presented in four parts. For the first, we focus on the precursors of the employment experiences of the participants, including their expectations and reasons for seeking temporary employment. This segues into a discussion of the employment profile of these student-migrant-workers, including the roles they occupy, in which sectors, the pay levels received, and their work and sundry factors which underpin these. In the second part, we dive deeper into the students' relationship with the atypical employment market, particularly TAW which is the prevalent employment form encountered. Here, we also consider the allure and negativities associated with temporary working for these student-workers. The third part of the chapter allows us to examine features which cause some of the students to maintain negative feelings towards work, including discrimination, exploitation and abuse they have faced. The final aspect of the chapter allows us to present a critical discussion of these findings through the frame of 'precarity'. Here we examine the various mediums of insecurity and disadvantage the student-workers are prone to encounter. This is followed by a discussion of their opinions of their employment situation and commentary on how this experience might be bettered. We conclude with a summary and discussion of the key findings.

Labour Market Inception: A Crash Course in Expectation Management

> I remember when my study visa just gotten approved, I was so excited … was hopeful, I thought I would come here, maybe get a part-time job in a law firm whilst studying. (Edet)

Although the sum of the narrative accounts as to the student-migrants' reception in the UK job market reveals a far-from-uniform portrait, Edet's sentiments are representative of the optimism and excitement for the opportunities that lay await for many students entering the country. Socioeconomic features mark the rationales behind students' decisions to migrate to the UK for higher education, ranging from the relative lack of quality educational facilities in their home country, to the relative affordability of living in the UK compared to other principal destinations such as the United States and Canada. More pertinently, the work privileges available featured as a prominent motivator behind their decisions to migrate to the UK for study. It is therefore unsurprising to report that gaining paid temporary, part-time work is often an imperative in these accounts, especially as most students indicate that this is their principal source of financial subsistence during their time studying in the UK. Nonetheless, 23 of the 37 participants indicated that they had initially expected to undertake part-time work within industries and contexts that fit or advance their vocational and academic interests:

> Before I got here and during those early times after I just came … I always thought I could get a part time IT job at a tech firm or even if that doesn't work do some freelancing, so I could get some international experience and also earn money, you know, kill two birds with one stone. (Adaeze)

Indeed, while some had hoped to secure employment related to their professional profiles, others had simply hoped for a kinder student job market reception. For example, Amina, a student undertaking an MA degree programme in Sociology, noted her desire to pursue ancillary employment on the basis of previous employment activity and the skills she had developed, but found this difficult to achieve:

> I always thought bad as e bad[1] I'll be able to make money from my hair stylist biz ... I can do everything, lace fronts, weaves, braids, you name it ... but I was not able to do that, I tried, I can't do it as a business on my own, at least not legally. (Amina)

While this expectation of a favourable, more amenable job market terrain can be considered as naïve, it was not totally unfounded. A resounding finding was that for some (12 participants), this expectation had been fuelled by university representatives and agents who, during overseas recruitment events, had remarked as to the potential opportunities for part-time work for international students in the UK.

> The university guy in Lagos told me that they usually do organise employment fairs where they put students in touch with employers in their discipline. (Uyi)

However, they soon found the reality to be quite different from the dream sold.

> It was so difficult. I even wrote to some firms asking to intern with them ... some wrote back saying they had no space for me, meanwhile some didn't even bother responding to my applications. (Edet)[2]

It is at this juncture that the documented difficulties of new job seekers, and especially recent migrants, associated with navigating the labour market unaided became apparent (see Benton et al. 2014; Brooks and Waters 2011; Hooper et al. 2017; Lodovici 2010). This hardship is particularly accentuated for the student-migrants who were seeking roles that required the applicant to be in possession of specific qualities i.e. those that allowed sufficient flexibility to fit in other commitments including academic study, immigration restrictions, or to even match their vocational interests. For most however, financial vulnerabilities soon inspired a more instrumental, purely transactional view of employment that resulted in the students settling for jobs purely for the income. The employment profile of these student-migrants is considered below.

---

1. Nigerian slang for 'worst case scenario'.
2. A student with a background in law who began with ambitions of seeking paid temporary work placements at law firms upon arriving in the UK. She failed to receive any offers of employment even after she lowered her expectations.

Employment Profile

We did not encounter considerable differences being identified as factors influencing the labour market location and job roles occupied by the student-workers across both study locations. Although participants often admitted to simultaneously holding multiple casual roles within different industries, no significant distribution in the sectors within which the student-migrants were employed was revealed. Albeit noting some overlaps, by far the most prevalent industry for the student-migrants' occupation was the social care sector (23), although the hospitality (12), food processing (6) and retail (5) sectors also featured prominently.

As it relates to job qualities, it is apparent that international students being precluded from full-time, permanent forms of employment effectively meant that they were only able to participate in the atypical or non-standard divide of the labour market – a market known for irregular, uncertain employment, often with high turnover rates. The portrait of the student-migrants' job profile encompassed mostly frontline, lesser-skilled, low pay roles.

As the pool of participants were all aged over 25, they were entitled to receive the statutory 'National Living Wage'. Thus, the average hourly wage applicable was just above the statutory minimum of £9 per hour. When accounting for regional disparities, wage levels between both study locations differed only slightly; Location A, situated in the North-East of the UK, averaged around £8 per hour, meanwhile Location B in the South-West of the UK, resulted in the student-migrants receiving pay of nearly £10 per hour.

> The first job I got was in a warehouse … I think I worked there only four times; it was too difficult … and having to stand for long hours all for like £7, minimum wage then … (Ife)

Job-hopping was a very common feature for the participants, especially in the periods immediately following migration. However, despite the intention of this being temporary in nature, sometimes this type of working lingered on well into their stay in the UK.

> I think I've done over 15 types of jobs and jobs are different jobs in this country. I've worked for cable companies, I've worked for mail companies, delivery mail companies, I've worked in restaurants, I've worked in bars. Like, I think I've done 15 different types of jobs, you understand? I've even done light construction… I followed a driver… a company's driver to deliver things. (Nnamdi)

More so, we can report of a prevalent skill-job mismatch. The participants, predominantly, were postgraduate students who tended to sit between medium-skilled and highly skilled workers when accounting for their existing academic qualifications. They were nonetheless placed in employment contexts that were incompatible with their professional portfolio for the most part, in roles for which they were obviously overqualified, and/or which presented little or no transferrable skill sets. This more so translated into underemployment and deskilling, occasioned by this mismatch between skills and available work opportunities (see Van Riemsdijk 2014; Kelly 2011).

Therefore, there was an occupational gradient in effect, corroborating the insights presented by Nyland et al. (2009) that international student-workers tend to be clustered in precarious job roles and those perceived as lowly in terms of stratification, skill, specification and pay.

The Role of Employment Intermediaries

As signposted earlier, a somewhat unexpected revelation from our study was of the high concentration of students in a single particular form of contingent employment relationship – TAW. Mirroring findings that alluded to an over-representation of recent migrants in TAW, as much as 80 per cent of the participants indicated that they were actively engaged for work through employment intermediaries (i.e. agencies) or did at some point during their time in the UK use such a service. For our participants at least, the allure of agency work can be distilled to a number of distinct, albeit related, factors. The first concerns the work agencies' role in providing initial access for new workers to the labour market (labour market integration); the second has to do with targeted recruitment efforts by these employment agencies; and finally, the third factor was that TAW affords to students a (much needed) degree of flexibility and control over their working lives. We explain the basis of these features below.

Labour Market Integration

The proliferation of student-migrants to this work can be directly attributable to their place as new job market candidates and student-migrants who possess neither the time, resources nor sociocultural means to participate in the labour market as fully active, autonomous job seekers. This insight directly corroborates previous findings including those from Biggs et al. (2006), Casey (1988) and Storrie (2004), among others, who have each documented the role of employment agencies as a means towards labour market integration for new job seekers. In this sense, the expedience and allure of agency work for students is intrinsically associated with the less tedious and near instantaneous route into paid employment it provides. This is especially relevant here given the structural disadvantage these subjects are documented to encounter while navigating the labour market.

> They call you. Yeah, you apply. So then, for that place, I rang them and then I told them I was interested. They sent me an application form immediately. (Uyi)

The opportunity cost present is one having to seek out employment independently or through some other forum, for example, the Job Centre. This prospect seemed unappealing to subjects due to the formalities associated with these alternative forums, unfamiliarity and time constraints:

> It's very straightforward, you could either go into the agency's office or better still sign up online, I did mine online … it is way better and faster than going to sit all day at the job centre applying for the same kind of low, low jobs. (Femi)

Following the fact that students are often in pursuit of the most convenient and fastest route into paid employment, these employment intermediaries usually operate akin to a one-stop-shop for everything employment related – from getting the students' prepared for entry into the labour market and sometimes even assuming the bulk of the costs associated with this endeavour, to mediating the minutiae of their working lives and monitoring their progress.

> Oh, I think it was quite easy. The recruitment process was not so tedious if I remember correctly, just provide a bank account, your NI and ID or BRP … I didn't really need to have prior work experience per se … when I went in, I did not even have an NI yet, they provided me with all the information I'll need to apply. Nana

> Everything, the health and safety training … is arranged by the agency, they pay for it as well and the cost is then deducted from your pay once you start picking up shifts (with the agency). (Ken-Saro)

This depiction is a perfect illustration of the value of the services employment intermediaries, including agencies, render. They enable the prospective student-migrant relatively easy access to the institution of work for all its socio-economic benefits and at minimal upfront cost, an important finding here is that these employment agencies often serve as the principal source of knowledge for accruable employment rights and responsibilities. While this is not ostensibly problematic, the seeming (over-) reliance on employment brokers for access to and knowledge of the labour market, however, sets the template for the exploitative conditions this study reports of in subsequent sections.

Targeted Recruitment

In addition to providing access into employment, a further reason for the concentration of international students in this work form is attributable to the targeted recruitment efforts on the part of employment agencies. It is often the case that these agencies adopt a range of strategic devises to tap into student-migrant networks within a specific location. For instance, it was not unusual to receive agency work advertisements through the mail, this we witnessed first-hand.

> That's how I got one of the agencies I work with now, they host events … they left a flier in my letterbox when I was in student halls … it was an okay offer, above minimum wage. (Nana)

The practices further include intensified publicity drives in student-populated areas, tailoring these recruitment pitches to appeal to newer, younger workers.

> Although the pay wasn't fantastic, I was sorta interested because they do usually provide catering, servers, for big, popular events … Cheltenham, you know, the horse race thing, and Wembley … I mean, these are places I had only heard of before coming here, not to talk of being paid to work there with free transport and accommodation … they said you keep all your tips, not all of that tip pooling rubbish some usually do, they also provide the uniforms and things like that. (Nana)

More pertinently, there were also reports of a referral system being utilised by various agencies wherein workers received a bonus for every subsequent worker they referred and who was subsequently recruited by the firm. Sub-delegating recruitment responsibilities in this way can be quite effective, not only does this enable a wider reach to a vast pool of potential workers, but more so it establishes a financial interest to recruits to further propagate the agency's services to other similarly situated actors. Thus, an indirect form of confirmation of the agencies' legitimacy was occurring which had a profound effect on the cohort. This makes it ever more noteworthy that approximately three quarters of the student-worker participants interviewed in this study indicated that they had learned out about the specific employment agencies they were engaged under through 'word of mouth' advertising or from within their respective social networks. This was as opposed to more formalised mediums including university organised employability events and Job Centre forums. More so, in each of the study locations, the student-migrants tended to be engaged with the same handful of recruitment agencies.

Flexibility

Certain phases and contexts of migration can be perceived to interlock with the temporal requirements of certain aspects of the labour market (Anderson 2014; Lodovici 2010). This is hypothesised to make for an employment relationship underscored by non-committal flexibility that works for all parties involved[3] – at least in theory. This is even more so where the worker is subject to institutional constraints on their labour participation ab initio. Thus, it was possible to anticipate from the onset that the degree of flexibility afforded through this working arrangement would feature as a principal motivation for student-migrants undertaking employment via temporary work agencies. Flexible working can be of the utmost importance, especially for student-migrants who often have other commitments, including, not least, their studies. Here, flexibility is enabled via the opportunity to exert control over one's working time, and the freedom to make decisions according to one's individual priorities.

> You're allowed to do what you want to do, work when you want to and stop when you don't want to work. (Tega)

> I cannot personally take up a job during my class hours or when I'm in the library doing my course work, even if they are offering me £20 per hour, I have my priorities you know … If I'm not available this week, then I'm not available. So, even if you call me, I will tell you I will do my assignment please or I'm in school. (Simbi)

> I think for me, as an international student, I think I can only work with agencies because of flexibility, the hours are okay for me, it's convenient for me. When I need to work, I work. When I don't need to work and I need to be in school, I'm in school. So, for a period of time when I was writing my dissertation last year about two, three months, I think I worked once a week about two, three months because I was focusing

---

3. Workers, third-party hiring firms and temporary work agencies.

on my dissertation. Whereas if it was a permanent job, you have your rota at beginning of the month, and you have to do those shifts. But for agency staff, if you don't want to work, you don't work. (Edet)

This freedom also enabled the participants to turn down or even cancel previously accepted assignments with relative ease;

> Sometimes you might accept a shift before realising its too far on the maps, or it's a place you don't like, then you can always call to tell them that you're ill or something came up and you can't make it … So, cancellation I have to do it from my own end because I only give out what I can offer. (Wale)

> If you don't feel up to it or something comes up you can just call and cancel to say you don't feel up to the shift … maybe you're uncomfortable or unhappy or you get a better shift somewhere else, you can without having to think twice. (Mensah)

More so, the lack of definite contractual commitments can also be leveraged for better terms (including pay) per work assignment. This is typically the case where the work assignment offered is either undesirable and/or inconvenient. It was not uncommon for subjects to negotiate higher than usual wage rates as incentives to accept work assignments they may not ordinarily have considered taking.

> Sometimes there are shifts no one wants to do … for example there is a care home in [redacted] where no one wants to go to because it's too far from town and they can be racist there. So they always struggle to fill that job and they know that … so they'll call and offer as much as £12 [per hour] … and sometimes you can even negotiate for more. (Simbi)

Although agency work is known for the proliferation of low pay and wage penalties, this finding seemingly illustrates the assertions advanced by the likes of Stanworth and Druker (2004) who found that agency workers tended to be better paid by the hour than permanent workers performing similar roles.

> When it comes to the issue of pay, I don't know for others but most of the agencies are – or most other places I've worked in, you notice that their main staff they pay them less. Maybe because of the benefits that they get, but we, they pay us higher, because we do usually negotiate for more where we can, theirs is fixed. (Simbi)

Furthermore, it has also been adduced that agency work provides workers with access to a variety of employment opportunities and experiences that can enhance their skill sets and overall employability (De Cuyper et al. 2009; Hays 2009). Although we found scant evidence to support this argument, it was noted by one participant:

> [The] agency actually gives you the chance to do a lot of things that being a direct employee wouldn't allow you to … you work in different places, meet new people. (Adama)

Of Seeking Definition Amidst Market Volatility

A somewhat ironic finding was that while TAW can be, by its nature, markedly insecure, this work form nonetheless provided a medium for the student-migrants to add greater definition into their work lives. This was amidst the intermittence and volatility that permeates the atypical labour industry on the one hand, and the insecurities brought on by migration structures on the other.

An inherent feature of contingent employment arrangements is that they are highly susceptible to fluctuations in the business cycle, the result being that work availability is increasingly dependent on market forces beyond the control of both the worker and employer. This tenurial insecurity is especially pronounced for workers engaged on 'zero-hour' terms, which happens to be the case for the majority of this study's participants. This volatility is apparent here as students admit to occasionally being beset with occasional stretches of unemployment due to shortages in demand or unsuitability of work assignments offered by the agency. To this end, the student-migrants tended to find a strategic workaround by engaging several work agencies simultaneously. In fact, it was never the case that a student-migrant was signed to just a single agency.

> Yes, I'm registered with more than one agency, I think everyone is … there are many reasons, maybe, you get more shift offers to pick from if you have several of them. (Femi)

> Just in case [the] agency does not have any shifts that suits your availability or there's an issue, or they misbehave here, you know all your eggs are not in one basket. (Amina)

By not limiting themselves to just one employer in this way, not only did the student-migrants amplify their chances of finding suitable work assignments, but they also mitigated the uncertainties brought on by zero-hour contracts. This often enabled just enough room to manoeuvre so they could effectively manage their work-life schedules. Doing this more so helped students who intended to maintain a position of adhering to the employment restrictions to which they were subject. This feature was apparent in the various arrangements through which participants had taken on work assignments from the various agencies. Although the minutiae of each might differ per agency, there were two broad arrangements through which workers obtained work assignments. For the first, some student-migrants indicated that they provided their availability for the working week to the agency in advance and subsequently were issued with available assignments that fitted with this. For the second, some were sent open work offers intermittently (as they became available), following which they indicated their interest through a process of bidding for the work. What we increasingly found was that participants often exploited these various arrangement to mitigate against uncertainties and according to their individual circumstances.

> I provide my availability with this one, that's like my main one, then these other ones send me shifts every other day [*sic*], I take them if I'm free for the time and its convenient for me, so it depends. (Amina)

For others with equally pressing commitments, the pliability afforded by agency work allowed them to more effectively maintain a work-life balance, this being the case at least for Simbi:

> I'm signed up to about four agencies but mostly work with only two ... I provide my availability for the week and [they] offer me shifts that match them ... they [the agencies] know I have childcare responsibilities to take care of, childminders are really expensive here you know, so me and my partner always plan to alternate work and babysitting duties for the week.

More so, it was not always the case that agency work presented the foremost means into paid work for all participants, yet for many, it was simply the most consistent.

> then would go from job to job, for different types of jobs, from one training to the next, looking online for job adverts on Groupon or Job Centre ... one of my mates even teased me that I spent more time training for jobs than actually doing the work I was training for ...

> I remember having no money and it was my turn to pay for light[4] in my flat then because as usual, I was in between jobs … She [the flatmate] later convinced me to register with an agency, at least that way I can get job offers straight to my phone without having to do too much, and at worst, on a bad week I would get at least one shift to do that I don't need to hustle for myself. (Adaeze)

In this illustration, agency work arrangements can thus present students with a means to cushion against some of the insecurities associated with contingent employment, and paradoxically presents a medium of stability and security that assists with effective time management, helping to instil a degree of definition in their working lives.

Nevertheless, the portrait of the student-migrants' engagement in this work form was not just of positive, accessible and flexible engagements. This study uncovered very negative consequences to temporary agency employment for the student-migrant, with all the structural constraints that comes with holders of this status.

Work Extents and Visa Rules

The highlighted socioeconomic vulnerabilities already raised in our study findings have shown how a not insignificant proportion of the participants engage in paid employment for hours in excess of those permitted in the terms of the study visa.[5] Although the interview guide used in our study, by design, excluded this explicit line of inquiry, the in-depth, intensive qualitative measures deployed here allowed for the inclusion of supplementary data by way of 'off the record' conversations and observations. The consequence being that this topic was broached in some form during those interactions. Subsequently, the majority of participants (23) alluded to working for 10–20 hours of work per week, especially during the recorded sessions. Albeit with the caveat that we had no means to verify such claims, these working hours fall within the legal limits imposed on their student visas.

Meanwhile, for about 12 participants, including 9 that participated in the ethnography, we were able to obtain a more definite understanding of their working hours and can conclude with a high degree of certainty that the

---

4. A euphemism for electricity.
5. That is in excess of 20 hours of work per week in term time (for full-time students studying at degree level).

extent of their workforce participation frequently exceeded the restrictions attached to their visa terms. These participants regularly engage in paid employment for periods between 25 and 50 hours per week during term time, with some maintaining hours that parallel and even surpass the conventional working week.

> I do usually work for like maybe 30–40 hours, I'll do my care work like twice, then I work as a salesperson at an African shop in town twice a week, then sometimes I also work at the stadium, but only when there's a football game. (Zamani)

More so, an interesting insight gleaned here was that students nearing the completion of their study programme and visa expiry dates were more open to discussing their illegal work extents. Their impending departure from the UK apparently meant that they had little concern in divulging this information during the course of the interviews due to reduced risk of potential repercussions from the authorities.

> I already have my certificate, even if I tell you I work more than 20 hours they cannot come and arrest me when I'm in my father's house in Accra, or deport me when I'm already deporting myself back to where I came from. (Tega)

This resonates with findings of Anderson et al. (2006) who, in a survey of Eastern European student-workers studying in the UK, found a large proportion of international students work a greater number of hours than their visa permitted. However, the only reason the participants in Anderson's study had been willing to admit to working in violation of their visa conditions was because they were surveyed soon before their home state acceded to the European Union, and thus they no longer feared law enforcement given their new EU-citizenship status and thereby no longer being the subject of immigration control.

For most participants, working in breach of visa terms is undertaken as a strategic response to mitigate against future economic precarity that follows from their social position as student-migrant workers. For instance, for Simbi, this tactic was adopted to afford to her the liberty to prioritise academic interests when it matters most.

> … per week … I typically work three shifts of say between 10–12 hours including breaks … with different agencies … Because sometimes you get a little bit of a break from school or when it is not so hectic with

> coursework, deadlines and all that, so you just want to work at least three shifts so that when it does get hectic, you know that you still have money saved up even when you can't work during that period. (Simbi)

This was a sentiment frequently reiterated, indeed flouting this restriction was predominately about the participants achieving financial security for present and future challenges. Indeed, some viewed working beyond the allotted hours strategically as a means towards achieving some semblance of balance amenable to their specific circumstance.

> … there are times when for like a month I don't pick shifts at all, like when I was writing my dissertation I did not work, I'm very sure if we calculate it, it might even balance out … the hours I worked versus the hours I did not … (Adama)

> … because if I don't work for say a week, I feel like I'm wasting the work hours on my visa, like I'm even losing money … (Ekong)

Then for at least two participants, working beyond the allotted hours was also a means to make productive the free time permitted by their less-than-demanding academic schedules.

> I get bored easily, I have classes only two days a week, and then I don't have exams to prepare for, just coursework and PowerPoint presentations … at least I could be making money with the time I would've spent faffing about, probably playing FIFA or something like that, you can't have too much money. (Adama)

Although it is largely undecided the extents to which juggling extensive work commitments with full-time study may detract from the academic performance and overall well-being of student-workers (Bradley 2006; Riggert et al. 2006), we find that this may well be the case at least for some of this study's participants, as self-reported.

> I don't care what they say but if we are being real, the time spent at work has to come from somewhere … that's time … the time that could be spent in the library you know, studying… (Nana)

> I try to do my best to take my notes and sometimes if it is a relaxed shift, I might even take my iPad or laptop to work, but I'll be lying if I said it doesn't affect my studies. (Ekong)

However, again it must be reiterated that this portrait was not monolithic as this is an inherently subjective query. It was not always the case that students readily admit that their extensive work commitments may detract from their academic performance.

> ... abeg[6] if you are smart you'll find a way to manage, look, I work at least four times a week but I'm still going to finish with a first, you just need to know what works for you, I don't need to spend two years in the library before I understand what I'm doing... (Abeo)

Apart from its effect on academic performance, this work practice effectively exposes the student-migrant to the harsher designs of the labour market which comes with lengthy, antisocial work hours, just as the perceived transience of tenure may engender social detachment and cause them to forego other pleasures and responsibilities in service of pursuing gainful employment solely for subsistence.

> I really need the money, so I just forget about these things, it's not like I'm happy doing it sef... I haven't had a social life, don't hang out or have fun, from school to work, work to school, like now I really wanted to have a summer break, but I couldn't, I was busy working all through summer. (Zamira)

> ... I'm always thinking of rent, and school fees ... (Adama)

Nonetheless, these insights reveal that student-migrants' behavioural patterns within the labour market are rarely static, but rather dynamic and evolve in response to situational variables. As a general finding, the bulk of evidence collated hints that this phenomenon can be quite detrimental for students' physical and mental health, it can detract from their lives as social actors, and also hinder their academic performance.

This sets the template for the ensuing section where we specifically address the more personally negative aspects of the student-migrant-worker experience.

Exploitation and Abuse at Work

The accounts of exploitation and abuse revealed by the study participants were mostly centred on remuneration provisions, and discrimination stemming

---

6. Nigerian slang meaning 'please'.

from a range of factors and demographical qualities. These are discussed in the sections that follow.

Remuneration

As previously noted,[7] these student-migrant-workers were typically in employment sectors known for low pay, and it was found in some instances that the low pay received was actually illegally so. While we find that all study participants, officially at least, earned an hourly pay at rates consistent with the National Living Wage, this was not always reflected in the actual pay received. This study uncovered evidence of exploitation, where workers are being underpaid by employers, and especially by employment agencies. Indeed, about a third of participants reported of confusing or bogus deductions in their payslips at some point during their time working on temporary contracts in the UK. This was operationalised through various underhanded practices on the part of employers, ranging from deductions for grossly overpriced uniforms, training events that never really happened, non-payment of 'overtime' work undertaken[8] and even blatant wage theft.

> … the amount of money I think is coming to me when I do my calculations isn't what comes on the payslip when they pay. It is either one deduction or the other, they deducted money for uniforms, for being minutes late, they'll clock you in for the exact time … (Adama)

> … there was a time we were deducted for lunch that we serve for free to attendees, it was an event hosting gig in the middle of nowhere, there was nowhere else to go eat and we got a lunch break, but they still charged us full price for food like we're meant to starve all afternoon… (Nana)

> … this agency, someone already warned me to run from them but I didn't listen … they provided transport to get to the care home, but no one told me that your work time begins as soon as you get on the bus, so when I put in my timesheet I only put in for hours I actually spent there, the agency supervisor signed off on it and said nothing … that lost almost two hours pay… (Ife)

Sometimes, apart from covert means like bogus pay deductions, instances of wage theft and exploitation can also be quite flagrant. One participant

---

7. See 'Employment Profile' above.
8. A euphemism for hours worked in excess of the legally mandated 20–hour weekly work limit.

reported of being offered 'under the table' lump cash payments at wage-levels that barely met the statutory minimum wage.

> ... this Ghanaian couple wanted me to look after their store from 10:00 a.m. to 6:00 p.m. for £50 per day on weekends, cash. They were saying its we-we so I'll just do it out of brotherly love ... I know I need the money but come on, I am not stupid, that comes down like less than £6 per hour, or even less I think ... I dunno why, it's like everyone is trying to cheat you here, even your own people, they think because you just came that means you don't know anything, they will not even dare suggest this with a UK-born citizen because they'll get in trouble. (Mensah)

Especially as it implicates 'overtime pay' and the 20–hour weekly work limits, student-migrants indicate that agencies and even employers may sometimes withhold wages for hours worked in excess of visa restrictions. They do this despite having prior knowledge of the student's legal status, a matter Abeo felt particularly strongly about:

> Most of them are thieves, big big thieves. They know what they're doing, they are very aware when they send you on two 12–hour shifts days apart, then time for payment they'll only pay for 20 hours, excuse me, like what happened to the remaining four hours?.. (Abeo)

Taking all of this into account, it may well be the case that the student-migrants' take-home pay often fell below statutory thresholds when the mass of hours worked, and payment received are tallied for discrepancies. However, while authors including Nyland et al. (2009) found that international student workers in Australia often needed to undertake employment for less than the legal minimum wage, especially as they were crowded in a narrower range of jobs, we find very little evidence to support this. Participants rarely indicated acquiescing to being paid below the legal thresholds, despite being disadvantaged by a crowded job market.

> If you are going to cheat me, at least try, don't piss on my leg and tell me its rain... (Mensah)

Discrimination and abuse

Accounts of discrimination and abuse are rife in the participants' recounting of their labour market experiences. We premise this by saying that this lies contrary to findings from Takeda (2005) and Nyland (2009) who both allude that difficulties encountered by international student-workers were more the result of market indices and less of racism and discrimination. However, those studies did not give a voice to the experiences of actors given to multiple intersecting forms of disadvantage and institutional violence, as this study does, nor did they utilise more critical and intimate methods of investigation. This perhaps accounts for the discrepancies in our respective findings.

> Trust me, there's a lot of racial discrimination, especially being a Black person … I've been called a monkey, told to go back to where I came from, spat at … but it's mostly from patients (in the care home) so you already know they are not right upstairs. (Abeo)

More than two-thirds of participants had at least one perceived discriminatory incident to report of, being dealt by a range of actors including clients, colleagues, line-managers, employers and recruitment officers. The accounts of discrimination featured in several distinct albeit often reinforcing respects – from differential treatment and micro-aggressions, to overt acts of bigotry and racist abuse. These experiences stem from a range of characteristics, from demographical features including ethnicity and gender, to more structural features like migrant status, their studentship, being temporary workers or, indeed, an intersection of all or some of these attributes.[9]

> … when you work with people that don't have the same colour with them, it is not always the best because they could be very racist – just the stupidest levels of racial stuff going on, you know? (Femi)

> There was one day I encountered the manager who was nasty and all that. She would say 'South Africa' when referring to me even when I told her I was Nigerian. And then when we would have to send my time sheets, she'll refuse to round up and put 10 hours 45 mins instead of just saying 11, when the remaining 15 mins is meant to be for hand-over as per normal practice. Then when I complain she'll say, 'If you don't want to work in this department, you stop coming here.' I never said anything to her… (Adama)

---

9. It should be noted that the legal consciousness and pluralism methodology adopted in this study meant that the participants self-described what they considered to be discriminatory. This, accordingly, referred to their subjective understanding as opposed to the imposition of an overarching definition in accordance with regulatory provisions or even our own definition.

Yet the extent of the participants' abuse was not limited to verbal attacks. There was the occasional case of physical abuse.

> I've been in a position where I was physically attacked by a patient and the patient was throwing racial abuse left and right … (Mikhail)

There are also reports of culturally underpinned differential treatment:

> There was this one time we got reported to the line manager by a colleague because we were speaking Yoruba at work, just because we were speaking Yoruba amongst ourselves, that became a problem. They said it made people uncomfortable because they couldn't understand what was being said, even though we were not speaking to them. (Ife)

Apart from these racially marked incidents, discrimination at work may yet involve other functions including the context of their employment position as temporary workers, who albeit expedient, are at best peripheral, and at worst, extraneous to a firms' organisational structure. Either way, there was little commitment from management towards these workers. Indeed, some participants reported of being assigned harder, grittier or unappealing tasks by work supervisors or managers.

> I was meant to be on break, and a patient in the home needed cleaning up, and my co-support worker was a permanent staff, and instead of her to do the cleaning up herself, because we basically do the same thing, she left the patient in their mess for almost an hour waiting for me to come back from break to do it. When I asked why, she said it's my job to provide help and not ask questions, but we do the same thing, she's just a full-time staff… (Edet)

More so, there were reports of workers being isolated and segregated according to their contractual status, with temporary staff often being identified by their uniforms and assigned workstations.

> If you go somewhere new, the first thing the supervisor they ask is if you are from an agency or full-time, because most times they don't even know themselves. When you say you are agency then they'll look at you funny and ask you to go do something where it will be only you or there'll be other agency staff working there… (Nnamdi)

This upholds Toms's (2012) assertion that agency workers are often segmented in workspaces in ways that may well engender social isolation. Again, their situation as recent migrants and students can present a source for differential treatment within workspaces. In this sense, it is somewhat ironic to find that these students often report of being stereotyped as being too 'well off' for the roles they occupy or assumed to be less committed workers who accept employment leisurely.

> Its many things, maybe it's because they think that you are a 'Johnny just Come'[10] or because you are a student you don't really need the money and you're doing it just because, so they treat you anyhow … like I don't have bills and responsibilities too, you know? (Abeo)

> And then I realised when I go talking with a very few of them, they were always asking me, 'What do you do? What do you do?' And then I'm like, 'I'm an international student.' 'What are you doing?' 'Master's?' And then they always ask me the question, 'Why are you here? Why are you here?' You know, like, 'Why? Why should you be doing your Masters' [degree] then you're working here? (Zamani)

Then there is the slight inconvenience of cultural novelty to contend with.

> … where I come from, when someone asks you 'are you alright?' it's usually meant as an insult, its fighting words, but here they ask you as a greeting, it's still weird. (Ekong)

Why We Do Nothing[11]

For the most part, those perceived violations were rarely ever actioned or overtly contested. This is due to a range of reasons; socioeconomic vulnerabilities; the participants' highly transactional view of employment, migration and labour market temporalities; and their overreliance on and fear of reprisals from employers which, collectively, result in the student-migrants lacking the time, resources and will to challenge and pursue recourse for unjust detrimental experiences.

---

10. Nigerian slang for inexperienced.
11. This is only a light-touch discussion as this topic is considered in detail in Chapter 6, where discussion of the subjects' claims-making behaviour in relation to legal mobilisation, especially drawing from ethnographic data, is offered.

> Before I came to this country, I was even starting working. I already made up my mind not to pay attention to discrimination or whatsoever. So, when people are talking about discrimination, racism and all that kind of thing, I'm like, I'm here to get my cash and I'm good. So, when they tell me: 'Go fuck off!' and I say same to you – I just smile and look very unmoved. It doesn't touch me. I don't feel hurt about it. (Simbi)

A number of participants admitted to being ill-equipped with a knowledge of how to seek recourse for these experiences. More so, the illustration presented by the participants can be quite cyclical, as discriminatory, unjust structures are often adduced as reasons for inaction in the face of an abusive experience. Especially for those in agency work, there was a recurrent understanding that the worker held the least leverage in the three-way relationship. It is in the recruitment agency and the user firm's financial interests to maintain an amicable business relationship with one another, and this can leave the worker in a truly disposable situation.

> Who will I report to ... Na them them[12] now, they'll always protect their own, just imagine I'm reporting you to your brother ... (Wale)

The Utterly Transactional Student-Migrant-Worker

The discussion here centres on the intersecting avenues for insecurity and disadvantage that mar the employment experiences of the study participants. It is divided into four main parts. We begin with a consideration of the subjective structural factors that underpin students' employment contexts through notions of socioeconomic inequities. Second, we discuss how these collated experiences satisfy the nomenclature 'precarious' in terms of their employment. Meanwhile, the third section focuses on the uncertainties brought on by the state-imposed constraints on the employment structures applied to international students. The fourth and closing section examines the subjects' appraisal of their employment experience in the UK.

Structural disadvantage

> It doesn't matter what your previous qualifications are, I am a certified civil engineer, but I work in a bakery. ... You do what you can get, that's just it. (Mikhail)

---

12. A Nigerian pidgin slang meaning 'it's between them...'.

The labour market position of these international students is effectively contoured by structural disadvantage and socioeconomic vulnerabilities that start to take effect, even prior to their arrival in the country for study, and more so lingers on throughout their residence.

> It even begins way before we get here, they, the British, colonised us and English is our official language but before we get here some of us may need to write IELTS to demonstrate our English level before we can even secure admission. (Abeo)

To start, participants directly attributed the inability to secure what they deemed as 'fitting work opportunities' to structural inequities that marked the entirety of the student migratory process. For one, the prevalent non-recognition of foreign qualifications and proficiencies, especially from developing states, in UK workspaces can prove detrimental for the student-migrant-worker. The fact that these students are, for the most part, unable to utilise existing qualifications and proficiencies obtained in their home states as an underpinning to them securing 'better' jobs in the UK effectively diminishes their job market prospects. This also predisposed them to underemployment and de-skilling occasioned by the apparent mismatch between possessed skills and available work opportunities (Kelly 2011; Van Riemsdijk 2014). It was a frequent occurrence for participants to reinforcement of these discriminatory structures by contrasting their circumstance to that of similarly placed EU-domiciled students.

> Now you think about it, we're all international students, but those from the EU can work for as long as they want, however they want and no one disturbs them for anything, and we from outside can only work 20 hours … Even though we are in the same class and do the same everything. (Abeo)

> Look at me now, I am a qualified legal practitioner back in Accra, I've passed the Bar, not even only as a solicitor, but am a barrister as well, but I can't even get a job as a paralegal here with all my degrees and experience, believe me I have tried … One rejection after the other meanwhile this Spanish chick that didn't even have a pure law background and hadn't practiced law before got several offers from big firms on her first time applying … (Edet)

This study corroborates the findings from the UK Council for International Student Affairs' (UKCISA) Report (2004), which highlighted how students from non-EU countries often experienced difficulties when navigating the UK employment market when compared to their EU-domiciled counterparts.[13]

In addition to the lack of amenable work opportunities for individuals in their position, other discernible reasons for this arduous labour market experience includes a lack of support with the recruitment process especially from their universities, and bureaucratic constraints.

> I attended one of those Uni employment fairs when I resumed but it was a waste of time, they were not really looking for part-time workers, it was more of work opportunities for after you graduate ... (Uyi)

> I had a course mate that had done his undergrad here, he told me not to wait for those people in the Job Centre or the Uni thingy, they'll only waste your time ... you are better off even looking online for vacancies on your own for anything you know you can do ... (Ken-Saro)

> I tried finding work with salons here, but they said I must get certified and do some tests like that. Ain't nobody got time for that ... (Amina)

Furthermore, their manifested employment situation also had much to do with time constraints and the uncertainties associated with transient forms of migration, including of students. For one, these are, after all, individuals on fixed term visas and as such may not have the luxury to either wait for better work opportunities, and further, they are also full-time students who, despite the stereotypes, are intent on succeeding in school and progressing academically. This circumstance is emphasised by real socioeconomic pressures, all of which deem a prolonged job search as impractical. This more so engenders a profoundly transactional view of employment where finding the perfect job seemed to matter less than, for example, paying tuition fees or rent. Indeed, akin to migrant labour theories, subjects indicate that their employment designation is underpinned by immediate socioeconomic necessity. This consequently meant that they tended to gravitate towards accepting readily available jobs on a contingent basis, solely for subsistence as opposed to holding out for more complementary roles. For instance, just under two-thirds of the participants indicate that they had begun searching for work opportunities only weeks after arriving in the UK, some even before they had been assigned National Insurance numbers.

---

13. Note, this view was expressed whilst the UK remained a Member State of the European Union. Following the UK's withdrawal since 1 January 2021, EU students are subject to more onerous immigration controls and no longer have the right to free movement or to non-discrimination as regards fees. They are thus treated as 'international' students.

> It feels like you're losing money, when you don't work up to your full potential if I can call it that ... I always budget, I've already done the maths that I'll work this long, earn this much, and it will last this long, anything other than that then I feel like I'm behind and need to make it up somehow ... (Uyi)

Socioeconomic inequities

Uyi's sentiments poignantly illustrates the archetypal 'the target wage earner' that makes for the majority of this study's participants. Contrary to findings documenting the benefits of international work experience for students as a motivation for seeking temporary employment while studying, for this study's participants, this was at best a peripheral consideration. Neither did the assertion that international students might opt for part-time work so to improve their English-language skills hold authority here. The participants, for this study at least, all came from Anglophone countries, which, through colonialisation, means they are already native English speakers. Quite simply, the principal reason for undertaking employment while studying was simply to be expressed in financial terms.

Turning to students who work in violation of study visa restrictions, that is, in excess of 20 hours per week during term time, this tactic is adopted mostly out of necessity. While scholars, including Ruhs and Anderson (2010), allude to a relationship between the individual's commitment to their immigration entry status and the likelihood for breaking the immigration terms attached thereto, this study finds that this is rarely ever the case. Most participants did not set out to work in breach of visa terms. For these respondents, working in breach of visa terms including the mechanisms adopted to effect this are mostly incidental, and deployed to cushion against socioeconomic insecurities as they navigate a novel terrain. And more importantly, despite their illegal working activities, most of these students are highly motivated and committed to excelling academically. In some instances, the portrait is quite cyclical, students often need to undertake more hours of paid employment to adequately cater to their individual needs and financial responsibilities (especially tuition fees), without which they may be withdrawn from their course and consequently lose the legal rights to remain in the country.

> What kind of stupid question is that, it's the money now, I need the money of course, rent, tuition, upkeep, they don't pay themselves ... (Abeo)

Although the argument can be made that this financial insecurity may have been pre-empted ab initio with more robust budgeting on the part of prospective students, their situations are rarely that linear. In some cases, financial insecurity may stem from external variables that exceed the control of the individual. An illustration of this can be witnessed through fluctuations in global economic forces and the dire inequities this perpetuates. Take for instance Abeo, a self-funded Nigerian PhD student, who had commenced study two years previously when the value of the Nigerian currency, the 'Naira', was worth significantly more than it is at present.[14] This downturn has resulted in financial resources held in the local currency at home losing much of its value once introduced and converted into the UK's currency.

> ... then when I just resumed for my undergrad, a pound was like roughly 200 Naira, now its risen to almost 500, I have to somehow pay tuition of almost 10 grand a year for three years, haba ...(Abeo)[15]

A substantial proportion of students directly ascribe the difficulties encountered in their labour market journeys as a direct consequence of both overt and institutional inequitable structures. It appears that such claims are not without substance given the numerous studies which point towards systemic discrimination as a persistent cause of disadvantage for ethnic and national minorities in the labour market. Studies have, for instance, demonstrated that when applying for jobs, ethnic and national minorities are less likely to receive an interview or job offer (Bertrand and Mullainathan 2004; Fix and Struyk 1993; Hirsh and Lyons 2010; Moss and Tilly 2001). And even when they are offered an interview, minorities are observed to be disproportionately clustered in the lower rungs of the employment hierarchy and on the peripheries of organisations (Stainback and Tomaskovic-Devey 2009; Tomaskovic-Devey et al. 2006). Here, there is a heightened resonance of the socioeconomic inequities associated with transnational student migration especially as it brings with it implications that transcend even their labour market station into other facets of their overall experiences. They note how the system is implicitly structured as if meant to reify disadvantage and exacerbate the hardships to which they are already beset.

---

14. The value of the Nigerian Naira declined by more than 100 per cent in this decade due to the fall in oil prices and other internal factors.
15. A Nigerian slang used to express disbelief or surprise.

The 'grapevine' of knowledge

The concentration of student-migrants in certain forms of work and occupying roles in specific sectors, and having formed relationships due to this circumstance, has significant effects on the informal social networks associated with the migratory process. This finding highlights the role of routine interactions in establishing the context of the student-migrant's placement within the labour market. These interactions are housed within mundane networks of information that historically precede the actor's arrival into the frame and exist independently of their input or decision-making. This also means they are prevalent in its dissemination. These networks serve as conduits through which experientially rooted knowledge on the expedience of specific employment agencies, organisations and employers gets transmitted. For instance, almost all participants to this study had no experience of agency work prior to their time in the UK and had only become aware of this form of working by friends and acquaintances within mostly homogeneous networks. More so, it is not coincidental that participants in each study location tended to be signed up to the same four to six employment agencies. These repeat agencies tended to be the ones specifically known and evidenced to be receptive of international student-workers. This insight reiterates evidence presented in the migration scholarship such as by Massey (1990) when demonstrating that networks of employment and immigration tend to take on dynamics of their own, negotiated over time. And more so, once these networks have become ingrained, they linger for time even when the socio-legal or economic framework is altered. However, just as this information gets freely disseminated, it may yet be amended when necessary, for instance where there is a new firm in town offering fairer terms, or when an agency ceases operations, or becomes particularly arduous to work with and so on.

Of course, the student-migrants' novelty to the UK labour market may well play a role here. A poignant finding is that for most of these student-migrant-workers, the employment agency itself was often the principal source for knowledge concerning their workplace rights and responsibilities. This can provide a motivated employer/agency with an avenue to surreptitiously exploit such workers, especially within remuneration contexts. For instance, there had seemed to be a myth circulating within the cohort at Location A that agency workers are not legally entitled to additional benefits including statutory sick pay, holiday pay and so on.

> I don't think we are entitled to sick pay, because I think you have to be a full-time employee to get it, or something like that … (Tega)

THE 'UTTERLY TRANSACTIONAL WORKER'   149

Another telling revelation here is that participants often expressed contrasting understandings of how accruable 'holiday pay' was being calculated, and work agencies were often at the centre of this confusion. A participant revealed they had seen a deducted percentage from their weekly wages for what was deemed as holiday pay contributions, which had been pooled into a purse remittable to the worker following a formal application to that effect. Meanwhile another reported of being informed by a work agency's representative that accruable holiday pay was being rolled up and paid out as a premium added to their hourly wage.[16]

Labour market uncertainties

The findings as presented here resonate with those of Stanworth and Druker (2004) and their proposition that

> the element of respectability and choice offered by tempting work must be set against the price paid at one and the same time by workers [*sic*], in terms of the transitory nature of the assignment, the marginal position in their assigned firms, their lack of employment rights and generally poor pay levels. (p. 67)

This much is very apparent here, especially following an application of Rodgers and Rodgers' (1989) thesis on the principal factors that make for precarious employment: (i) the degree of certainty of continuing employment; (ii) control over the labour process, and contractual status; (iii) the degree of regulatory protection; and (iv) wage levels (Rodgers and Rodgers 1989, 1). We consider these factors to the cohort of participants below.

Precarious contractual status

> I don't understand, I'm a worker, I work, that's all I know, the rest is long ... (Wale)

There was a prevalence of what can be conceived of as ambivalence on the part of participants towards the legal intricacies of their respective employment relationship, and more so of the rights and responsibilities that can flow

---

16. The practice of rolled-up holiday pay defies the express ruling of the Court of Justice of the European Union in Case (C-257/04) *Caulfield v Hanson Clay Products Ltd* [2006] ECLI:EU:C:2006:177 where it was held that this does not conform with the provisions of the Working Time Directive (Directive 93/104).

from this. More so, student-workers were generally apathetic to the prospects of broaching into the proscribed *self-employed* status.

For one, notwithstanding that it is legally mandated that employers furnish international students with a written document of their employment details to ensure they keep to the terms stipulated in their visas, it was rarely the case that these student-migrant-workers received this or indeed any formal contractual document from employers. Only five participants of the entire study population indicated that they had received formal contractual documents at any point in their work history in the UK. Meanwhile, as the subject of employment status is seldomly discussed or the matter for an underlying purpose (such as the assertion of a statutory right or benefit), for some, this had simply never come up or become relevant. Yet for others who had reasons to challenge work-related contractual issues and had sought some clarification of accruable rights, participants often reported of being ignored or provided with disingenuous information by their employers. For some who tried to pursue the matter, participants often reported of being directed to the firm's webpage containing its generic terms of engagement for clarification. This information was often very vague and left the individual no wiser for it. For instance, as this study includes data from intensive ethnographic observations, it was not uncommon for participants to seek the researcher's help (due to their legal background) to decipher some vague statement contained in formal correspondence from the agency. Sometimes these were seemingly intentionally vague to prevent the reader from fully understanding their meaning. Of course, this is only further obfuscated by the fact that participants were signed up to a number of employers and/or intermediaries, often with distinct organisational structures. This made pursuing the organisation for formal contracts in each work context an arduous task. Thus, it is unsurprising to find that these participants were, for the most part, oblivious of their employment status, on the worker, self-employed, or employee spectrum,[17] and particularly in respect to the accruable rights that are allocated to each class.

This uncertainty extends to the question of who assumes legal responsibility for the student-migrant-worker, and conversely who the individual felt responsible towards during work assignments. The subsequent responses to this line of enquiry varied between participants and work context, as might have been expected.

> It depends, like when I work as security for football matches, I feel like I am responsible to the stadium authorities and managers even though

---

17. Albeit with some notable exceptions, discussed in Chapter 6.

I'm with an agency, because they tell you exactly what you need to do and especially the safety measures because that it is very rowdy, and anything can happen, so you need to be more attentive and work more closely with your colleagues and supervisors. But when I work care, I feel more responsible to my agency, because they are the ones I know ... (Zamani)

Both, because the agency sent you there, whereas the supervisor tells you what to do for the day and how to do it, so it's both of them really ... (Ife)

I feel responsible to myself, I take care of myself, I don't wait for them, so if that's what you mean, I just make sure I am okay, and not hurt in any way wherever they send me to work ... (Abeo)

Although this ostensibly concurs with documented findings that more recent migrants (including students) and atypical labourers often present with poor knowledge of their employment rights and obligations, this portrait is far more nuanced. If anything, this has more to do with the context of the participants' employment position and the structural impediments, than an apathy for legal terminology. More so, contrary to documented insights that members of historically disenfranchised groups tend to avoid formal legal structures even in instances where it could be beneficial or provide reprieve due to an inherent distrust of formal institutions, our participants, for the most part, overlooked this simply because it is a potentially arduous exercise, it is unnecessary, or due to the structural impediments associated with acquiring this insight. The transactional and transient view of employment deems it farfetched that participants would challenge employers about their designated employment status as an abstract exercise, albeit that this could be critical to them adhering to their student visa terms. Yet, while it may not have been a contingent factor for most of the participants, these resultant confusions nonetheless stem from the porous regulatory frameworks that mark out atypical employment relationships in the UK.

The headaches of 'flexible' working on a student visa

This study finds truth in the documented advantage of transient employment relationships in respect of them allowing workers more flexibility and control over their working lives. This includes control over how, when, where and for how long they engage in paid employment. The reality, however, is that this advantage is not universally positive. Upon critical review, the value of flexibility can be severely dampened by several factors. The more pertinent of which includes the dynamics of their employment relationship, and the employment restrictions attached to students' work extents as subjects of migration control.

Zero-hour contracts

At both study locations there was a prevalence of one-sided, standard-form-esque employment relationships where the fundamentals were established exclusively by the agency. The individual's choice is simply to accept these terms or seek employment elsewhere. This sets the tone for the finding that the majority of participants were engaged on a zero-hour basis with no contractual guarantees. As many as 28 of the 37 participants indicated that they were usually engaged on zero-hour terms, and 5 other participants indicated that they had been so engaged at some point in their time in the UK. This, of course, meant that the availability and duration of work assignments varied greatly and were, generally, unpredictable. In fact, participants often expressed uncertainty about their work schedule in the short term;

> Yeah, I have for today, but I'm not yet sure about tomorrow, I haven't arranged anything yet, but I will probably get something before then … (Femi)

The detriments of zero-hour contracts, especially for the worker are well documented. For one, it engenders precarity and insecurity that can be perilous for the individual's mental health and overall well-being. Workers having this form of precarious relationship with the labour market are more prone to stress-related ailments, just as one's mental well-being is prone to suffer where there are lingering financial insecurities that cannot be assuaged by guaranteed work (Kamerāde and Richardson 2018). As this was in part an ethnographic study, we were able to witness the consequences of this uncertainty first-hand. It was not uncommon for students to dash from their residence to work at very short notice because they received an impromptu offer of a shift and they needed the money. At times, this meant that participants had to attend work contrary to their existing plans or even in times when they were ill.

> You don't get paid when you are sick, we don't get sick pay … I know I should be resting but who is going to tell that to the bills and the letting agents. Sickness is expensive, I can't afford it. (Adaeze)
>
> I get sick often because of the weather, it's always raining and so cold here, even when its sunny, it's still cold … And also because of what I do, I work with the elderly, most of them have compromised immune

systems, so it's easy to catch something, but I can't really help it, so except if it's really bad or I'm bedridden then I'll always take shifts ... (Adama)

They also undertook work assignments when doing so was detrimental to their academic study.

> ... I don't know yet, I might work tonight if I get sent a shift before the end of the day, but I'll first go to the library to work on my dissertation, I'll leave from there if I get a shift ... (Simbi)

Think twice before you say no

> You need to be sensible about it, you can't just be declining shifts like that, the agency will catch on and stop sending you shifts now, they might even think that you have gone back to your country that's why you are not picking shifts or responding to their messages ... (Wale)

Building on the proliferation of zero-hour contracts, the perceived flexibility for the worker in the sense that they retain the right to turn down assignments is true, but this is a two-way relationship. The agency, likewise, is not obligated to provide work assignments if it chooses. This can mean that employers may unilaterally withhold work, and this can occur following extended periods of inactivity and/or when the individual repeatedly declines shifts being offered. This was evident from responses collated at both study locations.

> If you don't pick shifts with some agencies like [redacted] for say two, three months, they may put you under review ... which basically means that they are about to delete your profile if you do not make yourself available, and you may have to reapply to pick shifts with them again in the future ... (Nana)

This is a poignant reflection given that there are a finite number of employers in any one region that will cater to student-migrant-workers' vocational peculiarities in an already crowded marketplace. This grounded the feeling expressed frequently by participants that they must maintain an active employment profile or risk the chance of being passed over for more eager workers.

> Oh, do you want to go over there? They just swap you for someone else. (Uyi)

> There are many of us looking for work and shifts and more are still coming every year, they know that's why they do what they like ... if you don't want the work, they can easily find another person that will grab it with both hands. (Tega)
>
> Sometimes there will be several people bidding for the same shift ... so if you don't do it, someone else will, it's that simple ... (Ken-Saro)

This in turn meant that in pragmatic terms, participants felt under pressure to accept work assignments in instances where they ordinarily would not, just to maintain the employment relationship.

> It's smart even if you find a better agency, you still pick shifts from the former ones from time to time, to keep them as backups. Except if you don't plan on ever working with them again, then you can totally ghost them ... (Mensah)
>
> Even if they are misbehaving, you should still keep them, because you may never know, you might need them in the future ... (Wale)
>
> If you don't want them to cut you like that, every now and then you can pick one or two shifts with them even you know they are not the best ... (Adaeze)

More so, the potential to be dropped by their respective employers can engender and/or exacerbate the insecurities that these students are all too familiar with.

> Nobody cares when you are sick or not doing well. Imagine, when I lost my dad, I told my agency that I'll be taking some time off for bereavement, the work planner at the agency, this lady asked if I'll be able to confirm when I'll be available again and how long I'll be mourning for because it is the agency's policy to deregister workers after 4 weeks absence. But they'll make an exception for me if I want. You can imagine, I just lost my dad and you are disturbing me with this ... (Edet)

Most of these insights corroborate those already present in the empirical research-based literature. Scholars including Forde (2001), Forde AND Slater (2005) and Smith (2016) each report of an uneven rendition of the flexibilities associated with this work form, especially noting how this is premeditated almost exclusively on terms established by the employer. Forde and Slater

(2005) note that it is often the norm for agencies to blacklist workers who turn down assignments on a regular basis, or relegate them to a lower tier of worker due to their presumed 'inflexibility'. More so, Forde (2001), Henson (1996) and Maroukis (2016) all indicate that contrary to the hypothesised benefit of mutual flexibility as the principal allure of temporary work, the seeming precarity associated with its non-committal nature often means that workers must be cautious of exercising their right to decline proposed assignments, especially if they intend to continue the employment relationship. After all, for employers, any negative effects of an increased staff turnover can be mitigated by accessing a pool of willing and available workers.

Migration constraints

However, what has not been contemplated explicitly in the existing literature is how this *weakened flexibility* can detract from the working lives of student-migrants for all the institutional constraints imposed on their employment rights by the state. More precisely, how these constraints may contour how subjects come to interact with the atypical labour market. In this vein, we conclude that the 20-hour per week work limit participants are subject to does not allow for the exertion of many of the perceived benefits of flexible working, at least for those intent on adhering to this restriction in the first place. This scenario can easily become a scheduling difficulty, especially as the duration of available work assignments often varies. In this way, a concerted effort is often required to adhere to the restrictions.

> I can say okay I'll do two 9- or 10-hour shifts in the week, and that's all. I'm done for that week, but most times you don't get it like that, you will rarely ever be two perfect shifts that will equal to 20 hours and keep you under this limit … (Mikhail)

This is why student-migrant-workers generally indicate a preference for overnight shifts that last between 8 and 12 hours.

> Because you can only get what comes (to the agency). If you go with what they say then you are not meant to do two overnight shifts from 9 to 9, because that will take you over, except you want to bust it … (Zamani)

While this may not appear to be, at first view at least, a significant problem, it can present profound implications, especially when nuanced by notions of one being a target wage earner whose employment participation is born purely out of socioeconomic necessity. For some, this may effectively impede their agency and decision-making in very specific ways.

> Sometimes when I'm broke, which is almost always, and I really need money, maybe I've worked twice for 16 hours already in the week, I'll have to now start calling agencies to see if they have any short shifts available to make up the remainder of my 20 hours… (Adama)

This also meant that the participant may have to either accept or decline work assignments in defiance of their individual circumstance, to be compliant with these work restrictions. In one of these instances, a participant agreed to take an emergency assignment (a three-hour shift), which involved an hour's commute on public transport.

> … I'll be home doing nothing anyways … maybe watching TV, at least I'll be making a profit. £30 that can pay for my groceries for like a week. It's not a bad deal really when you look at it that way. (Adama)

Some participants indicated that they generally intended to keep to the work limits per the study visa terms, but then these attempts were thwarted by the unpredictability of work assignments with the consequential result in them working over the 20-hour threshold.

> See like I said, I don't even think about it. I treat the 20-hour thing as a kind of advice, instead of something that is set in stone, because if you think about it too much you'll miss out on shifts when you need the money. So if you go over by 2–3 hours, it's understandable. I don't think they really care, its if you are busting it by like 20 extra hours, then there might be a problem … (Zamani)

These factors in sum demonstrate that it is often the student-migrant-worker who has to adjust their circumstances to adhere to the terms of flexibility prescribed entirely by employers and the broader labour market forces. This factor is further exacerbated by limited access to work assignments and the constraints on their working situations prescribed by immigration control.

Job (dis)satisfaction

> I hate it there, I really do… (Ife)

Considering the student-migrant-workers' perceptions of their temporary employment experiences, the overwhelming portrait is one of dissatisfaction. Indeed, most participants indicate profound displeasure about their situation within the job market and this underwhelming experience often required a critical adjustment process involving the tuning of individual standards, expectations and sociocultural values.

> ... but I've always hated the idea of doing care work and cleaning up after people's shit ... so even when my mates found work in care homes, I just couldn't see myself doing it ... (Ife)

We find that the participants deploy a range of sentiments in making sense of their *less than ideal* predicament in the UK labour market. Global socio-economic disparities play a critical role in shaping their perceptions of the respective labour market situation, in a multitude of ways. A recurrent theme, however, was for participants to draw comparisons between the standard of living and jobs accessible to them back home, and those to which they have had to endure while studying in the UK.

> Oh back home in Ghana, I'll never do this, I'll never see myself, working tills, serving drinks, how? I am a graduate ... Nana

For some, their newly found employment status was not particularly difficult to accommodate, even when it brought with it an occupational mismatch or deskilling. They were able to draw on a range of life skills and past experiences to ease this adaptive process. For instance, Edet, who worked as a care assistant, reports of how she quickly took to her role as a care worker due to the sociocultural nurturing roles women are accustomed with, especially in her country of domicile in communities suffused with patriarchal ideals.

> ... some people call it a dirty job and all that ... what made it easy for me to fit into care work, before my dad passed, he was ill for some time and we had to take care of him. So I had a bit of an experience of caring for a loved one that was incapable of helping themselves out with their basic needs ... I got an experience of how challenging it can be for most of these people despite their age, whether they're young or you're old, so I do my best to make their lives easier ... (Edet)

Some even make more explicit recourse to broader sociocultural norms from their country of residence in making sense of their situation.

> I am African, we take care of our elderly or sick relatives, we don't have care homes really, so I don't mind it really ... (Tega)

However, we should note that some participants' labour market reception was not replete of unmet expectations and gloom. For example, Ken-Saro's outlook had been informed at an early stage through insights that had helped curtail his expectations of the reality that awaits navigating the employment market as a student-migrant.

> … luckily for me, I had cousins schooling in Hertfordshire who had been here for a while. They already told me not to bother trying to find work through my university's employability blah blah blah, you simply do what is available and puts money in your pocket, you don't have to like it …

Then there were others who seemed indifferent about their experience in the employment market.

> I work tills, bars and events catering, those type of things … it is not the best, but it is not the worst either, I mean it pays the bills and it's not forever … (Nana)

Nana's sentiments demonstrate just how participants often turn the temporality associated with their individual circumstance into a source of respite that helps them get through the day.

But could employment be a steppingstone to something better?

The debate continues as to whether transient forms of employment may lead to better, more permanent job roles, for those that aspire to this at least. Booth et al. (2002) drawing from UK household data insist that temporary work can indeed provide an express path towards permanent employment. Meanwhile Storrie (2002) cautions against this assumption and asserts that the unavailability of comprehensive transitory data makes it practically impossible to confirm this with all certainty. While we can confirm assertions that agency work can provide a route towards gaining a foothold in the job market, especially for new job market candidates, the hypothesis that temporary work can provide a path towards permanent employment is effectively pre-empted here by migration constraints. This is because of visa terms that explicitly forbade the student-migrant-workers from undertaking full-time and/or permanent employment while studying. To accept permanent, full-time roles, these subjects must first secure a qualifying job opportunity with an accredited employer, and then go through the administrative route of making a visa application.[18] This process potentially makes it especially arduous for student-migrants to aspire to more stable, fitting employment relationships during and post study, and this is perhaps an outcome intended by policymakers (see Lomer 2018). This assertion is corroborated by the data. International student mobility data sourced from the Office for National Statistics report that for periods up to 2018, an average of 70 per cent of overseas students depart the UK upon completion of their study, while only approximately 14 per cent had successfully extended their visas for employment reasons. Then there is also the skills mismatch to contend with. These students, for the most part, occupied subsistence roles that had little to do with their future plans, and thus could not provide a pathway to better placed jobs. Consequently, this is one scenario where we can assert with a degree of certainty that temporary working for student-migrants does not lead to permanent or full-time employment.

> You know they say no knowledge is wasted, but why will I ever want to wait tables again in my life, or be a steward in the stadium, that's like going backwards, God forbid ... (Amina)

While it is also acknowledged that, for student-migrants, a benefit of temporary work is that it affords them an opportunity to frequently alternate work environments and experience new spaces, thus pre-empting the antipathy usually associated with being trapped in the same workplace for too long. This is also hypothesised to present them with the occasion to adopt an array of vocational specialties and improve their overall employability. These factors had very little bearing here as the frequent change of workplace was not a desirable quality for most of these subjects. More than three-quarters of participants indicating that they would much rather prefer a secure, predictable and less nomadic work context.

> Yes, I think I'll prefer that. I mean it's fun meeting new people and working in new places and all that, but that's what vacations are for. Always having to introduce yourself to people that don't really care gets tiring, or even having to ask where the restroom and kitchen is every

---

18. Then it is often the case, especially for roles outside the specified 'shortage occupations', there is a residents' labour test to contend with which provides that prospective employers of migrants must first advertise such roles specifically intended for workers with 'settled status' for a minimum period of 28 days.

time … if you have one place of work at least that way you know what you're expecting when you go in. (Nana)

I just want to do my shift and go to be honest, having a constant place will make it easier, especially for my transportation … For instance, I can be sent somewhere new today, where there's no bus service, maybe the bus doesn't stop there, and I'll have to walk, or call a cab, they will not even pay for the time spent transporting myself to get there. (Amina)

This rendition of events supports findings from the likes of Judge and Tomlinson (2016) that the majority of workers do not voluntarily engage in transient employment forms and would prefer more stable employment relationships. Most participants expressed a desire for more stable, better paid jobs that complement their professional profiles. They also expressed a desire for more institutional support towards achieving this, especially from their sponsors, the universities.

A Community Response

In this section we assess the framework which has led to the respondents' actions and their adoption of tactics, in direct response to the limitations on their economic freedoms and their experiences during employment, through a Therapeutic Jurisprudence (TJ) lens. In Chapter 5, we scrutinised the existing national employment laws along with the policies specifically attributed to restricting the economic engagement of international students, which establishes their anti-therapeutic effects. In light of this discussion, it is our finding that the communities of student-migrant-workers are already acting in a TJ-compliant manner, without their knowledge, in finding ways to manage their own situations and helping those new and entering members of this demographic to their group, which is perhaps the more interesting feature of our research. The cohort has adopted behaviours which promote positive and therapeutic results, and have readily appreciated the emotional needs of the members, and potential new entrants, and created a system which instils respect for the members, and mechanisms, which they justify and reinforce in each other, as an antidote to the unfairness they face (see Wexler 1990).

TJ has been widely discussed and critiqued from numerous standpoints and in an increasing range of disciplines and sectors. To name all those academics and disciplines here would be rather time-consuming and unnecessary given the task having already been ably undertaken by Yamada (2021) whose work, along with that of Hora and Chase (2003/2004), Hora et al. (1999), Kawalek (2020, 2021), Perlin (1993, 2019), Perlin and Lynch (2015), Wexler (1999,

2011), Winnick (1991, 1997) and Wexler and Winnick (1991, 1996) should be viewed as compulsory reading (and as a minimum) for those with an interest in this fascinating and developing field of enquiry. Essentially, however, TJ as its central constituent understands the psychological and emotional effects that the law has on those to whom it interacts and affects. Per Winick (1997),

> therapeutic jurisprudence is the study of the role of the law as a therapeutic agent. [...] Therapeutic jurisprudence builds on the insight that the law itself can be seen to function as a kind of therapist or therapeutic agent. Legal rules, legal procedures, and the roles of legal actors (such as lawyers and judges) constitute social forces that, whether intended or not, often produce therapeutic or antitherapeutic consequences. Therapeutic jurisprudence calls for the study of these consequences with the tools of the social sciences to identify them and to ascertain whether the law's antitherapeutic effects can be reduced, and its therapeutic effects enhanced, without subordinating due process and other justice values. (p. 185)

TJ has been allegorised by Wexler's use of the 'bottle' and 'wine' metaphor. The bottle being the actual law in place which is difficult to change or to manipulate, and the wine being the application of that same law which is susceptible to greater manipulation by an accommodating and understanding legal actor (in all their forms – judges, caseworkers, advisors, etc.). Yet, while as a heuristic, TJ facilitates a close inspection of the effects of the law and allows an appreciation of the very lived experiences of groups subject to the investigation, it is not without its critics. Indeed, the very words 'therapeutic' and 'anti-therapeutic' have caused scholars including Brakel (2007) and Slobogin (1995) to question the definitional accuracy of the terms and their meaning and application in the context of legal study. Ultimately for us, TJ as an investigatory lens provides a more nuanced understanding of the tactics used by the members of the student-migrant-worker group. This is, after all, a group of individuals in a new country who are subject to restrictions on their employment activities, expected to pay tuition fees, associated taxes and make other contributions to society, yet are often faced with discriminatory behaviour and rejections because of their race and background. The reactions to these situations, presented in this chapter and the next, have led to either a begrudging acceptance of this circumstance or a proactive response, where the group use their status, social capital and increasing knowledge of the social and economic structures in the region and sector, to alleviate these worst aspects. Dignity and the well-being of the members of the group resonate through their actions, even when these are on the periphery of legality (or perhaps even outright illegal), and are the drivers of the tactics employed by members of Cohorts at locations A and B.

Fundamentally, we cannot 'seriously write about or think about TJ without taking seriously the role of dignity in the legal process' (Perlin 2017, 1137). It is important in the context of the student-migrant-workers' reactions to the restrictions imposed on them that consideration is given to how the cohort react to being placed in this situation. As has been demonstrated, many of the respondents to this study were, at least somewhat, misled as to the employment situation they would enter when choosing to study in the UK. They were aware of the costs of study, the financial commitment that they and their families would be making, but were also reassured by advocates for universities that employment opportunities would be present to help support their academic endeavours, while further assisting their personal and professional development. In the event that these opportunities were more difficult to realise, and/or that those jobs available would be less likely to help the student-workers in their future professional careers, coupled with the restrictions on the manner in which they could work and the hours available to them to engage in employment (especially during term time – which for postgraduate students operates on a trimester basis), the students felt compelled to take action to redress this, perceived, unfairness and imbalance. This does bring us to the significance of dignity within the cohort's understanding and in how it is manifested in their actions. For Schopp (2016), human dignity is that

> uniquely human characteristic that renders humans capable of pursuing lives that manifest the worthy and honourable exercise of those characteristics. Such lives reflect the development and exercise of defensible principles of virtue and justice that distinguish honourable human lives from dishonourable human lives… This interpretation is consistent with the philosophical concept of dignity as a moral worth or status usually attributed to human persons. (pp. 75–76)

For these student-migrant-workers, the effects on their dignity through working in the UK have been profound. Throughout our study we have found evidence, to varying degrees, of discriminatory behaviour which has negatively affected the respondents. The sense of injustice in the treatment of student-migrants, and their responses presented here seeking to mitigate the worse effects of their status, are clearly demonstrated. These are individual and group-based tactics, and the mutual reinforcement that the actions taken are justified and 'fair' are the community responses to deal with these stresses. It is similar to, as Campbell (2021) writes, a 'community development to rethink how to remedy systemic inequity' (p. 2). The community has created its own resilience model (Ellis and Dietz 2017, S86–87) where the 'leaders', using their social capital (through their support networks and members of the community) sustain economic development within the community. This network facilitates a bidirectional transfer of information between the members of the community, the potential entrants (individuals who, in the countries of origin, are deciding whether to come to the UK to pursue their degree and post-degree-level studies) and those external bodies (such as firms of accountants and employers) who facilitate the breaches of the immigration rules and visa restrictions. The group supports its members through various forms of engagement and self-management, and in so doing it protects the health and social needs of the group and can introduce them to external actors and advocate on their behalf. The result is a strong and supportive community reacting to the inequitable effects of visa rules and treatment at employment in the face of a seemingly inaccessible formal legal system. Thus, this organisational architecture sees the dignity, its realisation and preservation, of the community as an overarching frame and the driver to circumvent the barriers imposed against this group and to ensure their economic mobility (see Kawachi and Kennedy 1997). Indeed, as evidenced in Cohort A, the social network was the primary mechanism for job placement and through their regular communications the student-migrants identified the 'good' employers from the 'bad.' They could learn where greater payments for work assignments were possible and how to negotiate with the employment agencies, and through this the individuals developed strong social bonds and an increasingly engaged community. This was fundamental to their success and acted as an antidote given that the finding of Wilkinson and Pickett (2009) that greater equality makes societies stronger was missing, at least for this societal group.

Words of Advice

Although prospective students can do better by exercising due diligence in seeking out information prior to and during mobility, universities must also accept some element of culpability in this often-detractive encounter for not equipping students with adequate, candid information pertaining to their employment rights and what to expect of the resident job market as student-workers. Towards the latter, universities must take a proactive approach to sanitise their overseas recruitment efforts by ensuring agents and representatives adopt a more honest and comprehensive account of the temporary job market that awaits student-migrants in the UK. Universities' renowned complacency and lack of proactivity in this regard gives room to agents with self-serving intentions (including employers and employment intermediaries) to muddy the waters and exploit international-student-workers in the workplace. We would go as far as urging universities to collaborate more broadly and intentionally with cross-sections of the private sector towards implementing a 'safe student-employer scheme' where student job seekers are put in touch with employers/organisations that have been vetted to ensure employment and immigration standards are effectively maintained. While most universities already do this by providing work placement opportunities tied to specific course provisions, we would suggest that this scheme is extended to sectors and roles outside of those that directly complement university programs. Schools should take a sentient approach by tuning their strategy to incorporate employers in sectors known to attract student-workers, for instance social care, hospitality and manufacturing. More so, they should collaborate with recruitment agencies as the labour market integration services they render can be an important source for prospective international students as workers. All of this should go towards promoting students' well-being and ensuring that they are only engaged with firms that provide a safe work environment, free from abuse and exploitation, and an adequate process for dealing with workplace concerns and incidents.

Summary and Conclusion

This chapter accounts for the employment experiences of international student workers through the frame of precarity. We can confirm that the bulk of international students' employment efforts was determined less by the trappings of individual agency, and more by broader specific institutional and circumstantial constraints, over which they have little control, and to which they are mostly reactive. These attested intersecting mediums of precariousness consequently ground the pervasive transactional outlook of employment this study reports of. These findings substantiate present migration, migrant labour and dual labour market theories which assert that more recent migrants – of which these students are – tend to wield a purely transactional view of employment, especially due to socioeconomic vulnerabilities and structural impediments (Bloch and McKay 2015; IOM 2020; Doeringer and Piore 1971). We find that these students encounter significant difficulties in navigating the UK labour market and are especially inclined to gravitate towards jobs that are deemed as precarious, low status and low paid. More so, their place in the labour market is pre-set by barriers brought on by market forces and migration structures that take effect before they arrive in the UK, and effectively push them to the insecure employment forms while they are here. They resort to seeking employment through agencies due to the inherent difficulties they encounter navigating the labour market unaided as new entrants and as recent, transitory migrants who often lack the requisite sociocultural understanding, time and resources to be fully independent job seekers. Indeed, temporary agency work can be beneficial for these students as it affords to them an expeditious route into paid employment, flexibility and a degree of control that renders a semblance of certainty into their working lives. However, most of these benefits are dampened by the insecurities associated with their employment position and again, migration structures. Flexibility for one is increasingly dictated by the employers' terms, which are subject to fluctuations in broader market forces including labour demand. This precariousness is exacerbated by the imposition of the 20-hour weekly work limit which effectively does not leave much scope to exercise true freedom over their working lives. However, for some, the socioeconomic frailties they are encumbered by meant that they often had to accept employment assignments for durations well in excess of the mandated limits.

The sum of these temporalities, structural constraints and socioeconomic vulnerabilities may well cause other aspects of their lives as social actors to suffer, including their studies. In particular, we found that the bulk of the participants self-reported as being subjected to multiple intersecting forms of discriminatory, exploitative and abusive work conditions, and expressed profound discontent about their experiences in the temporary employment market. Although the student-migrants' heightened reliance on specific employment relationships for subsistence was in some ways beneficial in the short term, this also engendered exploitation and docility in the face of abuse. This takes into account that the student-migrants' employment options were effectively limited to a narrow spectrum of job roles, especially as their labour market prospects were institutionally bound in forms that pre-empted them from aspiring to more coveted and/or rewarding employment environments. This consequently meant that large numbers of student job seekers are actively being crowded into a limited market, and thus more prone to exploitation and maltreatment from employers, employment brokers and service users. Frequently iterated sentiments of disposability and exploitation corroborate insights from the, admittedly sparse, literature on international students working by the likes of Nyland et al. (2009) and Takeda (2005). These academics attributed the dismal employment conditions students encounter to the fact employers and employment brokers alike are aware of the available pool of student-migrant-workers, and due to their abundance individuals are easily replaceable. This may be just one of the reasons that push some members of the student-migrant cohort into semi-legal forms of working.

Chapter 7

SEMI-LEGAL WORKING?

Introduction

In this chapter we begin by documenting our findings of the various formations of semi-legality recognised within both cohorts of student-workers, while noting the protections and insecurities peculiar to each group. Second, we analyse these issues through the framework of legal mobilisation and 'claims-making'. This latter framework is chosen to help make sense of the various manifestations that semi-legality may have and how it impacts the emergence and transformation of disputes, as actors respond to potentially injurious and justiciable experiences in the workplace. In the final aspect of the chapter, we address the issues raised by the participants through the schema of legal consciousness, in particular as this impacts on the students' lived experiences of migration rules which restrict and impact their employment opportunities while studying. This segues into a broader discussion of the varied semi-legal patterns of behaviour used as a medium for exerting socio-legal resistance, and a critique of semi-legality in the reification and continuation of legal hegemony. The findings presented here are founded on data collated from ethnographies[1] of two cohorts of international students, identified here as Cohort A and Cohort B (see Chapter 6). This evidence is supplemented with data from interviews where necessary to verify and/or to expand upon the issues raised during the ethnography data collection phase.[2] In reporting these findings in this chapter, participants from each cohort are tagged 'A' and 'B', respectively, followed by a number designating their (anonymised) identity.

---

1. See Chapter 2 for details of the methodology adopted in this study.
2. It is important to state that this tranche of study findings rely less on direct quotes from participants and more of insights from our fieldnotes and interactions. This is as a result of concessions made during the fieldwork phase in response to participants' apprehension of being digitally recorded conversing about conduct that may consider breach of the terms of their student visas.

Part One: Semi-Legality as a Dynamic Devise

The devises of semi-legality refer to the various mediums through which student-migrants blur the lines between legal and illegal conduct in respect of the state-prescribed restrictions on their employment while studying. This empirical undertaking is nuanced by the inherent precariousness that stems from being subjects of immigration control, engaging in what may be conceived as risqué behaviour. This is also contextualised by the risk of detection posed by the state through institutions including law enforcement, the Home Office and Her Majesty's Revenue and Customs (HMRC). In respect to 'the whole government approach',[3] these institutions are tasked to work hand in hand so as to pre-empt and/or bring to account actors responsible for 'illegal' migrant labour (see Fudge 2018).

Subsequently, we find that there are distinct tactics adopted by these subjects to dually enable and avoid detection for employment activities in breach of visa restrictions peculiar to each study cohort. These strategies more so are present with varying degrees of protection and exposure for the student-migrants involved, and may implicate a range of external individual and institutional actors – from employers and employment intermediaries, to Companies House and freelance accountants. Before discussing these various strategies, it is useful to recap the relevant Tier 4[4] student visa conditions in respect of paid work, and which extend throughout the life of the application of the visa. International students must not work more than 20 hours per week in term time (working full-time during vacations is permitted), set up a business, work as self-employed or pursue a career by filling a permanent full-time vacancy. The restriction on working also extends to voluntary works, and any work undertaken on this basis contributes to the 20-hour threshold.

Rendered into a spectrum, semi-legality can be graded according to the number of work restrictions the student violates and the tactics adopted in so doing. On this basis, we begin our discussion of the participants to this study, and the categorisation of the devises used by each study cohort to circumvent the employment visa restrictions.

Cohort A: The Nomads

In this cohort, the prevalent devise to facilitate their semi-legality involved the participants undertaking work assignments with several employers and/or

---

3. See Chapter 3.
4. On 5 October 2020, the government changed the immigration route for students. The 'Tier 4' route is now the 'Student' route; however, most of the changes are not of practical significance in respect of participants to this study.

employment intermediaries, while not exceeding 20 hours of work per week with any single employer. Hence our designation of them as 'nomads'. This is notwithstanding that the total sum of hours worked per week may regularly be in excess of the mandated limits. In this way, the student-worker ostensibly keeps within the limits of visa restrictions (and by extension, the law), per each work context, but clearly not when the total number of hours worked are collated. Participants in this cohort typically worked two to four work assignments per week, lasting anywhere between 20 and 40 hours in total. This consequently means that subjects in this cohort present with only *one strike of semi-legal behaviour* for working in excess of the mandated weekly limits.

The perceived benefit of this tactic is the observation that alternating work contexts in this way makes it more arduous for state authorities, and the employers, to track the true extent of employment undertaken by the student-worker. Further, and more significantly, it is also seen as a mechanism to limit exposure of their 'wrongdoing' as the student-worker retains control of the entire process. Negatively, the participants who engage in such activity tend to be much more mobile and transient than their counterparts in Cohort B, having to regularly seek out new assignments and transit between different work contexts, perhaps as frequently as every other week. As a consequence, this has the effect of making their working lives erratic and precarious. To this end, one of the participants recounted a light-hearted narrative of how, unknowingly, he wore the wrong uniform to a work assignment and was threatened with a sanction.

> ... since that happened, I always take all my uniforms in my bag pack, just in case ... (A1)

More so, this stratagem is far from fool proof as the entirety of their work extents may yet be detected through an examination of their National Insurance records. But as we discovered in the course of the study, this ploy was used more as a vehicle for the student-worker to protect themselves, somewhat surprisingly less from the attentions of the state, but more from parochial employers, especially considering the potential for exploitation and abuse this can engender.

> You have to be smart, if they know you are working more than 20 hours, they can use that as an excuse to treat you anyhow they like... (A4)

This seeming wariness was not something which lacked a basis in fact. The participants often recounted narrative experiences of them starting their working relationships in connivance with specific firms in order to circumvent the student visa rules. This typically involved employers who would record due wages and hours worked in ways that concealed or distorted the student's true employment extents. This arrangement had been reliant on what one might call a 'gentleman's agreement' where the employer was expected to act in good faith and make accurate payments for hours worked, even if these were to be made in arrears. However, the reality experienced by the participants was that employers often failed to adhere to their end of this bargain. Wage payments were habitually short of the correct sum, and subsequent attempts to enforce the payment was reacted to with silence or further diversionary tactics by the employer.

They are all thieves… (A4)

As these were fairly homogenous networks, it was unsurprising to find that students in this cohort all reported a similar ordeal and often implicated the same group of employers for this underhanded practice. This consequently necessitated a shift by the students to working alone while maintaining a fleeting relationship with several employers.

Cohort B: The Pseudopreneurs

In the second cohort, the tactics adopted by the participants took on a different, more sophisticated turn, albeit with some parallels with Cohort A. The students in Cohort B contracted for work assignments through a limited company which they had incorporated for this express purpose. Thus the designation 'pseudopreneurs' in allusion to the fact that they are ostensibly classed as self-employed, albeit misleadingly so. Here, the legal trappings of limited companies, by way of the separate legal identity and the metaphorical veil of incorporation, operate to shield the students' true employment status from immediate scrutiny. Indeed, it would likely require legal proceedings against the company and its directors for the veil to be pierced and the true nature of the undertaking to be revealed.[5] While this scheme is not original, as it is commonplace for individuals to contract for work using their own

---

5. Several instances exist which justify a court raising/piercing the corporate veil to ascertain the true working relationships with a corporation. The most pertinent in the situation discussed here would be that either the company had been established as a fraud/sham (such as *Re Darby ex p Brougham* [1911] 1 KB 95) or that it is a construction to avoid legal obligations / duties (such as demonstrated in *Prest v Petrodel Resources Ltd & Others* [2013] UKSC 34). *Prest* is interesting in this respect as Lord Sumption remarked how English law enables the piercing of the veil 'when a person is under an existing legal obligation or liability or subject to an existing legal restriction which he

limited companies especially for tax advantages, this act expressly breaches visa rules barring students from engaging in business activity or work as self-employed: *strike one*. Further, there is also the fact that this cohort of students present with the most active labour market profiles of all. They tend to undertake work comparable to full-time employment, that is, in excess of 40 hours per week during term time: thus, *strike two*.

It is imperative to note that developing such a plot, and executing its plan, relies on complicit actors and structural loopholes. Firms, on the one hand, which are complicit in contracting with students through a limited company; disregarding the legally mandated 'right to work' checks of which they are obligated to be cognisant, and ignoring the work restrictions affixed to students' migrant status. On the other hand, this tactic is symptomatic of lax regulatory oversight in respect of corporations in the UK. Incorporating a limited company is a relatively easy and inexpensive process, which can be completed online via the Companies' House website and at the modest cost of £12. Meanwhile it has since been acknowledged that the vast volume of applications received means that Companies' House does not possess the requisite resources to scrutinise every single item of information provided by prospective company promoters. This scenario provides for the necessary obfuscation of details to hide the identity of those undertaking the work and the employer which is happy for the work to be undertaken in this manner. This, however, does not address the issue of taxation. As the students performing the work are ostensibly designated as self-employed, taxes due to HMRC are subsequently administered via the self-assessment route. To this end, students in this cohort often engage the services of freelance accountants, also familiar with the business structure and the rationale for its operation, to avoid problems and audits. Here, it is interesting to note that members in this cohort each used the same accountant.

... Ohh we have accountants for that, don't worry yourself ... (B5)

This cohort also tended to have the most stable employment relationships of all. Here, there was no need to shuttle between different employers or work assignments, as they only contracted with specific firms that were complicit in this scheme, whom they relied on to keep sending work assignments their way. This consequently meant that these participants often had their work schedules planned out for months in advance. However, as a negative to this employment structure was the involvement of external agents who exacerbated the

---

deliberately evades or whose enforcement he deliberately frustrates by interposing a company under his control' (35).

students' anxieties for working in violation of visa conditions. This aspect of the employment tactics deployed by those in Cohort B becomes ever more apparent during the course of this chapter.

Furthermore, in parallel to Cohort A, we find that this *semi-legal* scheme evolved in consonance with the students' lived encounters in the job market. For instance, B1, who takes credit for introducing this employment scheme to the rest of the cohort, initially began working in excess of the mandated limits through a colleague's limited company. He, however, separated his involvement with this colleague following a dispute over accruable wage payments. B1 proceeded to incorporate his own limited company through which he contracts for work.

> … that is the only way, to do your own thing, everyone is trying to cheat you because they think say you be JJC [Johnny just come]… (B1)

Albeit by way of Cohort A's pivot towards a nomadic work pattern bereft of any connivance with the external actors, or indeed, Cohort B's move to incorporate limited companies in connivance with employers, we find in both study cohorts that the participants must often contend with the unfriendly motions that go with working in breach of visa conditions. While they reluctantly yield to the teeming vulnerabilities associated with life in the semi-legal arena, this resignation is, however, not absolute. It is followed by informed action to circumvent a repeat performance where possible. This especially demonstrates the fluidity and dynamism of semi-legality as an empirical phenomenon, a nuance lost on the existing corpus of knowledge.

Between the Gradations of 'Semi-Legality' and Precarity

Actions have consequences, and upon appropriating the frame of precarity, it is the case that the various devises of semi-legality employed by the participants has differentiated impacts on the measure of insecurity to which they are consequently exposed. This is especially relevant here, as we will soon see that the demarcations between the actors' journeys within the labour market and their broader social realities crumble. For one, we find that the 'nomads' (i.e. Cohort A) who attempt to maintain their sanity by alternating between work contexts, tend to have the most erratic employment profile but nonetheless retain a greater level of autonomy over their working lives. Save for an underlying need for financial security, the nomads felt less need to remain committed to any one employer, neither did they feel responsible to anyone but themselves as far as their work pattern was concerned. Whereas for the pseudopreneurs (i.e. Cohort B), where actors contract via their own limited companies, besides the fact that they presented with a more stable employment profile, they more or less lack concrete agency in critical aspects of the labour process, including with whom, where and for how long they work. In addition to running preference for contracting with specific employers who will act in collusion with the students, work assignments are usually planned out for weeks in advance and are so intensive that it often takes centre stage in their everyday lives. This consequently meant that students in this cohort had to move commitments, including study, around their work schedules.

However, the extensive economic activity undertaken by subjects in Cohort B meant that they were significantly financially better off than their counterparts in Cohort A; they worked longer hours and they earned more. However, as exemplified in analyses of employment status, the results of this study corroborated the established view that while these 'entrepreneurs' felt quite secure in employment, this was less so within the context of their broader social lives as transient migrants. This is illustrated when recounting the encounters during the ethnographic fieldwork in this location. In a phone conversation with B1, clarifying some information pertaining to the project, when a sensitive topic was broached, he suddenly ended the call. Some minutes later, B1 contacted one of the research team members again through the instant messaging app, *WhatsApp*, expressing how he felt more secure talking about work through that medium as opposed to regular phone calls. When pressed about this, he noted a rumour circulating that the 'authorities' (read as the Home Office) had been tapping phones as part of an ongoing investigation into suspicions of illicit migrant labour within the region. In this regard, he emphasised the enhanced encryption of the app when compared with the use of phone calls. Another instance of this manifest insecurity involved the use of, or more precisely the non-use of the car park adjoining the participant's residence. Where possible, students in this location had the unusual habit of parking their vehicles some distance away from the car park specifically available as part of the rent of their apartment. When prompted as to why this was, they indicated it was a tactic to enable them to 'slip under the radar' and so as not to rouse any suspicions from the neighbours as to the source of their 'wealth'.

> Better safe than sorry ... B3, and You can't trust these white neighbours, they're so nosy ... (B4)

While we are unable to confirm the substance of this manifest paranoia, such a disposition is indicative of the much more 'guarded' countenance discernible in this location that is seemingly brought on by the extents of semi-legal behaviour. Albeit phone calls or car parks, in Cohort B, there was a manifest distrust of 'outsiders' and precariousness that seeps into mundane contexts of their everyday lives.

Meanwhile these apprehensions can be starkly contrasted with the disposition discernible in Cohort A, where there exists only one strike of semi-legal behaviour. While there was a similar wariness of outsiders, and especially the authorities, this was on a much subtler basis and nowhere as extreme. This can be illustrated in a similar exchange. Housemates in this location mundanely discussed concerns about immigration enforcement officials being sighted within the vicinity of the flat. This was a very light-hearted conversation, and one which did not cause undue concern amongst housemates, at least according to our observations. This cohort was quick to dispel any emerging anxieties as indeed they believed the Home Office had more important things to do than chase up international students who have the habit of working 'a little' more than permitted on their visas.

> I think they have better things to do than to be looking for international students who are working too much … (A2)

> I don't think it's us they are after to be honest … maybe it's those people that come here illegally or overstay that they are after, not us … (A4)

These statements, although made in passing, resound to an alarming degree. We see subjects unwittingly internalise and appropriate the state's 'degrees of harm' agenda towards combatting illegal migrant labour as a source of respite. Semi-legality, except where it involves significant breaches of employment restrictions attached to immigration status, which apparently is not the case here, is considered to entail relatively low harm and correspondingly low consequence. For example, while 'bogus' educational institutions and migrants on student visas, albeit with no intention of studying at all, are deemed to generate substantial harm, students who are studying but working for a greater number of hours than legally permitted are deemed to be less harmful to the state's interests (Ruhs and Anderson 2010).

Succinctly, what we see in effect across both cohorts is a subjective frame of gravity where it would seem that the extent of violations regarding student immigration rules correlate with the degree of paranoia and insecurity encountered by actors both in and outside of their work lives. Although the sum of the resultant precariousness that stems from working in breach of visa regulations may not seem as grave as, for example, someone who is an 'illegal' migrant labourer (Calavita 1998; Gleeson 2010), these uncertainties nonetheless subsist and contour the actors' social realities, albeit in a tempered fashion. Semi-legality in itself represents a blurring of legally sanctioned behaviour and thus inspires notions of insecurity spanning from fears of detection due to the frailty of one's tenure in the state as an unsettled migrant. It is this inherent insecurity that inspires the highlighted schemes to evade the rules and pre-empt detection and vulnerabilities that emanates therefrom. More so, for these respondents, working in breach of visa terms including the mechanisms adopted to effect this are for the most part incidental, dynamic and are deployed so to protect against socioeconomic and legal uncertainties as they navigate a novel employment market. However, the choice of entering semi-legal employment distinctively contours the individuals' claims-making behaviour and legal consciousness disposition.

Part B: Claims Making in the Semi-Legal Arena

Participants were questioned about a broad range of work issues pertaining to conditions, incidents and experiences they deemed particularly problematic, based entirely on their subjective assessment. Just as scores of literature from both the migration and employment scholarship indicate (see Gleeson 2010; Ying et al. 2007), these stories were replete with commentaries of instances of injurious and potentially justiciable experiences, nearly all of which failed to mature into formal claims-making or actual mobilisation of the law. Albeit the limitedness of the study restricts claims of generalisability, our findings ostensibly resonate with established socio-legal outcomes presented in other studies, including those of Ewick and Silbey (1998) and Nielsen (2000) that members of historically disenfranchised groups know better than to seek recourse in the law for problems encountered in their everyday lives. Yet this is overly reductive, the discourses employed by subjects in their reconstruction of events in respect of the socio-legal meaning-making process reveals a far more nuanced portrait.

This empirical analysis entails four principal agendas: first we question what student-workers identify as problematic experiences/incidents within employment contexts. Second, we consider the participants' subjective interpretations of these grievances including with whom to place the blame. The third agenda centres around what actions had been taken to address this, including the registration of formal complaints, and informal approaches at resolution or, conversely, their decision to simply accept the status quo. Meanwhile, the fourth consideration entails the participants' estimate of justice and the fairness of the processual outcomes that follow from the aforementioned problematic encounters. This is all nuanced by the participants' semi-legal exploits in terms of the student visa rules on employment.

The incidence and features of grievances

As the finding from the participants of 'perceivable justiciable experiences' was for the most part subjective, this invariably meant that the students had determined a range of experiences as being injurious. This means that the first stage of the dispute pyramid, the naming stage wherein the (Un)Perceivable injurious experience ((Un)PIE)[6] is processed and transformed into a PIE, is effectively bypassed. The subjects' expression of these incidents was sometimes prompted specifically and, at other times, flowed freely as the interviews progressed. In both situations, the naming and recollection of experiences deemed as injurious did not require much effort on either the part of the interviewer or that of the interview subjects. Participants were often bemused as to the limits of what makes for an 'injurious experience' once informed of the entire subjectivity of the line of enquiry.

The accounts of injurious experiences elicited were quite varied, the location of these exchanges ranged from work sites, to residential settings and law offices. Participants more so implicated a range of actors, from the employers and employment intermediaries, to clients and work colleagues, as being complicit in some way for a specific ill suffered, or indeed playing a part in its exacerbation. The more cited instances of problematic experiences had to do with inconsistencies in payments for due wages and exploitative work conditions involving employers, and discrimination stemming from altercations with other actors while at work.

Consequently, we found that participants retained heightened consciousness of the law in respect of identifying the extent of injury which afforded legal protections, and how they might proceed with claims-making. They were assertive of their entitlement to better treatment on relevant fronts, albeit they rarely pursued a resolution through the application of the law. This inclination to accept grievances can be attributable to factors associated with their structural location as recent migrant-workers, and all the sociocultural, economic and legal implications deriving from this. This disposition can, however, be whittled down under scrutiny to a handful of reasons, namely the overdependence of certain work relationships, their socioeconomic and legal precariousness, and their relative powerlessness and marginalisation.

I do not want trouble

First, when subjected to indiscretions in the workplace, any form of outward claims-making will entail the worker drawing attention to themselves.

---

6. (Un)PIE stands for (Un)Perceivable Injurious Experience.

This is not a situation to be relished, especially when one is engaging in forms of proscribed conduct and is in a precarious socioeconomic position. Here, the risk of detection, coupled with the fiscal utility of employment, makes it so that student-migrant-workers are increasingly reluctant to disturb their already delicate realities by pursuing legal recourse for perceived wrongs suffered on the job. In this way, we find again that these individuals' inaction was less the application of fecklessness, and more of strategy. More so, there is an understated acknowledgement of the participants' relative disadvantage within the employment relationship, albeit aloofness or intimacy, they are all the same – a disposable resource with potentially more to lose should they pursue formal claims-making through legal channels.

Furthermore, this decision to refrain from invoking the machinery of the law even in instances where this might prove expedient is also in part due to the perceived unpredictability of the law as an institutional resource. The law as a normative reserve is nevertheless more accessible to better positioned actors in terms of their socioeconomic status. Thus, the available legal structures that provide potential avenues for recourse are in essence perceived as a foreign, inaccessible and even potentially treacherous terrain that one must avoid at all costs. This dreary regard for the law engendered a tactile docility that endured even in the face of maltreatment. For instance, not only were the participants quite reactive to name an injurious experience, they more so tell their inaction in a way that can best be described as a performance of *wilful naivete*.

> I just look at them and laugh, I know what you're doing, but I just choose to keep quiet, I'm not a fool. (A4)

This naivete is strategically gamed out in utter awareness of their precarious circumstance, and what they perceive as a transient phase in their exploits. This seeming transience dually provides a source for reprieve and a reason to endure unfairness for the time.

> So, I was just like, 'Well, I just can't be bothered. Say what you want.' Like I have my career ahead of me. I'm not going to be there in the next five [years], you know. In the next two, three years, I knew I wasn't going to be there. (B3)

By keeping their heads down in this way and avoiding conflict, these students opted against asserting their knowledge of workplace rights and entitlement to better treatment so to retain a measure of certainty and normalcy in their lives. That being the case, this was already an established practice. Insights from the extant socio-legal scholarship on migrant labour explains just how legally tenuous the situations of migrant-workers (read as undocumented) tend to be as precarious, target wage-earners. This, coupled with them being 'outlaws' in some sense, can deter them from turning to legal redress for whatever cause (see Gleeson 2010; Doeringer and Piore 1971). While we do see this here to an extent, especially as the bulk of accounts of injurious experiences narrated by the participants mostly went unresolved in any meaningful way for this very reason, yet again, the portrait here is far more nuanced, especially when contemplating their semi-legal exploits. Not only is there a line to be drawn between semi-legality and *outrightly illicit* migrant labour with regard to claims-making behaviour, but there are also more intricate distinctions between the two distinct semi-legal devises uncovered in this study regarding the trajectory of disputes. We expand upon this in the following subsections.

The gradations of semi-legality and the dispute pyramid: naming, blaming, claiming

It is interesting to note that the entails of the specific semi-legal devise employed by the participants often had profound effects on the trajectory of grievances according to the dispute pyramid. Cohort A comprised the nomadic student-workers who embark upon semi-legality independently and bereft of any form of connivance with external agents. For this cohort, there was little trouble identifying a specific experience as injurious (i.e. the naming stage), neither did they have any difficulty with attributing blame to the party deemed responsible, the employers, clients, colleagues, and so on (i.e. the blaming stage). However, actors in this cohort rarely ever proceeded beyond the 'blaming' stage. In this regard, once responsibility or blame is externalised, they tended to stop short of tabling said grievances or outwardly communicating a claim to the relevant party deemed responsible. For instance, when faced with a potential case of wage theft, A2 responded by bequeathing to 'divine forces' what could have well been a formal grievance or claim even.

> I leave them for God … (A2)

This tendency is often informed by past experiences where one might have moved to stake a claim over an injurious experience, but to no avail. A4, for instance, who had been repeatedly called an 'ape' by clients at an adult care facility where she worked, had raised this issue with her managers who were reluctant to take any action.

> I kept complaining, I sent two letters. No response... No one called me to ask how I am faring ... I was affected mentally, and it was quite depressing ... now I just do my thing when something happens to me at work, nothing will come of it if I take action, so why bother ..? (A4)

Whereas if the perceived wrong is particularly distressing from the subject's point of view, rather than attempt to resolve it with their employers or line managers as the case may be, this cohort would often opt to terminate the employment relationship altogether. They consequently chose to accept this as a learning experience.

> Surprisingly, that turned out to be my last *chuckles* It turned out it was going to be my last time working there ... I just left; it became too much you know ... (A4)

But even then, their highly nomadic work pattern meant that they had little means or time to fixate upon any one injurious experience emanating from one employment context out of the several they juggled at the time.

> Abuse me, call me a black cunt all you want, what's my business. I may not even get a shift here again for months ... if it is too much, I'll reject shifts there, tell them that I don't want to work there anymore, no time to even check time ... (A2)

With Cohort B, where semi-legal labour was implemented via limited companies and, more pertinently, in cahoots with employers, the students were more assertive, resolute actors, who tended to progress further up the dispute pyramid than their counterparts in Cohort A. In addition to a heightened propensity to name an experience as injurious and assign blame to the parties deemed responsible, they tended to progress on to the claiming stage much more frequently when compared to those in Cohort A. This apparent disparity can be attributable to the intimate dynamics of their employment relationship with the employer, and especially said employers' complicity in breaching the visa conditions. More precisely, we find that the co-complicity of the employers in semi-compliant behaviour enabled a more secure, intimate relationship that emboldened the student-workers in this cohort to voice discontent for perceived wrongs meted out on them in the workplace.

These actors tend to more readily approach the firms' management in seeking redress for grievances.

Here, we see that while semi-legality and vulnerabilities effectively pre-empted actors in Cohort A from proceeding to the claiming stage of the dispute pyramid, this had a somewhat opposite effect in Cohort B where the intricacies of semi-legality effectively equalise the moral balance that exists between both parties to the employment relationship. This emboldening capacity of semi-legality was evident in an instance where B5 summoned a formal meeting with her de facto employers in a dispute over 'complicated' pay deductions.

> I felt I was being … I don't want to use – but maybe being tricked or something but it was really, really confusing for me. It was a face-to-face meeting … The boss actually was trying not to be in the meeting, I had to send for him because he had to at least respond to the question that I had … (B5)

While this effectively sees to it that both parties' interests were aligned towards dealing with issues in-house (and in hushed tones), this neutrality nonetheless empowers actors in Cohort B to increasingly seek remedies for perceived injurious experiences. This capacity is however not unfettered. In synonymy with Cohort A, these events rarely culminated in formal claims-making or mobilisation of the law, albeit for different reasons. There was more or less a stagnation in dispute transformations beyond the point of being emboldened to voice discontent over perceived injurious experiences, especially where the voiced concerns remained unresolved or inconclusive following these deliberations. Thus, we concluded that this morally neutral terrain had negligible effects on the overall processual outcome of grievances. In Cohort B, the portrait was increasingly one where there exists an understated understanding that going above and beyond seeking redress via formal, legal means invites the manner of external attention and scrutiny antithetical to their circumstance as semi-legal workers. While this specific semi-legal terrain in respect of claims-making might be morally neutral, it is more so nuanced by socioeconomic disadvantage. Here, there is a lingering unwillingness to disrupt a valuable work relationship highly amenable to their circumstance over a perceived wrongdoing, if it can be helped that is. This is an even more pertinent consideration because finding a replacement, co-complicit employer might not be easy.

Therefore, the principal difference in claims-making between the cohort locations increasingly had much to do with the question of when as opposed to if they decided simply to accept the situation. In Cohort A, this was immediately after the apportioning of blame, whereas in Cohort B, this was after the claim had been communicated to the relevant parties.

They said to come with clean hands ...

It is worthy to note that the findings of this study contradict the hypothesis of attributions which identify self-blame as an inhibitor to the emergence of disputes, especially plaguing the 'have nots' and 'marginalised' in the 'naming' and 'blaming' stages of transformations. This is not quite the case for this study's subjects as while they on occasion own up to their roles in the causation and/or aggravation of a grievance, these sentiments did not deter or inhibit the perceptions of these events as unjustly injurious due to the act or omission of another. At least not in the way the likes of Felstiner et al. (1980) and Kelley and Michela (1980) envision. Here, self-blame is increasingly rendered through semi-legality, especially in the claiming stage. Actors often name an experience as injurious, apportion blame to others deemed responsible, and even go as far as to communicate a claim to the relevant party. Self-blame, however, creeps in during the claiming stage, and for reasons unconnected to the grievance itself. Here, the actors' breach of visa conditions increasingly dissuade them from proceeding to formally mobilise the law. They do this reflexively, while noting the potential for an alternate, more legalistic route towards dispute resolution, if only they had been wholly compliant with the various work restrictions, that is. In this way, self-blame becomes significant during the latter parts of the dispute transformation process as the consequences of the actors' indulgence in respect of semi-legality becomes increasingly apparent to them, and this deters them from seeking a legal resolution.

'Deserving of' versus the 'need for' redress

We find that there is an often-understated distinction in effect between distressing incidents deserving of redress, and those that are particularly in 'need' of redress. Actors' resignation to their vulnerable socioeconomic circumstance, coupled with the inherent difficulties and consequences that goes with formal claims-making for their already precarious realities, made it so that there is in effect a high threshold to be met for an event, albeit problematic and unjust, to actually need to be 'resolved'. On the one hand, it was easy for the participants to see just how unfair and justiciable an experience is, however, actioning these concerns on the other often requires concerted time and effort by the individual. This is as if to say the injurious event itself did not constitute enough interference into their increasingly insecure working lives, raising attention in the pursuit of rectifying these injurious experiences might very well exacerbate this distortion to their subjective ecosphere. Claims-making in this sense potentially brings with it real implications that may detract from their earning capacity and subsistence. This makes it so that there is no capacity, by way of time, the will and the resources, to do more than acknowledge a wrong has been done to them, save for exceptional circumstances where this threshold for action is breached. This level is inherently subjective and takes into consideration mundane features including the gravity of the grievance, the potential for its recurrence and the parties implicated. B4, for instance, recounts hitting this breakpoint in a problematic ordeal that threatened his very means of sustenance and his reputation. This had to do with a malpractice claim entered against him before an occupational regulatory body by a disgruntled service user. In a bid to resolve this, he went to the lengths of engaging the services of a solicitor for the formal inquiry that soon followed. Here, the potential repercussions of inaction or internalising the issue seemed to outweigh any other consideration.

> At the end of the day I came out not guilty, the truth came out, but I won't get the £600 I paid the solicitor in regard to that … money I can't get back … (B4)

Even then, this threshold is never static, and is instead constantly being revised in real time as the event unravels. This dynamism can be illustrated, taking the case of A3, who initially started being unrelenting of his rights when he was physically assaulted at work by an unstable service user. He suffered a broken jaw and a resultant significant dental bill. When his employers failed to accept liability, he proceeded to engage the services of a personal injury solicitor on a contingency fee basis. The solicitor initiated formal correspondence with the employer on A3's behalf, but was forced to conclude the matter early when negotiations stalled and a formal claim to a court was the next step. In this way, although there was sufficient will power initially to engage official legal actors, this enthusiasm soon waned as the matter ventured into an unfamiliar, uncertain and more legalistic terrain. He, just like the majority of this study's participants, acts this way especially for the sheer invasiveness the formal legal process may enable, which is antithetical to their social structure. This is especially underlined by the inconspicuousness and prevarication engendered in response to the vulnerabilities ascribed to their marginal location as transient migrant-workers who need to earn a wage to subsist, and more so exacerbated by their involvement in semi-legal employment. In this portrayal, the formal machinery of the law and the state's brand of justice are deemed as chaotic, disorderly designations that become even more unappealing when reified by the participants' specific circumstances, which in itself is an ongoing process. Their plural reality is one where ideals of justice are subjective and dependent on the social cost of mobilising the law. Contrary to its stated intents of maintaining order and exerting justice, the formal legal avenues with respect to dispute resolution are deemed as disruptive and intransigent.

'Semi-legal' versus 'illegal' migrant labour

Finally, there are some noteworthy distinctions to be made between claims-making behaviour contoured by semi-legal (student)-migrant-labour as an empirical phenomenon rendered in this study, and the accounts of outright illegality with unauthorised migrant labour contained in the literature on the subject. Scholars including Avendaño and Hincapié (2008) and Gleeson (2010) find that predatory employers often weaponise the threat of detection and law enforcement against undocumented migrant workers as a means of keeping them subservient and to dissuade them from seeking redress for exploitative work conditions. While this indeed was a stated concern for this study's participants (especially for those in Cohort A), semi-legal migrant labour does not present such extreme vulnerabilities. Participants across both study cohorts never reported the employers explicitly leveraging the violations of immigration conditions as a means to impede claims-making. Reasons for this are likely to include that the participants were either unaware of this fact (Cohort A), or because they too were complicit in this process, (Cohort B).

Another avenue where claims-making in the semi-legal sector fares relatively better here is the dependence on a specific employer for employment, especially as this is shown to curtail workers' ability to leave exploitative and abusive employment relationships and contest any maltreatment emanating from same (Gleeson 2010). We find that there was a degree of dependence on specific employment contexts for Cohort B where there was active connivance with specific employers, albeit less so for Cohort A with the prevalence of nomadic workers. Yet either way, even though the law was not perceived as immediately helpful towards providing a remedy for wrongs committed against them, it did not follow that these events always went untended, uncontested or unactioned. This lies in contrast to the docility and vulnerability often associated with outrightly proscribed migrant labourers, as participants here were kept neither wholly docile or submissive by the power imbalance in the employment relationship. In the semi-legal arena, there is always the implicit potential for actors to simply walk away from an unfavourable or exploitative employment relationship (Cohort A), or to voice their discontent to the relevant party (Cohort B). For these participants, there is just enough room to manoeuvre effectively within the labour market. That said, we now turn to address the impact of semi-legal behaviour on the workers' legal consciousness disposition.

Part Three: Gradations of Semi-Legality and Legal Consciousness

In this section of the chapter, we use the analytical framework of legal consciousness to assess semi-legality as reflected in what these workers do, think and say in respect of the work restrictions attached to their status as subjects of migration control. These restrictions can be delineated as a form of 'legality' (Ewick and Silbey 1998) in this deployment. Upon a cursory application of Ewick and Silbey's (1998) legal consciousness archetypes – 'before the law', 'with the law' and 'against the law' it is apparent that students who act 'before the law', where legality is construed as sacred and objective, will generally not deviate from these visa rules under any circumstance. Those acting 'with the law', where legality is viewed as a game that can be manipulated for personal advantage, will usually seek to manipulate these rules in some way to suit their individual objectives. Finally, those acting 'against the law' will feel trapped by these conditions and thus seek ways to manage its effect on their lives through acts of distancing and/or resistance. More so it is hypothesised that these actors, as they present with marginalised identities, are more given to an 'against the law' legal consciousness disposition and will generally look to resist the rules.

However, legal consciousness is just as indefinite and inchoate as it is intrinsic. We find that it is rarely ever the case that these actors neatly fit into one of these predetermined categories. By implication, semi-legality represents a tainted replication of legality, as it essentially marks an adulteration of the legally sanctioned tenets. This ostensibly curtails the possibility that those working in violation of visa terms can be classed as 'before the law', but yet this is only in theory. In this framing, Cohort A's nomadic arrangement involves traversing the legal territory alone, absent of any connivance with external actors. It can thereby be deemed as an act of distancing and, by extension, an illustration of 'against the law' strand of legal consciousness. Conversely, Cohort B's entrepreneurial route can be deemed as 'gaming the system' by experimenting with the rules and exploiting loopholes, all for personal benefit. This consequently deems them as 'with the law' per legal consciousness readings. But yet again, this study finds, in respect of Ewick and Silbey's proposition and indeed a good number of emergent legal consciousness scholars, that actors' attitudes towards the law are hardly ever determinate, neither are these categories fixed or immutable. We discuss this while illuminating the participants' self-reflections on their semi-legal conduct through the immigration rules and the law more broadly.

Rationalising dissent

The meaning-making in respect to semi-legal behaviour is discernible from the various discourses used by the participants within both cohorts, in an attempt to rationalise and justify their semi-compliance, that is, working in breach of study visa terms. These discourses could be grouped under three broad, albeit interrelated, heads: the case for exceptions and apportioning of victimhood, sentiments that subjects are 'bending' as opposed to outrightly breaking the law and, last, a recourse to the hostile broader sociopolitical terrain in respect of migration as a defence and justification for their 'errant' behaviour.

Exceptionality and victimhood

This justification head centred on, in one respect, the sentiments of the exceptional nature of the participants' circumstance, and on the other, the embrace or rejection of victimhood – as the case may be. It is interesting to note that we find marked distinctions between both study cohorts on how they appropriate these discourses in making their case for 'reprieve' for semi-legal conduct.

Cohort A: I'm sorry but you leave me no choice ...

In Cohort A, the case was increasingly made for the exceptional direness of the individual's socioeconomic circumstance as the principal rationale for transgressing the study visa rules. Here, the prevalent inclination was for subjects to attempt to justify their erstwhile proscribed behaviour by admitting to falling foul of the law, while simultaneously making a case for empathy by portraying themselves as near helpless victims at the mercies of its dire, unanticipated consequences for their newly found realities.

> ... what they don't tell you about before coming are all the many bills and taxes ... (A2)

For most, working in breach of visa terms was undertaken as a strategic response to mitigate against future socioeconomic vulnerabilities that follow from their status as 'have nots'. Meanwhile, in doing so, this rhetoric is further fine-tuned for poignancy where actors in this cohort often allude to the detriments of juggling between their studies and their extensive work commitments.

> I really need the money, so I just forget about these things, it's not like I'm happy doing it ... I haven't had a social life, don't hang out or have fun, from school to work, work to school, like now I really wanted to

have a summer break, but I couldn't, I was busy working all through summer. (A4)

They do this specifically to situate themselves as the only true victims of this circumstance, while demonstrating their aversion for this predicament.

> … I don't think anyone would really go through everything to come out here just for work on a student visa … (A3)

In this sense, embracing the discourse of victimhood is appropriated as an emotive rationalisation of their dissenting behaviour.

Cohort B: Sorry not sorry, I'm special …

Whereas in Cohort B, the responses took a different, somewhat methodical turn. In contrast to the embracing of victimhood, as increasingly discernible in Cohort A, the discourse invoked here to justify semi-legal work patterns hinged more on the subjects' heightened estimation of self, and a more purposive, implied approach to deconstructing these employment restrictions. Subjects in this cohort were far more likely to extol affirmative distinctions as grounds for why they ought to be exempted from visa rules.

> I get what they are trying to do with the whole 20 hours thing, maybe they think it's for our own good so we can concentrate on our academics … but it's not like I am only working and not minding my studies, you can even check my academic records, I'm one of the best performers in my class … I'll probably even get awards in my department at grad, so … (B4)

Not only were members of this cohort more inclined to view this entire ordeal as indeed victimless, they more so tended to take more ownership of the circumstances of their decision to derogate from these employment restrictions. This rejection of victimhood was so staunch that the participants rarely admitted to being susceptible to the documented detriments of undertaking extensive work commitments while in full-time study.

> Abeg[7] if you are smart you'll find a way to manage. Look, I work at least four times a week but I'm still going to finish with a first [class

---

7. Nigerian slang meaning 'I beg' or 'please'.

degree] … you just need to know what works for you, like me, I don't need to spend two years in the library before I understand what I'm doing (Abeo)

Some participants in this cohort furthered this argument while alluding to the economic value of their employment for the state.

The more I work, the more taxes they collect, I know some people that are British where I work with that don't even bother to pay tax … (B1)

This position was adopted drawing from symbols of legality, including the payment of due taxes and National Insurance contributions, itself portraying an institutional endorsement of their half-compliance with these employment conditions. Such findings corroborate those of Young's (2014) in the ethnographic study on illicit cockfight rings set in a rural Hawaiian community. Young finds that participants maintained a brand of informal orderliness that mirrored the state-sanctioned conception and proceeded as though this 'neutralised' some of the adverse effects that their illegal behaviour might otherwise have on a bird owner's ability to perceive himself as law-abiding.

Of course, the discrepancies apparent between both cohorts in this regard can be partly explained by the inherent distinctions in their semi-legal designations. In Cohort A, it is possible to see how subjects here can position themselves outrightly as victims of circumstance, as indeed this was a primary reason for why they pivot to being nomadic, lone actors in their working engagements. More so, their semi-legal devise entails just one strike of violation, and this leaves just enough moral stock for them to make the case that they are merely being responsive to the socioeconomic uncertainties with which they are beset. This consequently renders them 'before' and 'against' the law in the same breath. Meanwhile in Cohort B where there are two strikes of semi-legality, this circumstance denotes proactivity and a manifestation of wilful agency if anything. Working in excess of 20 hours per week during term time is one thing, but going further by incorporating a limited company for this express purpose requires concerted effort. This devise can hardly be explained away as simply a *knee-jerk reaction* to pre-empt socioeconomic insecurity. Thus, as hypothesised, members of this cohort align more with the 'with the law' legal consciousness disposition where the law is seen as a game to be played in a morally neutral terrain.

Legitimacy, Bending Not Breaking the Rules, and Attitudes to Reform

Notwithstanding the aforementioned distinctions between cohorts, there was a lingering propensity for students to readily acknowledge the legitimacy of these legal precepts, albeit while taking exception to its restrictive and debilitating impact for their earning potential and socioeconomic security. On a base level, most participants readily admit to the inherent appropriateness and substance of these rules, as some form of restriction on student working is warranted. For instance, they commented how it operates as a means to mark the purpose of one's admission into the country and sets them apart from other migrant groups. In this way, the legitimacy of these restrictions was hinged on its service as a symbolic *aide-mémoire* of the objects of their international mobility; academic pursuits, albeit that they often deviated from this express purpose.

Following this admission, it was also often the case for the participants to expressly rationalise their erstwhile deviant behaviour as merely 'bending the rules' as opposed to outrightly transgressing the law. While a strict application of the law may result in these student-migrant-workers as being culpable *outlaws*, the perception of the law in their minds (i.e. legal consciousness) assumes a more flexible, fluid interpretation, one that can well be adapted to suit their notions in a way that does not cognitively impugn or detract from its normative function. Some even go as far as recasting their behaviour as a virtuous trait that should be embraced.

> It's not like we are stealing … (A4)

> … what are they going to do? Arrest me for being too hardworking…? *Chuckles* (B3)

Another apt illustration of the variability of legal consciousness with the participants is apparent in the responses to discussions relating to the reform to the substance of employment restrictions. Here we find the majority of respondents inclined to maintain the status quo; this is despite the problems it brings them, and the resources and effort they expend towards evading the impending consequences. However, it is noteworthy that some in Cohort B express discontent over being proscribed from undertaking work as 'self-employed' and from engagement in business activities. Needless to say, this had more to do with their specific work context as they contract for work via a limited company structure and are consequently considered as self-employed de jure. If this specific restriction ceases, then their complicity in unauthorised work is ameliorated to all but one strike of working in excess of the mandated

20-hour work limit. However, although they indicate discontent with this aspect of the visa rules, they nonetheless subscribe to the holistic resonance of these restrictions.

> I understand it, if they don't make this rule, then there's no difference between student visas and work visas to begin with. 20 hours seems fair, because the law for everyone is like forty something hours I think, so twenty is kind of like half of that, you can't really complain. (A3)

> It is reasonable, you know … if you work by yourself, as self-employed … then you can just lie and report that you did not do more than 20 per week, there's no way for them to know … (B2)

The sum of these attitudes to reform indicate an acquiescence to law that is frequently associated with a 'before the law' strand of legal consciousness, where the law is deemed as objective and rational. Again, this portrait was, however, not entirely uniform. Some subjects expressed consternation at the potential value of an alternative approach by way of legal reform to the student immigration rules. As the historically marginalised subjects, which most have grown to self-identify as, they know not to retain stock in the brand of fairness and rightness possible through the formal legal structures.

> … I think if they try to change anything, they'll probably make it worse, maybe even say we cannot work at all, so I don't know, you can't trust them … (A1)

Succinctly, the legitimacy of these visa rules for these students was inherent in the fact that it objectively marks a reasonable middle ground enabling the effective administration of employment, education and migration as interrelated socio-legal institutions. It is not as though the law by way of mandated restrictions do not matter, simply that it must be tempered by the individual and for the individual, so to account for the intricacies of their peculiar circumstance. There is an implicit endorsement of the legitimacy and practicality of these immigration rules, the inherent complication is in the socioeconomic hardship it presents when applied to their specific context and interests, that is, *the law in action*. As this inclination is discernible within both cohorts, it becomes apparent that there is a functional understanding that the rules can be reimagined, and are malleable, a perception consonant with the 'with the law' strand of legal consciousness. This also speaks to the renditions of legal pluralism, that what makes for law and order may well be dependent

Structural Inequities and Resistance: Ojoro Cancel Ojoro

A further source of meaning that contoured the perceptions of the participants' errant behaviour of the law on student migration precepts had to do with the lopsided distribution of power and resources between them and the UK state, its institutional might and broader social structures.[8] This was viewed as a powerful, antagonistic force acting to mar the student-migrant-workers' everyday mobility and social ascendancy. This rhetoric implicated their socioeconomic vulnerabilities and the inequities that plague this cohort of workers, especially those from sub-Saharan Africa. The transactional outlook of international education as an industry, more broadly, and the hostile sociopolitical terrain in the UK with regard to migration were impeding structures which were simultaneously externalised and internalised. The participants perceived these to be external forces to which they must strive to prevail against, and internally as an inherent rationale for why they 'must do what they must'. Here, there is a framing of semi-legal behaviour as carved out of resistance to the motions that be, albeit indistinct, and notions of self-serving entitlement.

As it concerns the increasingly transactional nature of international higher education, we can report of a seeming entitlement amongst some subjects built around the notions that their presence in the country was duly bought and paid for.[9] This through the capital expended by the student to make study abroad possible in the form of tuition payments, time spent in the country, living costs incurred and so on. The utility of their presence in the country bestows them the right to gainful employment, however needed, and the opportunity to at least equalise their investments in terms of human and financial capital. This is highly relevant for student-migrant-workers in their situation, particularly those coming from developing states where there are significant and palpable levels of socioeconomic inequity. This perception is only exacerbated by the hostile political terrain surrounding contemporary migration, and especially the politicisation of international students. For instance,

---

8. Ojoro: a Nigerian slang which means 'to cheat, usually by manipulating the outcome of a certain event'. In this context, the expression 'Ojoro cancel Ojoro' is used to denote two equally complicit actors each guilty of attempting to mislead one another.
9. Until the new rules are introduced, most international students were subject to a four-month time limit to leave the UK after the expiry of their visa. Since October 2019, students on Tier 4 student visas, and studying at degree level or higher, were able to switch to a Tier 2 visa within three months of the expected date of the completion of their course and benefit from greater flexibility in seeking employment in the UK.

the fact that international students are required to leave the UK soon after the completion of their studies merely serves to reify these notions.[10] For most, this equation just did not fairly balance out when the argument was simplified to the sums of money paid, the irredeemable time and effort spent, and the resultant degree being awarded.

> The way I see it, it is not a fair deal at all, that you'll pay all that money to come to school abroad, then they'll kick you out once you're done and then you'll go back home poorer than you came … (A3)

One participant went as far as accusing the British state of being bad-faith actors, for which they see the remedy as derogating from the sociopolitical contract (as they see it) they have with the state upon admission into the country.

> they are cheating us if you look at it, they don't want us here, they just want our money, that's why it's so hard for students like us to remain after we finish our course, why it's so hard to get a job … and they only make it harder by the day, so you better make the best use of the little time you have here is all I can say. Don't let a piece of paper stop you, as they say back home, Ojoro cancel Ojoro … (B4)

By extension, the fact that most students worked in excess of the 20 hours threshold was out of necessity, and to be able to afford their continued legal residence in the state only deems this action as fair. In this portrayal, semi-legality is dually enacted as not only resistance of, but also as a medium towards retaining legality. A2 best explained this, drawing an amusing analogy involving a tenant who mowed the lawn of a slum landlord as a deductible on (already unreasonably high) rent.

> They treat us like criminals anyway … really, they make the university monitor our every move, our attendance … and report to the Home Office. We miss class for too long, they can even deport you if care is not taken … (B5)

---

10. Note, these interviews were held prior to the changes introduced from 2021 (previously, international student graduates were permitted a maximum of two years' extension to remain in the UK, through a work visa, before having to leave). Per the British Council, 'from summer 2021, international students who have successfully completed an undergraduate or master's degree will be able to benefit from two years' work experience in the UK upon graduation, through the new Graduate Route. Students who complete their PhD will be able to stay for three years.' https://study-uk.britishcouncil.org/after-your-studies/post-study-work.

Here we see how the sociopolitical structure may well engender normative implications and provide a discursive resource through which student-migrant-workers attempt to justify their engagement in illicit behaviour. This, even more so, when it is located in what they perceive as an unwelcoming terrain. This was an overtly transactional portrait and one that provides students a justification to engage in proscribed conduct, one where employment beyond the mandated limits is portrayed as an equaliser of sorts given the perceived structural inequities to which they are subject. In conclusion, the participants would much prefer a *zero-sum* equation if anything, and this places them 'with the law', where legality is actively gamed out in a morally neutral, yet self-serving, terrain.

Semi-Legality, Legal Consciousness and Everyday Resistance

While semi-legality can be conceived of as resistance in the broader sociological sense, it does beg the question whether it satisfies a form of socio-legal resistance. The defining features of everyday resistance in respect of legal consciousness is outlined as encompassing an awareness of one's relative lack of power, a sense of the possibility of turning a situation to one's advantage and an implicit 'justice claim' that the current conditions are unfair and that those with more power are responsible for this unfairness (Ewick and Silbey 1998, 183). Further, resistance is often 'institutionally indecipherable'; that is, there are few 'rules' or 'standard operating procedures' for handling the ways in which actors resist. Per Scott (1989), when actors within a social location lack power, they will often resist in small ways that cumulatively make it difficult for those with the power to control them.

We can advance a view that semi-legality as enacted by this study's subjects fulfil each of these components. First, these actors increasingly acknowledge their relative powerlessness, not just within the employment relationship, but more so in general, stemming from several reinforcing social locations and identities, as migrants from less well-off states and 'have nots', ethnic minorities, historically marginalised and politically victimised. They overtly and implicitly demonstrate perceptions of their inherent powerlessness through the stories they tell, the justifications they give for deviating from legally sanctioned behaviour, and more so, for their inaction in the face of abuse and exploitation in the workplace. They also make implicit claims about justice and fairness as they ascribe differential experiences to their structural location within the fibres of society, and more so the role of the law, the state and other social actors in perpetuating these injustices. Indeed, as indicated earlier, semi-legal employment is undertaken as an avenue to equalise the inequities perpetuated by their structural disadvantage and powerlessness.

And last, the distinct strategies adopted to resist these rules, from the nomads of Cohort A, to the entrepreneurs within Cohort B, parallels the hypothesis that resistance is indistinct and institutionally decipherable. These are for the most part covert schemes, where actors, albeit at various locations dually appropriate and reject notions of victimhood, just as they despise and resist these rules, yet do not concertedly call for structural reform of the legal provisions surrounding student migration in the UK. Indeed, these slight, covert acts of resistance through semi-legality are not designed to enact broader social change, rather they are demonstrably inspired by self-serving intents. This more so allows subjects to assert a degree of individual agency and autonomy in a lived reality marked with multiple, intersecting avenues for vulnerability and precariousness.

Indeed, we find some consonance in Ewick and Silbey's (1998, 2003) assertions that especially within subordinated groups in society, resistance in legal consciousness is underpinned by tinges of dignity, underground justice and moral superiority. But where we soon start to see cracks in this model is the correlation of resistance with the 'against the law' strand of legal consciousness. This may, to an extent, speak to the findings in Cohort A, given that the *nomads* actively pivot to a more transitory, aloof work pattern to pre-empt future victimhood and distance themselves from the law. But, when actors deploy semi-legality as a medium of resistance towards these rules, there was not a staunch rejection of legality as envisaged by Ewick and Silbey (1998, 2003). Especially in Cohort B where the *entrepreneurs* who appropriate corporate doctrines towards shielding non-compliant work extents are situated, this marks an outward embrace of legality as a means of resistance, while simultaneously implicating a 'with the law' typology of legal consciousness.

Yet it must be contemplated that their disputing behaviour also suggests that there are elements of resistance in both a 'with' and an 'against' the law form of legal consciousness. Similar to other marginalised groups, they tend to distrust the law and legal institutions. Knowing at what transition to leave the dispute pyramid, especially with knowledge that one is engaging in proscribed conduct, can be conceived as resistance to the potential insecurities presented by formally approaching the law while having *skeletons in your cupboard*. This presents a gamed-out response in spite of the law. Here, actors dictate the parameters of their engagement with legality as they decide when to embrace, and when to oppose and resist.

Thus, our findings corroborate the remarks of Hull (2003, 655) as to whether the concept of resistant legal consciousness must be redefined to allow room for the fact that actors may be 'against the law' in important ways, and simultaneously embrace rather than reject legality as part of their resistance in some other.

Semi-Legality and Legal Hegemony

A fitting point to close this analysis is to speak to the effectiveness of semi-legality as medium of contestation towards legal hegemony. After all, the contemporary legal consciousness scholarship's inattention to the issue of legal hegemony – that is, how law manages to retain its hegemonic hold on society despite its historic failings to produce a more egalitarian society – is one of the principal reasons Silbey (2005) had condemned the concept to academic antiquity.[11] Semi-legality as enacted by this study's participants, albeit effective in the short term for their immediate social, legal and economic security, does little to impugn on the overarching resonance and institutional might of the law as the principal institution for social order and mediator of their presence in the country. Notwithstanding the participants' venture into the hazy, albeit proscribed terrain of semi-legality, this is a direction that is, for the better part, being mediated on terms established by the law and its constituted institutions. Even when they vehemently protest its implications for their lives and deviate from its standards, the law yet presents the foremost resource through which the participants measure their decision-making and behaviour. And then, resistance to law via semi-legality takes almost as much as it gives – Whether it is by way of mundane insecurities that linger surreptitiously within both locations, an apprehension for legal symbols, or docility in the face of potentially justiciable injustices. There is a constant deference to the law in all of these designations.

This, however, only establishes the existence of legal hegemony within this population. Indeed, we must explain the 'why' of it if we are ever to meet the standards set by Silbey (2005) in her critique of the emergent scholarship. Halliday (2019, 871) makes an interesting analogy that we find pertinent here. The easiest way to unravel the law's endurance will be to conduct a simple thought experiment of what a society, truly alienated from the law, would look like.

> It would be a society that is governed through open and widespread repression, rather than largely through consent. It would be a totalitarian or authoritarian state, rather than a liberal one.

Now, conversely, we would like to imagine what a wholly compliant society would look like, devoid of resistance and socio-legal struggles between the haves and have nots, the marginalised and the institution. The portrait that comes to mind is one similar to that depicted by Halliday – repressive,

---

11. See Chapter 4.

totalitarian, zombie-esque and monolithic. Why then legal hegemony? Quite simply, the law is all we know, and more poignantly, all we have been made to know, courtesy of years of profound social programming. The law is ideological more than anything, akin to default operating system software where we, social actors, make up the hardware upon which it runs. Our experiential meaning-making represents every key stroke entered, towards producing command prompts that may yet only be rendered through the law, as this is the default system. This is not to say social actors do not possess the ability to go rogue, as a matter of fact we do, and often so. We could argue that it is impossible to be a law breaker in every legal facet imaginable, just as it is practically impossible for one to be utterly compliant with the law in the entirety of one's existence. Again, using a technology metaphor, much like an iPhone or Android mobile telephone device can be jailbroken from its default operating system, we too can remain compliant, just as we can as well stray away from the confines of preset norms, albeit from state law or indeed other coexisting cultural repertoires of normative order in the manner of legal pluralism. Each of these possibilities presents socio-legal implications. But, however, for law to maintain its hegemonic hold and resonance, there has to be overwhelmingly more actors compliant and acquiescent to its provisions and institutions, even under duress, than there are breaking or resisting within a spatio-temporally bounded location. All the same, 'legality' is the default 'ideal' state, through which everything else gets filtered, and for which a majority of actors revert to when assessing their situation and the implications of their decision-making and manifestation of agency.

The constitutive theory of law must thus be sentient to the fact that law is inherently an arena for often contrasting possibilities, where everything and nothing happens all at once, where acquiescence and resistance coexist indistinctly in an enduring state of tension. There is a middle ground somewhere between these distinct, contrasting possibilities. Semi-legality as an empirical schema illustrates this point perfectly. The sum of these findings buttresses the indeterminacy and variability of legal consciousness as an empirical phenomenon. These otherwise marginalised actors can be seen to embrace, reject, resist and game the law as they deem fit. Here, we find all three strands of legal consciousness within both locations in respect of the legal restrictions affixed to their work patterns during study. They are 'before the law' as they increasingly submit to its legitimacy and stop short of advocating for reform of the student visa conditions. They are 'with the law' especially and even as they appropriate legality towards evading the stated study visa rules and equalising the socioeconomic and political disadvantage they were presented with. And 'against the law', when they decry the structural hardship that pushes them towards the semi-legal terrain.

Underpinning this all is the frequently iterated sentiment that student-migrant-workers labour beyond the mandated limits, not simply for immediate subsistence, but more so they can afford to pay tuition. Both of these assertions encompass the primary conditions in the social contract between the students and state/HEIs prior to entry, and failure to adhere to these terms can be dire. The student-migrant-workers can be removed from their course and consequently lose their right to remain in the country. Ergo, they engage in semi-legal employment in the short term, so to keep to legality within the broader contexts of their residence. Thus, we can see how these actors resist legality in some way by embracing legality in another, yet in the service of legality in the 'bigger picture'.

We close this chapter by contending that the critical hypothesis of legal consciousness charted within individuals and society, as multifaceted and fragmented, provides the very recourse through which the law endures and retains its hegemonic hold. Social actors overarchingly place unrelenting faith in the law and its institutions because it is the principal measure of a peoples' value system and normative ideals, and for which there are no cogent alternatives.

Summary and Conclusions

This chapter has reported the findings derived from ethnographic data collated from two distinct cohorts of student-migrant-workers of sub-Saharan African descent in the UK. Here, we considered semi-legality as applied to student-migrants through the employment restrictions to which they are subject while studying in the UK. Semi-legality is used here to refer to the employment of student-migrants who are legally resident, but who are working in contexts that breach the employment restrictions affixed to their migration status. As a notional schema, semi-legality represents a contested space of (il)legality. This concept has been largely ignored in the existing socio-legal scholarship on migration, and thus we take this opportunity to explore it as a multifaceted, dynamic construct that can have distinctive implications for the actor's relationship with the law. As an empirical phenomenon, we find that it allows student-migrants to manage the socioeconomic and legal insecurities presented by their circumstance as disadvantaged actors.

In order to better understand its various manifestations in respect of student-migrant labour, it was first pertinent to explore its formations and consequences beyond the binary legal/illegal demarcations, and more so centre on the student-migrant-workers' strategic agency in creating their own working relationships, in spite of the state's bureaucratic frameworks. As a lived phenomenon, we find that there are a number of ploys used by the participants towards enacting and concealing semi-legality in the labour market. In Cohort A, we find more nomadic student-workers who alternate between various work contexts and employers so to conceal employment in excess of the mandated 20-hour weekly work limits. Meanwhile the students in Cohort B enact semi-legality by contracting for work through limited companies which they incorporated for this express purpose and in connivance with their respective employers, all while working well in excess of the mandated limits. These distinct gradations of semi-legality are subsequently filtered through three socio-legal frameworks: precarity, legal mobilisation (as seen in claims-making behaviour) and legal consciousness.

In seeking the relationships between these distinct renditions of semi-legality in respect of precarity, we find some pertinent disparities between both cohorts. The students in Cohort A were more given to insecure employment, both in terms of job tenure and wages, but fared better than those in Cohort B who tended to be more insecure in their everyday lives outside of work, but nonetheless enjoyed a more stable, favourable employment relationship in terms of tenure and pay.

As it impacts their legal mobilisation, our findings demonstrate that indulging in semi-legal employment effectively impedes the subjects' claims-making prospects. Students within both cohorts had little trouble 'naming' a particular incident as problematic and ascribing 'blame' to the party deemed responsible. However, students in Cohort A tended to leave the dispute pyramid prior to communicating a claim to those deemed responsible and seeking recompense. They often would rather discontinue the employment relationship than take this action. This is due to a cumulation of factors; lingering wariness of outsiders, distrust of employers who could potentially weaponise this information against them, the fleeting relationship they maintained with said employers to whom they ordinarily would communicate any grievances, the fear of detection from the authorities, and a heightened sense of independence. Conversely in Cohort B, the co-complicity of employers effectively neutralises the moral terrain in a way that emboldened the student-migrant-workers to increasingly communicate any grievances and seek redress. However, in instances where the grievance went unresolved following these deliberations, they rarely moved to a formal claim in law. This is because they were similarly discouraged by the complications that could flow from this line of action due to their semi-legal employment relationships. Those in this cohort tended to continue with the employment relationship, despite ills suffered, due to the socioeconomic benefits and the distinctiveness of their semi-legal design which made it arduous to find alternative employment commensurate in value. It is our conclusion that claims-making in both designations often culminates in legal alienation as actors increasingly refrain from engaging the law.

For the final part of the chapter, we examined semi-legality in light of legal consciousness in an illustration of the concept's inherent indeterminacy and the plurality of socio-legal actors. While semi-legality as an 'adulterated' form of (I)legality in theory pre-empts a 'before the law' form of legal consciousness, and as marginalised actors they are hypothesised as typically being 'against the law', the portrait is however far more nuanced than this. We find elements of all three forms of legal consciousness within this population. They are mostly 'with the law' with regard to reform and the legitimacy of the aforementioned visa rules, they are nonetheless against its implications for their socio-legal and economic realities and overarching claims-making prospects. They are 'with the law' as they seek out ways to resist and evade the aforementioned repercussions. Yet in all of these renditions, legality suffuses the arena through which all of these variant exchanges occur. This aptly illustrates the constitutive resonance and endurance of the law and legal hegemony. Quite simply, the law endures because there are no fitting alternatives which will command the manner of institutional acquiescence and normative foundation it reserves within society.

The findings presented here both enrich our theoretical understanding of legal consciousness, claims-making behaviour and the marginalised. It illustrates just how much there is to explore in the grey areas that linger beyond the binary 'legal' and 'illegal' divides of the socio-legal scholarship in respect of migration, and more so the lived experiences engendered by the bureaucratic and sociopolitical structures associated with contemporary migration. It also speaks to those problems outlined in Chapter 5 of the legal definitions of employment status, the rights aligned to same, and how poor definitional practices contributed to the precarious status of the student-migrants as workers. It further confirms the additional work needed in this field to explain and then remedy the problems that exist for all parties if the UK wishes to continue to attract international students – particularly given the changes from 2021 to the immigration system and the rights for international student graduates to remain in the UK in search of employment.

Chapter 8

CONCLUSIONS

Introduction

This concluding chapter draws together the main findings from the study. We present an answer to the question we posed in the first chapter regarding the lived experiences of student-migrants with respect to the legal restrictions affixed to their employment rights while studying in the UK. As a supplementary, we reiterate the ways through with this study offers a contribution to the existing body of literature, before, finally, we identify areas for further research which build on the insights generated from our study.

The Lived Experiences of Student-Migrants with Respect to Their Employment Position

It will be remembered that in Chapter 1 we posed the overarching question on which our study was based. To this end, we wished to examine the lived experiences of student-migrants as workers in relation to the legal restrictions affixed to their employment rights while studying in the UK. This question was premised on the designation of international students as subjects of immigration control. In respect of Tier 4 study visa conditions, international students have generally been restricted to a maximum 20 hours of employment per week during term time, and also proscribed from undertaking work autonomously as independent contractors or self-employed. These restrictions were aimed at keeping students true to the purpose for their admission into the country, protecting them from burnout that can follow from having to juggle extensive employment with study commitments, and finally (argued by some at least), protecting domestic workers from undue competition. This agenda also implicates the state's efforts towards ensuring students keep to these employment restrictions and the codified proscription of illicit migrant labour. These efforts were marked by the 'whole Government', the 'degrees of harm' approach and the provisions of the Immigration Act 2016.

In an effort to address the issue of student-migrants working, we reviewed the current and available literature on student migration, migrant labour with regard to insecure employment, and migration as a socio-legal phenomenon. In so doing we identified the ways through which this book consolidates the, albeit, limited empirical investigations into this phenomenon, while highlighting the underlying justifications for its empirical agenda. The data required for this study was garnered through the use of qualitative methods by way of semi-structured interviews and ethnographic observations involving cohorts of international student-workers of sub-Saharan African descent. However, it is pertinent to note that the limitations inherent in our study sample design means that its findings are not ideally representative of the broader population.

This limitation being acknowledged, the study offers a contribution to the body of knowledge in two principal ways.

The Status of the Student-Migrant-Worker and Precarity

For the first, we account for the employment experiences of the student-workers as rendered through the analytical frame of precarity. Precarity is a concept deployed by contemporary sociologists within the industrial relations scholarship to denote the spread of insecure employment, and more so to question the lived experiences of workers who are given to this manner of employment (the precariat). Here, the object is to examine the various ways through which employment restrictions may engender insecurity and precariousness into the lived experiences of these students, and consequently, to assess their agency as they move to respond to, counteract and resist these erstwhile limiting legal structures. The pertinence of this empirical agenda is based on the existing scholarship's failure to incorporate this group (the students) into the discourse surrounding precarious work, or indeed to contemplate them as a distinct subset of *precariat* subjects. We argue that this positioning defies the de facto and de jure circumstances surrounding their labour market participation which is steeped with the potential for manifold and intersecting forms of socioeconomic and legal insecurities, and our empirical evidence illustrates just this.

In respect of this objective, our study accounts for the employment experiences of international student workers *from the ground up*. The findings here confirm that international students' employment journeys are determined less by the trappings of individual agency, and more by broader specific structural and circumstantial constraints over which they have little control, and to whose circumstances they are mostly reactive. These attested intersecting mediums of precariousness consequently ground the pervasive transactional outlook of employment this study reports of. These findings substantiate existing migration, migrant labour and dual-labour market theories that intimate that recent migrants – including these students – tend to wield an often purely transactional view of employment, especially due to socioeconomic vulnerabilities and structural impediments (Bloch and McKay 2015; IOM 2020; Doeringer and Piore 1971).

Further, we discovered that these students encounter significant difficulties in navigating the UK labour market and are consequently given to jobs that are deemed as precarious, low-status and low-paid. More so, their employment context is preset by barriers brought on by market forces and migration structures that start to take effect before they arrive in the UK, and while resident, they are effectively directed towards insecure employment forms. They resort to finding occupations through employment agencies due to the inherent difficulties they encounter navigating the labour market unaided as new entrants and as recent, transitory migrants who often lack the requisite sociocultural understanding, time and resources to be fully independent job seekers. Indeed, TAW can prove beneficial for these students as it affords them a relatively expeditious route into paid employment, flexibility while engaged, and affords limited control that renders a degree of certainty into their working lives. However, most of these benefits are severely dampened by the insecurities associated with their employment status and again, migration structures. Flexibility, as one criterion, is increasingly dictated by the terms outlined by the employer, which is, itself, subject to fluctuations in broader market forces including labour demand. This precariousness is further exacerbated by employment restrictions and especially the 20-hour weekly work limit. The culmination of the structural impediments does not leave students much flexibility to exercise true freedom over their working lives. More so, for some, the socioeconomic frailties they are encumbered with means they often have to undertake employment for durations well in excess of the mandated limits. The sum of these temporalities, structural constraints and socioeconomic vulnerabilities may well cause other aspects of their lives as social actors, including their studies, to suffer.

Although the students' heightened reliance on specific employment relationships and intermediaries can be beneficial in the short term, this can very well engender exploitation and docility in the face of abuse. This takes into account the fact that students' labour market prospects are institutionally bound in forms that pre-empt them from aspiring to more coveted and/ or rewarding employment contexts. This effectively limits their employment prospects to a meagre spectrum of job roles, with populations of student job seekers being crowded into an already saturated market. This market saturation effectively reifies students' susceptibility to exploitation and maltreatment within employment contexts. Frequently iterated sentiments of disposability and exploitation here corroborate the insights found in the, albeit sparse, literature on the experiences of international student-workers offered by the likes of Nyland et al. (2009) and Takeda (2005). These authors attribute those dismal employment conditions encountered by some student-workers to the fact that employers and brokers know how easily replaceable this segment of the workforce is.

As far as lived employment experiences go, we find that the bulk of students are subject to multiple, intersecting vulnerabilities in the labour market. They are increasingly subject to acts of discrimination, exploitative and abusive work conditions, and they typically indicate discontent regarding their situatedness within the temporary employment market. Furthermore, the students' reliance on informal networks, and employers and employment intermediaries as a principal source of information concerning the local labour market terrain and accruable employment rights, exacerbates their inherent vulnerability and the potential for exploitation. We close by asserting that universities could do more to forearm international students with candid insights on what to expect of the temporary employment market, including the quality of jobs they may have to undertake for subsistence while studying. Such institutions must also do more to provide students with comprehensive knowledge of accruable employment rights and proactively ensure that students are engaged with *decent* employers – Those employers who provide a safe work environment free of exploitation and abuse, and with thorough and effective processes for dealing with workplace concerns, queries and incidents (not limited to grievances).

Student Migrants, Semi-Legality, Legal Consciousness and Mobilisation

Second, this book adopts a socio-legal paradigm where the empirical schema of 'semi-legality' as it applies to student-migrant labour is centred. Semi-legality has been described as the employment of student-migrants who are legally resident but working in contexts that breach the employment restrictions affixed to their migration status. As an analytical tool, the concept marks a middle ground between outrightly illegal/unauthorised activities and utterly legal/compliant student-migrant labour. The students are operating legally in the sense that they do reserve the right to gainful employment while studying, but contemporaneously illegally as they defy the conditions imposed on the manner in which they are entitled to exercise this right. This concept has been largely ignored in current socio-legal scholarship in respect of migration, and as such we take this opportunity to expand on the phenomenon as a multifaceted, dynamic construct that often has distinct implications on the actor's relationship with the law, broadly defined. This insight is predicated by the dearth in the socio-legal scholarship on the intricacies that exist within variations/gradations of legality. How these variations may come to impact on the actors' relationship with the law is crucial given that while it is quite apparent that the manner of engagement with the law may differ between someone who is totally acquiescent of the law, and an 'outlaw' who habitually defies it, this begs the question of what distinctions can be expected of actors that engage in processes that effectively straddle between spectrums of legality and illegality? Here, we examined the various devises of semi-legality as they impact the students' subjective perceptions of the legal conditions that regulate their employment in the state, that is, legal consciousness, and claims-making behaviour as it concerns the dynamics of their engagement with the law and its institutions, in response to injurious experiences in the workplace, that is, legal mobilisation.

In order to better understand its various manifestations within student-migrant employment, it was first pertinent to explore its formations and consequences beyond binary legal/illegal demarcations, and more so centre on the students' strategic agency in navigating their own course, despite the state's bureaucratic frameworks. As a lived phenomenon, it allows student-migrants to manage the socioeconomic and legal insecurities presented by their circumstance as disadvantaged actors. In fulfilling these empirical objectives, we first focused on the empirical renditions of semi-legality as applied to student-migrants through the employment restrictions to which they were subject while studying in the UK. We discovered a number of ploys towards enacting and concealing semi-legality in the labour market being adopted, these correlating within each study location and, more so, implicating the extents of the violations of the student-migration rules. For instance, with Cohort A, we typically found nomadic student-workers who alternate between various work contexts and employers so to conceal employment in excess of the mandated 20-hour weekly work limits. This we considered as *one strike of semi-legality*. Meanwhile in Cohort B, the student-migrants enacted semi-legality by contracting for work through their personal limited companies which they incorporated for this express purpose. Further, as this activity was undertaken in connivance with their respective employers, all while working well in excess of the mandated limits, it resulted in action we considered as *two strikes of semi-legality*. These distinct gradations of semi-legality being subsequently filtered through three frameworks, precarity, legal mobilisation (evidenced through claims-making behaviour), and legal consciousness.

In pursuit of the connexions between these distinct renditions of semi-legality in terms of precarity, we found pertinent disparities between both cohorts. The student-migrants in Cohort A were more given to working in insecure employment, both in terms of job tenure and wages, but largely faring better than those in Cohort B who tended to be more insecure in their everyday lives outside of work, yet simultaneously enjoying more stable, favourable employment relationships with respect to tenure and pay.

As it impacts their legal mobilisation, we discovered that indulging in semi-legal employment effectively impedes subjects' claims-making prospects. Students within both cohorts had little trouble 'naming' a particular incident as problematic and ascribing 'blame' to the party deemed responsible. However, students in Cohort A tended to 'fall off' the dispute pyramid prior to communicating a claim to those deemed responsible, rather choosing to discontinue the employment relationship than pursue a remedy. We uncovered various factors which led to this action including their lingering suspicion of outsiders, distrust of employers who could potentially weaponise this information against them, the fleeting relationship they maintained with said employers to whom they ordinarily would communicate any grievances, the fear of detection from the authorities and a heightened sense of independence. Whereas in Cohort B, the co-complicity of employers effectively neutralises the moral terrain in a way that emboldened the student-migrants to increasingly communicate any grievances and press for reparation. However, in instances where the grievance went unresolved following these deliberations, the student-migrants rarely moved to formally invoke a resolution under the law. In large part it seemed that they were similarly discouraged by the complications that could flow from this line of action due to their semi-legal employment endeavours. Members of this cohort more so tended to continue with the employment relationship, despite ills suffered, due to the socioeconomic benefits this brings, and the distinctiveness of their semi-legal design which makes it arduous to find alternative employment, at least in respect of the alternatives being commensurate in value. We further made comparisons between claims-making in respect of semi-legal and illegal migrant labour. Here, semi-legality acts as a mediated, less profound form of illegality. One where actors are not outrightly condemned to the underground and can still interact with state institutions to engage in formal legal mobilisation wherever necessary, especially if a subjective threshold for action is met. Nonetheless, it is our conclusion that claims-making in both designations often culminates in legal alienation as actors increasingly refrain from engaging the law.

Further, we considered the concept of semi-legality through legal consciousness in an illustration of the concept's inherent indeterminacy and the plurality of socio-legal actors. While semi-legality as an 'adulterated' form of (I)legality in theory pre-empts a 'before the law' form of legal consciousness, and as marginalised actors they are hypothesised as typically being 'against the law', the portrait we formed is, however, far more nuanced than this. Elements of all three forms of legal consciousness were found within this population. They were mostly with the law with respect to reform and the legitimacy of visa rules, yet nonetheless against its implications for their socio-legal and economic realities and overarching claims-making prospects. They were with the law as they sought out ways to resist and evade the aforementioned repercussions. Still in all of these renditions, legality suffuses the arena through which all of these variant exchanges occur. This aptly illustrates the constitutive resonance and endurance of the law and legal hegemony. Quite simply, the law endures because there are no fitting alternatives for which will command the manner of institutional acquiescence and normative pedestal it reserves within society.

The findings presented both enrich our theoretical understanding of legal consciousness, claims-making behaviour and the marginalised, and illustrate just how much there is to explore in the grey areas that linger beyond the binary 'legal' and 'illegal' divides of the socio-legal scholarship of migration. And more so, the lived experiences of the bureaucratic and sociopolitical structures associated with migration today.

Recommendations for Further Research

Comprehensively, we believe that the findings produced from this study ably address the empirical objectives outlined in Chapter 1 and make a contribution to the pool of existing knowledge. Yet, there is still much work to be done towards situating student-migrants as distinctive socio-legal/economic actors and their everyday mobility in the host state. While a considerable body of knowledge has been developed around migration as a social phenomenon and for specific migrant populations, student-migrants are rarely centred in the existing scholarship. Therefore, we take this opportunity to advance two empirical agendas which build upon the insights generated from our study of the student-migrant-worker population, which might help further understandings of this demographic.

Precarity and the student-migrant-worker

First, although this study has examined the insecurities inherent in the employment relationships of student-migrants, we find an overwhelming concentration of international students engaged in one specific sector, social care. Although this study highlights some of the factors that ground this proclivity, we believe this phenomenon is worthy of more in-depth, critical empirical attention. Not only do most of this study participants indicate discontent to find themselves working in care homes, especially given the abuse they are prone to encounter from the residents, it is their palpable belief in there being no tangible alternatives to employment and nothing better to which they should aspire which is particularly interesting. While we have concluded those matters which direct the student-migrants into TAW, we believe that there are distinct rationales that predispose them to social care work. It is yet the case that ethnic minorities and migrants are documented to disproportionately populate frontline roles in the care sector generally (NHS 2020; Oung et al. 2020), but we know less how these tendencies and their underpinnings extend to student-migrants of sub-Saharan African descent, especially as nuanced by global inequities.

This agenda brings together the 'industry-specific' and 'sending country' analytical approaches towards situating the precarity-migration-agency nexus as hypothesised by Paret and Gleeson (2016, 284). The 'industry specific' approach assesses the dynamic interactions between precarity and agency among migrant-workers within specific sectors of the economy. The sending country approaches centres on migrants' home countries, albeit with more emphasis on the socioeconomic circumstance in developing states, where most international migrants originate. This approach consequently looks to account for the socioeconomic implications this transition brings for the individual.

When amalgamated, both approaches can present us with a more holistic insight into student-migrants' interpretation of precarity. For instance, while migrants in economically well-off states often have access to a variety of employment opportunities – albeit in precarious work within low-pay sectors – they also come from regions where jobs are scarce and unemployment is rife. This can consequently make them view low-paid, precarious jobs in the host state more favourably (see Paret and Gleeson 2016). However, Murphy-Lejeune (2002) suggests that international students can be understood as a new migratory 'elite within an elite' considering it as one of the more capital-intensive forms of transnational mobility. These contradictions can present with distinct implications that can be deployed towards examining the intricacies of student-migrants' agency when operating in specific sectors within the labour market. Here, the focus is on particular workplace contexts, precarious legal status with respect to migration precepts, and notions of socioeconomic insecurity and inequities (Paret and Gleeson 2016).

Semi-legality, legal consciousness and student-migrant-workers

A second avenue through which our findings might be developed in the socio-legal sphere is through empirical research on the manifestations of semi-legality and legal consciousness as they impact on student-migrant workers. Of course, we have in this study examined the subject from the student's point of view, and concluded that semi-legality in some contexts cannot be undertaken without the active connivance of employers and employment intermediaries. While our study's empirical objective excludes a focus on the legal consciousness of employers that wilfully participate in violating students' migration conditions, what might be termed 'semi-legal employers', this is a subject worthy of further evidence-based study.

For instance, while we discovered that student-migrants' justifications for violating employment laws tied to their immigration status include socio-economic disadvantage and insecurity, victimisation and exceptionality, along with a malleable perception of the 'law', how many of these factors apply to 'semi-legal' employers remains to be seen. There are pertinent empirical questions here such as how do semi-legal employers perceive the visa rules, and how does semi-legality impact on the dynamics of the employment relationship and claims-making and grievance administration from an employers' point of view? After all, such employers are ostensibly in a better socio-economic and legal position relative to student-migrant-workers. They are better resourced, often do not share similar migration insecurities and are the beneficiaries of the students' claims-making behaviour. The culmination of these factors ground the employers' position as privileged actors in this context, and it would be incredulous to expect the same legal consciousness disposition to exist for the marginalised as for the privileged. If the marginalised are hypothesised to present with an 'against the law' form of legal consciousness, then privileged actors are ostensibly either with or before the law, but then again, how does semi-legality as a half-way point between utter illegality and semi-legality affect this entire process? This insight could enrich our understanding of semi-legality as a multidimensional phenomenon with sentient moving parts and actors.

Finally, we would like to draw the attention of the burgeoning sub-scholarship on migration as a socio-legal phenomenon to depart from a framing of illegality as an end to itself for migrants' relationship with the law. Our use of semi-legality illustrates the need for further study and a nuanced understanding that can be garnered when we increasingly look towards the legality of acts, as opposed to of persons.

BIBLIOGRAPHY

Abraham, Katharine G. 1990. 'Restructuring the Employment Relationship: The Growth of Market-Mediated Work Arrangements'. In Katherine G. Abraham and Robert B. McKersie, eds. *New Developments in the Labor Market: Toward a New Institutional Paradigm*. Cambridge, MA: MIT Press.

Abrego, Leisy. 2008. 'Legitimacy, Social Identity, and the Mobilization of Law: The Effects of Assembly Bill 540 on Undocumented Students in California'. *Law & Social Inquiry* 33, no. 3: 709–34.

Abrego, Leisy J. 2011. 'Legal Consciousness of Undocumented Latinos: Fear and Stigma as Barriers to Claims-Making for First- and 1.5-Generation Immigrants'. *Law & Society Review* 45, no. 2: 337–70.

Abrego, Leisy J. 2018. 'Renewed Optimism and Spatial Mobility: Legal Consciousness of Latino Deferred Action for Childhood Arrivals Recipients and their Families in Los Angeles'. *Ethnicities* 18, no. 2: 192–207.

Abuosi, Aaron, and Abor, Patience. 2015. 'Migration Intentions of Nursing Students in Ghana: Implications for Human Resource Development in the Health Sector'. *Journal of International Migration and Integration* 16: 593–606.

Adepoju, Aderanti, and Van der Wiel, Arie. 2010. *Seeking Greener Pasture Abroad*. Ibadan: Safari Books.

Adepoju, Aderanti, van Naerssen, Ton, and Zoomers, Annelies. 2007. *International Migration and National Development in sub-Saharan Africa: Viewpoints and Policy Initiatives in the Countries of Origin*. Leiden: Brill.

Agarwal, Parwan, Said, Mohsen E., Sehoole, Molathlegi, Sirozi, Muhammad, and Wit, Hans. 2008. 'The Dynamics of International Student Circulation in a Global Context: Summary, Conclusions, and Recommendations'. In Hans de Wit, Pawan Agarwal, Mohsen Elmahdy Said, Molatlhegi T. Sehoole and Muhammad Sirozi, eds. *The Dynamics of International Student Circulation in a Global Context*, Volume 11. Leiden: Brill.

Alberti, Gabriella. 2020. 'Migrant Labour in London's Hospitality. Ethnographic Reflections on Subjectivity, Transiency, and Collective Action After a Decade'. *Etnografia e ricerca Qualitativa* 1: 79–101.

Alberti, Gabriella, Bessa, Ioulia, Hardy, Kate, Trappmann, Vera, and Umney, Charles. 2018. 'In, Against and Beyond Precarity: Work in Insecure Times'. *Work, Employment and Society* 32, no. 3: 447–57.

Alberts, Heike C. 2007. 'Beyond the Headlines: Changing Patterns in International Student Enrollment in the United States'. *GeoJournal* 68, nos. 2–3: 141–53.

Albiston, Catherine R. 2005. 'Bargaining in the Shadow of Social Institutions: Competing Discourses and Social Change in Workplace Mobilization of Civil Rights'. *Law & Society Review* 39, no. 1: 11–50.

Ali, Syed. 2007. '"Go West Young Man": The Culture of Migration Among Muslims in Hyderabad, India'. *Journal of Ethnic and Migration Studies*, 33, no. 1: 37–58.

Allison, Christine. 2015. 'Law in Books Versus Law in Action: A Review of the Socio-legal Literature'. In Imbeau, Louis and Jacob, Steve eds. *Behind a Veil of Ignorance? Power and Uncertainty in Constitutional Design*. New York: Springer.

Anderson, Bridget. 2010. 'Migration, Immigration Controls and the Fashioning of Precarious Workers'. *Work, Employment and Society* 24, no. 2: 300–317.

———. 2013. *Us and Them? The Dangerous Politics of Immigration Control*. Oxford: Oxford University Press.

———. 2014. *Precarious Pasts, Precarious Futures*. Oxford: Oxford University Press.

Anderson, Bridget, Ruhs, Martin, Rogaly, Ben, and Spencer, Sarah. 2006. *Fair Enough. Central and East European Migrants in Low-Wage Employment in the UK*. York: Joseph Rowntree Foundation.

Appleyard, Reginald T. 1988. 'International Migration in Asia and the Pacific'. In Reginald T. Appleyard, ed. *International Migration Today: Trends and Prospects*, Volume 1. UNESCO, Paris, and Centre for Migration and Development Studies, University of Western Australia, 89–167.

Arrigo, Bruce. 2004. 'The Ethics of Therapeutic Jurisprudence: A Critical and Theoretical Inquiry of Law, Psychology and Crime'. *Psychiatry, Psychology and Law* 11, no. 1: 23–43.

Atkinson, Anthony B., and Hills, John. 1998. 'Exclusion, Employment and Opportunity'. Centre for Analysis of Social Exclusion. London: London School of Economics and Political Science, *Research Paper no. CASE004*.

Atkinson, John. 1985. *Flexibility, Uncertainty and Manpower Management*. Brighton: University of Sussex, Institute for Employment Studies.

Atkinson, Rowland, and Flint, John. 2001. 'Accessing Hidden and Hard-to-Reach Populations: Snowball Research Strategies'. *Social Research Update* 33, https://sru.soc.surrey.ac.uk/SRU33.html.

Autor, David, and Houseman, Susan. 2005. 'Temporary Agency Employment as a Way Out of Poverty?'. Upjohn Institute Working Paper No. 05–123. Kalamazoo, MI: W.E. Upjohn Institute for Employment Research.

Avendaño, Ana, and Marielena, Hincapié. 2008. 'The Rollback of Immigrant Workers' Civil Rights'. AFL-CIO. http://www.aflcio.org/mediacenter/speakout/aa_mh.cfm.

Baas, Michiel. 2010. *Imagined Mobility. Migration and Transnationalism among Indian Students in Australia*. London: Anthem Press.

Bacon, David. 2008. *Illegal People: How Globalization Creates Migration and Criminalizes Immigrants*. Boston, MA: Beacon Press.

Baláž, Vladimir, and Williams, Allan M. 2004. ' "Been There, Done That": International Student Migration and Human Capital Transfers from the UK to Slovakia'. *Population, Space and Place* 10, no. 3: 217–37.

Baldwin-Edwards, Martin. 1998. 'Where Free Markets Reign: Aliens in the Twilight Zone'. *South European Society and Politics* 3, no. 3: 1–15.

Ball, Malcolm, Hampton, Colin, Kamerade, Daiga, and Richardson, Helen. 2017. 'Agency Workers and Zero Hours – The Story of Hidden Exploitation'. Project Report (unpublished) http://shura.shu.ac.uk/16682/.

Banakar, Reza. 2000. 'Reflections on the Methodological Issues of the Sociology of Law'. *Journal of Law and Society* 27, no. 2: 273–95.
———. 2015. *Normativity in Legal Sociology*. Switzerland: Springer.
Beck, Uirich. 1992. *Risk Society: Towards a New Modernity*. London: Sage.
Beech, Suzanne E. 2018. 'Adapting to Change in the Higher Education System: International Student Mobility as a Migration Industry'. *Journal of Ethnic and Migration Studies* 44, no. 4: 610–25.
Beine, Michel, Docquier, Frederic, and Schiff, Maurice. 2013. 'International Migration, Transfer of Norms and Home Country Fertility'. *Canadian Journal of Economics/Revue canadienne d'économique* 46, no. 4: 1406–30.
Beine, Michel, Noël, Romain, and Ragot, Lionel. 2014. 'Determinants of the International Mobility of Students'. *Economics of Education Review* 41: 40–54.
Belous, Richard S. 1989. *The Contingent Economy: The Growth of the Temporary, Part-Time and Subcontracted Workforce*. Washington, DC: National Planning Association.
Benach, Joan, Muntaner, Carles, Delclos, Carlos, Menéndez, Maria, and Ronquillo, Charlene. 2011. 'Migration and "Low-Skilled" Workers in Destination Countries'. *PLOS Medicine* 8, no. 6: e1001043. https://doi.org/10.1371/journal.pmed.1001043.
Benton, Mehgan, Sumption, Madeleine, Alsvik, Kristine, Fratzke, Susan, Kuptsch, Christiane, and Papademetriou, Demetrios G. 2014. *Aiming Higher: Policies to Get Immigrants into Middle-Skilled Work in Europe*. Migration Policy Institute. https://www.migrationpolicy.org/research/aiming-higher-policies-get-immigrants-middle-skilled-work-europe.
Bernhardt, Arnette, Milkman, Ruth, Theodore, Nik, Heckathorn, Douglas D., Auer, Mirabai, DeFilippis, James, and Perelshteyn, Jason. 2009. *Broken Laws, Unprotected Workers: Violations of Employment and Labour Laws in America's Cities*. Russell Sage Foundation. https://www.russellsage.org/awarded-project/broken-laws-unprotected-workers-violations-employment-and-labor-laws-americas-cities.
Berrey, Ellen, and Nielsen, Laura B. 2007. 'Rights of Inclusion: Integrating Identity at the Bottom of the Dispute Pyramid'. *Law & Social Inquiry* 32, no. 1: 233–60.
Berthélemy, Jean-Claude. 2006. 'Aid Allocation: Comparing Donors' Behaviours'. *Swedish Economic Policy Review* 13: 75–109.
Bertrand, Marianne, and Mullainathan, Sendhil. 2004. 'Are Emily and Greg More Employable Than Lekisha and Jamal? A Field Experiment on Labour Market Discrimination'. *American Economic Review* 94, no. 4: 991–1013.
Bessey, Donata. 2012. 'International Student Migration to Germany'. *Empirical Economics* 42, no. 1: 345–61.
Biernacki, Patrick, and Waldorf, Dan. 1981. 'Snowball Sampling: Problems and Techniques of Chain Referral Sampling'. *Sociological Methods & Research* 10, no. 2: 141–63.
Biggs, David. 2003. *Employment Agency Workers, Their Job Satisfaction and Their Influence on Permanent Workers*. PhD Thesis, University of Leicester.
Biggs, David. 2006. 'The Decline of the Temporary Worker: A Regional Perspective'. *Local Economy* 21, no. 3: 249–63.
Bilecen, Başak, and Van Mol, Christof. 2017. 'Introduction: International Academic Mobility and Inequalities'. *Journal of Ethnic and Migration Studies* 43, no. 8: 1241–55.
Blair, Tony. 1999. 'Attracting More International Students'. [Speech to London School of Economics launching Prime Minister's Initiative], June 18. London.
Blandy, Sarah. 2014. 'Socio-Legal Approaches to Property Law Research'. *Property Law Review* 3, no. 3: 166–75.

Bloch, Alice. 2013. 'The Labour Market Experiences and Strategies of Young Undocumented Migrants'. *Work, Employment and Society* 27, no. 2: 272–87.

Bloch, Alice, and McKay, Sonia. 2015. 'Employment, Social Networks and Undocumented Migrants: The Employer Perspective'. *Sociology* 49 no. 1: 38–55.

Boeri, Tito, Brücker, Herbert, Docquier, Frederic, and Rapoport, Hillel, eds. 2012. *Brain Drain and Brain Gain: The Global Competition to Attract High-Skilled Migrants*. Oxford: Oxford University Press.

Boittin, Margaret L. 2013. 'New Perspectives from the Oldest Profession: Abuse and the Legal Consciousness of Sex Workers in China'. *Law & Society Review* 47, no. 2: 245–78.

Bonet, Rocio, Cappelli, Peter, and Hamori, Monika. 2013. 'Labour Market Intermediaries and the New Paradigm for Human Resources'. *Academy of Management Annals* 7, no. 1: 341–92.

Bonner, Ann, and Tolhurst, Gerda. 2002. 'Insider-Outsider Perspectives of Participant Observation'. *Nurse Researcher* 9, no. 4: 7–19.

Booth, Alison L., Francesconi, Marco, and Frank, Jeff. 2002. 'Temporary Jobs: Steppingstones or Dead Ends?'. *Economic Journal* 112, no. 480: 189–213.

Borrie, W. D. 1959. *The Cultural Integration of Immigrants: A Survey Based Upon the Papers and Proceedings of the UNESCO Conference*. Paris: UNESCO.

Bosniak, Linda. 2008. *The Citizen and the Alien: Dilemmas of Contemporary Membership*. Princeton, NJ: Princeton University Press.

Boswell, Christina, and Straubhaar, Thomas. 2004. 'The Illegal Employment of Foreign Workers: An Overview'. *Intereconomics: Review of European Economic Policy* 39, no. 1: 4–7.

Boulin, Jean-Yves, Lallement, Micheel, Messenger, Jon C., and Michon, Francois, eds. 2006. *Decent Working Time: New Trends, New Issues*. Geneva: International Labour Office.

Bourdieu, Pierre. 1984. *Distinction: A Social Critique of the Judgement of Taste*. Translated by Richard Nice. Cambridge, MA: Harvard University Press.

———. 1987. 'What Makes a Social Class? On the Theoretical and Practical Existence of Groups'. *Berkeley Journal of Sociology* 32: 1–17.

———. 1993. *Sociology in Question*, Volume 18. London: Sage.

Bradley, Graham. 2006. 'Work Participation and Academic Performance: A Test of Alternative Propositions'. *Journal of Education and Work* 19, no. 5: 481–501.

Brakel, Samuel Jan. 2007. 'Searching for the Therapy in Therapeutic Jurisprudence'. *New England Journal on Civil and Criminal Confinement* 33: 455–500.

Brewster, Chris, Mayne, Lesley, and Tregaskis, Olga. 1997. 'Flexible Working in Europe: A Review of the Evidence'. *MIR: Management International Review* 37: 85–103.

Bridges, David. 2001. 'The Ethics of Outsider Research'. *Journal of Philosophy of Education* 35, no. 3: 371–86.

British Broadcasting Corporation (BBC). 2004. *The University 'Market' Is Here*. http://news.bbc.co.uk/1/hi/education/3595049.stm.

———. 2018. *Anger as 'Windrush Generation' Face Deportation Threat*. https://www.bbc.co.uk/news/uk-politics-43726976.

Bronstein, Arturo S. 1991. 'Temporary Work in Western Europe: Threat or Complement to Permanent Employment?'. *International Labour Review* 130, no. 3: 291–310.

Brooks, Rachel, and Waters, Johanna. 2009. 'International Higher Education and the Mobility of UK Students'. *Journal of Research in International Education* 8, no. 2: 191–209.

———. 2010. 'Social Networks and Educational Mobility: The Experiences of UK Students'. *Globalisation, Societies and Education* 8, no. 1: 143–57.

———. 2011a. 'Fees, Funding and Overseas Study: Mobile UK Students and Educational Inequalities'. *Sociological Research Online* 16: 1–9.
———. 2011b. *Student Mobilities: Migration and the Internationalization of Higher Education*. Basingstoke: Palgrave Macmillan.
Brown, Lorraine, Edwards, John, and Hartwell, Heather. 2010. 'A Taste of the Unfamiliar. Understanding the Meanings Attached to Food by International Postgraduate Students in England'. *Appetite* 54, no. 1: 202–7.
Bryman, Alan. 2016. *Social Research Methods*. Oxford: Oxford University Press.
Bryson, Alex. 2013. 'Do Temporary Agency Workers Affect Workplace Performance?'. *Journal of Productivity Analysis* 39, no. 2: 131–38.
Bullough, Robert V. 2007. 'Ali: Becoming A Student – A Life History'. In Dennis Thiessen and Alison Cook-Sather, eds. *International Handbook of Student Experience in Elementary and Secondary School*. Dordrecht: Springer, 493–516.
Bumiller, Kristin. 1987. 'Victims in the Shadow of the Law: A Critique of the Model of Legal Protection'. *Signs* 12, no. 3: 421–39.
Burchell, Brendan, Deakin, Simon, and Honey, Sheila. 1999. *The Employment Status of Individuals in Non-Standard Employment*. Great Britain, Department of Trade and Industry.
Büthe, Tim, Jacobs, Alan M., Bleich, Erik, Pekkanen, Robert J., and Trachtenberg, Marc. 2015. 'Qualitative & Multi-Method Research Journal Scan: January 2014–April 2015'. *Qualitative & Multi-Method Research* 13: 65–75.
Butler, Judith. 2006. *Precarious Life: The Powers of Mourning and Violence*. London: Verso.
Calavita, Kitty. 1998. 'Immigration, Law, and Marginalization in a Global Economy: Notes from Spain'. *Law & Society Review* 32, no. 3: 529–566.
———. 2007. 'Immigration Law, Race, and Identity'. *Annual Review of Law and Social Science* 3, no. 1: 1–20.
Calavita, Kitty, and Jenness, Valerie. 2015. *Appealing to Justice: Prisoner Grievances, Rights, and Carceral Logic*. Berkeley: University of California Press.
Calhoun, Patrick, and Smith, William P. 1999. Integrative Bargaining: Does Gender Make a Difference? *International Journal of Conflict Management* 10, no. 3: 203–24.
Cameron, David. 'Speech on Immigration'. [Speech to Conservative Party Members], New Statesman, April 14. https://www.newstatesman.com/2011/04/immigration-british-visas-work.
Campbell, Amy T. 2021. 'Addressing the Community Trauma of Inequity Holistically: The Head and the Heart Behind Structural Interventions'. *Denver Law Review* 98, no. 1. https://repository.law.uic.edu/facpubs/806.
Campbell, C. M., and Wiles, Paul. 1976. 'The Study of Law in Society in Britain'. *Law & Society Review* 10, no. 4: 547–78.
Cantwell, Brendan. 2015. 'Are International Students Cash Cows? Examining the Relationship Between New International Undergraduate Enrollments and Institutional Revenue at Public Colleges and Universities in the US'. *Journal of International Students* 5, no. 4: 512–25.
Carlin, Jerome, and Howard, Jan. 1965. 'Legal Representation and Class Justice'. *U.C.L.A. Law Review* 12: 381–437.
Casey, Bernard. 1988. *Temporary Employment: Practice and Policy in Britain*. London: Policy Studies Institute and the Anglo-German Foundation.
Casey, Catherine, and Alach, Petricia. 2004. '"Just a Temp?": Women, Temporary Employment and Lifestyle'. *Work, Employment and Society* 18, no. 3: 459–80.

Castelli, Francesco. 2018. 'Drivers of Migration: Why Do People Move?'. *Journal of Travel Medicine* 25, no. 1: 1–7.

Castles, Stephen. 2000. *Ethnicity and Globalization: From Migrant Worker to Transnational Citizen*. London: Sage.

Chauvin, Sebastien, and Garcés-Mascareñas, Blanca. 2012. 'Beyond Informal Citizenship: The New Moral Economy of Migrant Illegality'. *International Political Sociology* 6, no. 3: 241–59.

Chavez, Christina. 2008. 'Conceptualizing from the Inside: Advantages, Complications, and Demands on Insider Positionality'. *The Qualitative Report* 13, no. 3: 474–94.

Chen, Liang-Hsuan. 2007. 'Internationalization or International Marketing? Two Frameworks for Understanding International Students' Choice of Canadian Universities'. *Journal of Marketing for Higher Education* 18, no. 1: 1–33.

Chiang, Shiao-Yun. 2014. 'Cultural Adaptation as a Sense-Making Experience: International Students in China'. *Journal of International Migration and Integration* 16, no. 2: 397–413.

Chiswick, Barry R., ed. 2011. *High-Skilled Immigration in a Global Labor Market*. Washington, DC: AEI Press.

Choonara, Joseph. 2019. *Insecurity, Precarious Work and Labour Markets: Challenging the Orthodoxy*. Camden: Palgrave Macmillan.

Choudaha, Rahul, and de Wit, Hans. 2014. *Internationalisation of Higher Education and Global Mobility*. Oxford: Symposium Books.

Clark, Nick, and Sedgwick, Robert. 2005. *International Students: It's a Buyer's Market*. World Education News and Reviews. https://wenr.wes.org/2005/07/wenr-august-2005-international-education-its-a-buyers-market.

Coghlan, David. 2003. 'Practitioner Research for Organizational Knowledge: Mechanistic- and Organistic-Oriented Approaches to Insider Action Research'. *Management Learning* 34, no. 4: 451–63.

Cohen, Nissim, and Arieli, Tamar. 2011. 'Field Research in Conflict Environments: Methodological Challenges and Snowball Sampling'. *Journal of Peace Research* 48, no. 4: 423–35.

Collins, Francis L. 2012. 'Transnational Mobilities and Urban Spatialities: Notes from the Asia-Pacific'. *Progress in Human Geography* 36, no. 3: 316–35.

Connolly, Catherine. 2002. 'The Voice of the Petitioner: The Experiences of Gay and Lesbian Parents in Successful Second-Parent Adoption Proceedings'. *Law & Society Review* 36, no. 2: 325–346.

Connolly, Catherine E., and Gallagher, Daniel G. 2004. 'Emerging Trends in Contingent Work Research'. *Journal of Management* 30, no. 6: 959–83.

Cordova, Efren. 1986. 'From Full-Time Employment to Atypical Employment: A Major Shift in the Evolution of Labour Relations?'. *International Labour Review* 125, no. 6: 641–57.

Corlett, Adam, and Gardiner, Laura. 2015. *Low Pay Britain 2015*. Resolution Foundation. https://www.resolutionfoundation.org/publications/low-pay-britain-2015/.

Cornelius, Wayne, Martin, Philip, and Hollifield, James. 1994. *Controlling Immigration: A Global Perspective*. Palo Alto, CA: Stanford University Press.

Costa, Daniel, and Martin, Philip. 2018. *Temporary Labor Migration Programs: Governance, Migrant Worker Rights, and Recommendations for the U.N. Global Compact for Migration*. https://www.epi.org/publication/temporary-labor-migration-programs-governance-migrant-worker-rights-and-recommendations-for-the-u-n-global-compact-for-migration/.

Costello, Cathryn, and Freedland, Mark R. 2014. *Migrants at Work: Immigration and Vulnerability in Labour Law*. Oxford: Oxford University Press.

Cotterrell, Roger. 1998. 'Why Must Legal Ideas Be Interpreted Sociologically?'. *Journal of Law and Society* 25, no. 2: 171–92.

———. 2002. 'Subverting Orthodoxy, Making Law Central: A View of Sociolegal Studies'. *Journal of Law and Society* 29, no. 4: 632–44.

Coutin, Susan B. 2000. 'Denationalization, Inclusion, and Exclusion: Negotiating the Boundaries of Belonging'. *Indiana Journal of Global Legal Studies* 7, no. 2: 585–93.

———. 2011. 'The Rights of Noncitizens in the United States'. *Annual Review of Law and Social Science* 7, no. 1: 289–308.

Cowan, Dave. 2004. 'Legal Consciousness: Some Observations'. *Modern Law Review* 67, no. 6: 928–58.

Creed, Peter A., French, Jessica, and Hood, Michelle. 2015. 'Working while Studying at University: The Relationship between Work Benefits and Demands and Engagement and Well-Being'. *Journal of Vocational Behavior* 86: 48–57.

Creswell, John W. 1998. *Qualitative Inquiry and Research Design: Choosing among Five Traditions*. Thousand Oaks, CA: Sage.

———. 2003. *Research Design: Qualitative, Quantitative, and Mixed Methods Approaches*. Thousand Oaks, CA: Sage.

———. 2009. *Research Design: Qualitative, Quantitative, and Mixed Methods Approaches*, 3rd ed. Thousand Oaks, CA: Sage.

———. 2012. *Educational Research: Planning, Conducting and Evaluating Qualitative and Quantitative Research*, 4th ed. Boston, MA: Pearson Education.

———. 2014. *A Concise Introduction to Mixed Methods Research*. Los Angeles, CA: Sage.

Cronin, Constance. 1970. *The Sting of Change: Sicilians in Sicily and Australia*. Chicago: University of Chicago Press.

Cully, Mark, Woodland, Stephen, O'Reilly, Andrew, Dix, Gill, Millward, Neil, Bryson, Alex, and Forth, John. 1998. *The 1998 Workplace Employee Relations Survey: First Findings*. Department of Trade and Industry.

Curtis, Susan, and Lucas, Rosemary. 2001. 'A Coincidence of Needs? Employers and Full-Time Students'. *Employee Relations* 23, no. 1: 38–54.

Cvajner, Martina, and Sciortino, Giuseppe. 2010. 'Theorizing Irregular Migration: The Control of Spatial Mobility in Differentiated Societies'. *European Journal of Social Theory* 13: 389–404.

Dadush, Uri. 2014. 'The Effect of Low-Skilled Labour Migration on the Host Economy'. KNOMAD Working Paper Series. https://carnegieendowment.org/files/Effect-of-Low-Skilled-Labor-Working-Paper-1.pdf.

Dako-Gyeke, Mavis. 2015. 'Exploring the Migration Intentions of Ghanaian Youth: A Qualitative Study'. *Journal of International Migration and Integration* 17: 723–44.

Davidov, Guy. 2004. 'Joint Employer Status in Triangular Employment Relationships'. *British Journal of Industrial Relations* 42, no. 4: 727–46.

———. 2005. 'Who Is a Worker?'. *Industrial Law Journal* 34, no. 1: 57–71.

Davies, Anne C. L. 2009. *Perspectives on Labour Law*, 2nd ed. Cambridge: Cambridge University Press.

De Cuyper, Nele, Notelaers, Guy, and De Witte, Hans. 2009. 'Job Insecurity and Employability in Fixed-Term Contractors, Agency Workers, and Permanent Workers: Associations with Job Satisfaction and Affective Organizational Commitment'. *Journal of Occupational Health Psychology* 14, no. 2: 193–205.

De Genova, Nicholas P. 2002. 'Migrant "Illegality" and Deportability in Everyday Life'. *Annual Review of Anthropology* 31, no. 1: 419–47.

De Grip, Andries, Hoevenberg, Jeroen, and Willems, Ed. 1997. 'Atypical Employment in the European Union'. *International Labour Review* 136, no. 1: 49–71.

de Wit, Hans. 2008. 'The Internationalization of Higher Education in a Global Context'. In Hans de Wit, Pawan Agarwal, Mohsen E. Said, Molatlhegi T. Sehoole and Muhammad Sirozi, eds. *The Dynamics of International Student Circulation in a Global Context.* Rotterdam: Sense.

———. 2011. 'Globalisation and Internationalisation of Higher Education'. *Revista de Universidad y Sociedad del Conocimiento* 8, no. 2: 241–48.

de Wit, Hans, Hunter, Fiona, Egron-Polak, Eva, and Howard, Laura, eds. 2015. *Internationalisation of Higher Education: A Study for the European Parliament.* http://www.europarl.europa.eu/RegData/etudes/STUD/2015/540370/IPOL_STU(2015)540370_EN.pdf.

Deakin, Simon. 2013. 'What Exactly Is Happening to the Contract of Employment? Reflections on Mark Freedland and Nicola Kountouris's Legal Construction of Personal Work Relations'. *Jerusalem Review of Legal Studies* 7, no. 1: 135–44.

Deakin, Simon, and Morris, Gillian. 2009. *Labour Law,* 5th ed. Bloomsbury Oxford: Bloomsbury Academic.

Dean, Hartley. 2018. 'EU Citizenship and "Work": Tensions between Formal and Substantive Equality'. In Sandra Seubert, Oliver Eberl, and Frans van Waarden, eds. *Reconsidering European Citizenship: Contradictions and Constraints. Interdisciplinary Perspectives on EU Citizenship.* Cheltenham: Edward Elgar.

Delsen Lei. 1995. *Atypical Employment: An International Perspective-Causes, Consequences, and Policy.* Groningen: Wolters-Noordhoff.

DeLyser, Dydia. 2001. '"Do You Really Live Here?" Thoughts on Insider Research'. *Geographical Review* 91 nos.1–2: 441–53.

Denzin, Norman K., and Lincoln, Yvonna S. 2011. *The Sage Handbook of Qualitative Research.* Los Angeles, CA: Sage.

De Cuyper, Nele, De Jong, Jeroen, De Witte, Hans, Isaksson, Kerstin, Rigotti, Thomas, and Schalk, Rene. 2008. 'Literature Review of Theory and Research on the Psychological Impact of Temporary Employment: Towards a Conceptual Model'. *International Journal of Management Reviews* 10, no. 1: 25–51.

Doan, Nguyen Q. T. 2015. 'Neoliberal Capitalism, Transnationalism and Networked Individualism: Rethinking Social Class'. MSc Thesis. LSE, London. https://www.lse.ac.uk/media-and-communications/assets/documents/research/msc-dissertations/2015/Nguyen-Quynh-Tram-Doan.pdf.

Docquier, Frederic, Lowell, B. Lindsay, and Marfouk, Abdeslam. 2009. 'A Gendered Assessment of Highly Skilled Emigration'. *Population and Development Review* 35, no. 2: 297–321.

Docquier, Frederic, and Rapoport, Hillel. 2012. 'Globalization, Brain Drain, and Development'. *Journal of Economic Literature* 50, no. 3: 681–730.

Dodani, Sunita, and LaPorte, Ronald E. 2005. 'Brain Drain from Developing Countries: How Can Brain Drain Be Converted into Wisdom Gain?'. *Journal of the Royal Society of Medicine* 98, no. 11: 487–91.

Doeringer, Peter, and Piore, Michael. 1971. *Internal Labour Markets and Manpower Analysis.* Lexington, MA: DC Heath.

Domingo, Pilar, and O'Neil, Tam. 2014. *The Politics of Legal Empowerment. Legal Mobilisation Strategies and Implications for Development.* London: Overseas Development Institute.

Dreher, Axel, and Poutvaara, Panu. 2005. 'Student Flows and Migration: An Empirical Analysis'. IZA Discussion Paper No. 1612, CESifo Working Paper Series No. 1490. https://ssrn.com/abstract=731765.

Drever, Eric. 1995. *Using Semi-Structured Interviews in Small-Scale Research. A Teacher's Guide.* SCRE Centre.

Dupret, Baudouin. 2007. 'Legal Pluralism, Plurality of Laws, and Legal Practices: Theories, Critiques, and Praxiological Re-Specification'. *European Journal of Legal Studies* 1, no. 1: 296–318.

Durkheim, Emile. 1933. *The Division of Labour in Society*. Translated by George Simpson. Illinois: Macmillan.

———. 1997. *The Division of Labor in Society*. United Kingdom: Free Press.

Dustmann, Christian, Fabbri, Francesca, and Preston, Ian. 2005. 'The Impact of Immigration on the British Labour Market'. *Economic Journal* 115, no. 507: F324–F341.

Dustmann, Christian, Frattini, Tommaso, and Preston, Ian P. 2013. 'The Effect of Immigration along the Distribution of Wages'. *Review of Economic Studies* 80, no. 1: 145–73.

Düvell, Franck. 2008. 'Clandestine Migration in Europe'. *Social Science Information* 47, no. 4: 479–97.

Edelman, Lauren B., Erlanger, Howard S., and Lande, John. 1993. 'Internal Dispute Resolution: The Transformation of Civil Rights in the Workplace'. *Law and Society Review* 27, no. 3: 497–534.

Edelman, Lauren, Fuller, Sally, and Mara-Drita, Iona. 2001. 'Diversity Rhetoric and the Managerialization of Law'. *American Journal of Sociology* 106, no. 6: 1589–641.

Edwards, James. 2019. 'Theories of Criminal Law'. In Edward. N. Zalta, ed. *The Stanford Encyclopaedia of Philosophy*. Stanford, CA: Metaphysics Research Lab, Stanford University.

Efionayi, Denise, and Piguet, Etienne. 2014. 'Western African Student Migration: A Response to the Globalisation of Knowledge'. *Education, Learning, Training: Critical Issues for Development* 5: 174–94.

Ellis, Wendy R., and Dietz, William H. 2017. 'A New Framework for Addressing Adverse Childhood and Community Experiences: The Building Community Resilience Model'. *Academic Paediatrics* 17, no. 7: S86–S93.

Emberson, Caroline, and Trautrims, Alexander. 2019a. 'How Might Modern Slavery Risk in Adult Social Care Procurement be Reduced?'. *Public Procurement Global Revolution IX*, June 16–18, University of Nottingham.

———. 2019b. 'Public Procurement and Modern Slavery Risks in the English Adult Social Care Sector'. In Olga Martin-Ortega, and Claire Methven O'Brien, eds. *Public Procurement and Human Rights: Opportunities, Risks and Dilemmas for the State as Buyer.* Cheltenham: Edward Elgar, 180–91.

Emerson, Robert M., and Messinger, Sheldon L. 1977. 'The Micro-Politics of Trouble'. *Social Problems* 25, no. 2: 121–34.

Emir, Astra. 2020. *Selwyn's Law of Employment*. Oxford: Oxford University Press.

Engel, David. 1998. *How Does Law Matter in the Constitution of Legal Consciousness?* Evanston, IL: Northwestern University Press.

Engel, David M., and Steele, Eric H. 1979. 'Civil Cases and Society: Process and Order in the Civil Justice System'. *Law & Social Inquiry* 4, no. 2: 295–346.

Engel, David M., and Munger, Frank. 2003. *Rights of Inclusion: Law and Identity in the Life Stories of Americans with Disabilities*. Chicago: University of Chicago Press.

Ettlinger, Nancy. 2007. 'Precarity Unbound'. *Alternatives* 32, no. 3: 319–40.

Ewick, Patricia, and Silbey, Susan. 1998. *The Common Place of Law: Stories from Everyday Life*. Chicago: Bibliovault OAI Repository, University of Chicago Press.

———. 2003. 'Narrating Social Structure: Stories of Resistance to Legal Authority'. *American Journal of Sociology* 108, no. 6: 1328–72.

Faist, Thomas. 2016. 'Cross-Border Migration and Social Inequalities'. *Annual Review of Sociology* 42, no. 1: 323–46.

Faris, John. A. 1995. 'An Analysis of the Theory and Principles of Alternative Dispute Resolution'. Doctoral Thesis, University of South Africa. http://uir.unisa.ac.za/bitstream/handle/10500/16772/thesis_faris_ja.pdf?sequence=1&isAllowed=y.

Favell, Adrian, and Recchi, Ettore. 2011. 'Social Mobility and Spatial Mobility'. In Adrian Favell, and Virginie Guiraudon, eds. *Sociology of the European Union*. Palgrave Macmillan: Basingstoke, 50–75.

Feldman, Penny H. 1994. '"Dead End" Work or Motivating Job? Prospects for Frontline Paraprofessional Workers in LTC'. *Generations: Journal of the American Society on Aging* 18, no. 3: 5–10.

Felstiner, William L. F. 2001. 'Synthesising Socio-Legal Research: Lawyer-Client Relations as an Example'. *International Journal of the Legal Profession* 8, no. 3: 191–201.

Felstiner, William L., Abel, Richard L., and Sarat, Austin. 1980. 'The Emergence and Transformation of Disputes: Naming, Blaming, Claiming'. *Law & Society Review* 15, no. 3: 631–54.

Ferber, Marianne A., and Waldfogel, Jane. 1998. 'The Long-Term Consequences of Non-Traditional Employment'. *Monthly Labour Review* 121: 3–12.

Fernández-Reino, Marina, and Rienzo, Cinzia. 2020. *Migrants in the UK Labour Market: An Overview*. Migration Observatory. https://migrationobservatory.ox.ac.uk/resources/briefings/migrants-in-the-uk-labour-market-an-overview/.

Fields, Mark. 2014. In 'International Students and the UK Immigration Debate' August 2014' British Future and Universities, UK. https://www.britishfuture.org/wp-content/uploads/2014/08/BRFJ2238-International-Students.WEB-FINAL.Embargo-25.8.14.pdf.

Financial Times. 2018. 'UK Urged to Ease Limits on Foreign Students' Right to Work'. https://www.ft.com/content/69582712-b5a1-11e8-bbc3-ccd7de085ffe.

Findlay, Allan M. 2011. 'An Assessment of Supply and Demand-Side Theorizations of International Student Mobility'. *International Migration* 49, no. 2: 162–90.

Findlay, Allan M., King, Russell, Smith, Fiona M., Geddes, Alistair, and Skeldon, Ronald. 2012. 'World Class? An Investigation of Globalisation, Difference and International Student Mobility. *Transactions of the Institute of British Geographers* 37, no. 1: 118–31.

Findlay, Allan, King, Russell, Stam, Alexandra, and Ruiz-Gelices, Enric. 2006. 'Ever Reluctant Europeans: The Changing Geographies of UK Students Studying and Working Abroad'. *European Urban and Regional Studies* 13, no. 4: 291–318.

Findlay, Allan, King, Russell, Geddes, Alistair, Smith, F., Stam, Alexandra, Dunne, Malread, Skeldon, Ronald, and Ahrens, Jill. 2010. *Motivations and Experiences of UK Students Studying Abroad*. Project Report. London: Department for Business, Innovation and Skills.

Fiske, Susan T., Cuddy, Amy J., Glick, Peter, and Xu, Jun. 2002. 'A Model of (Often Mixed) Stereotype Content: Competence and Warmth Respectively Follow from Perceived Status and Competition'. *Journal of Personality and Social Psychology* 82, no. 6: 878–902.

Fix, Michael, and Struyk, Raymond. 1993. 'Clear and Convincing Evidence: Measurement of Discrimination in America'. EconPapers. The Field Experiments Website. https://econpapers.repec.org/paper/febnatura/00241.htm.

Fletcher, Anthony. 1999. *Gender, Sex and Subordination in England, 1500–1800*. London: Yale University Press.
Fleury-Steiner, Benjamin. 2004. *Jurors' Stories of Death: How America's Death Penalty Invests in Inequality*. Ann Arbor: University of Michigan Press.
Flick, Uwe. 2014. *An Introduction to Qualitative Research*, 5th ed. London: Sage.
Forbes-Mewett, Helen, Marginson, Simon, Nyland, Chris, Ramia, Gaby, and Sawir, Erlenawati. 2009. 'Australian University International Student Finances'. *Higher Education Policy* 22: 141–61.
Forde, D. Chris. 2001. 'Temporary Arrangements: The Activities of Employment Agencies in the UK'. *Work, Employment and Society* 15, no. 3: 631–44.
Forde, Chris, and Slater, Gary. 2005. 'Agency Working in Britain: Character, Consequences and Regulation'. *British Journal of Industrial Relations* 43, no. 2: 249–71.
Foucault, Michel. 1971. 'Orders of Discourse'. *Social Science Information* 10, no. 2: 7–30.
Fredman, Sandra, and Fudge, Judy. 2013. 'The Legal Construction of Personal Work Relations and Gender.' *Jerusalem Review of Legal Studies* 7, no. 1: 112–22.
Freedland, Mark R. 2003. *The Personal Employment Contract*. Oxford: Oxford University Press.
Freeman, Michael D. A. 2006. *Law and Sociology*. New York: Oxford University Press.
Freeman, Michael. 2008. *Lloyd's Introduction to Jurisprudence*. London: Sweet and Maxwell.
Freeman, Michael. D. 2014. *Lloyd's Introduction to Jurisprudence*. London: Sweet & Maxwell.
Fudge, Judy. 2018. 'Illegal Working, Migrants and Labour Exploitation in the UK'. *Oxford Journal of Legal Studies* 38, no. 3: 557–84.
Gabbatt, Adam. 2010. 'Alan Johnson Announces Crackdown on Student Visas'. *The Guardian*. https://www.theguardian.com/education/2010/feb/07/student-visas-cuts-points-system.
Galanter, Marc. 1974. 'Why the "Haves" Come Out Ahead: Speculations on the Limits of Legal Change'. *Law & Society Review* 9, no. 1: 95–160.
Gayle, Damien. 2018. 'UK Has Seen "Brexit-Related" Growth in Racism, Says UN Representative'. *The Guardian*. https://www.theguardian.com/politics/2018/may/11/uk-has-seen-brexit-related-growth-in-racism-says-un-representative.
Geddes, Andrew. 2008. *Immigration and European Integration: Beyond Fortress Europe*. United Kingdom: Manchester University Press.
Geddie, Kate. 2013. 'The Transnational Ties That Bind: Relationship Considerations for Graduating International Science and Engineering Research Students'. *Population, Space and Place* 19, no. 2: 196–208.
———. 2015. 'Policy Mobilities in the Race for Talent: Competitive State Strategies in International Student Mobility'. *Transactions of the Institute of British Geographers* 40, no. 2: 235–48.
Genn, Hazel. 1999. *Paths to Justice: What People Do and Think about Going to Law*. Oxford: Hart.
Ghosh, Bimal. 1998. *Huddled Masses and Uncertain Shores: Insights into Irregular Migration*. Leiden: Martinus Nijhoff.
Gibbs, Jack P. 1968. 'The Issue in Sociology'. *Pacific Sociological Review* 11, no. 2: 65–74.
Gilliom John. 2001. *Overseers of the Poor*. Chicago: University of Chicago Press.
Glaser, Barney, and Strauss, Anselm. 1967. *The Discovery of Grounded Theory: Strategies for Qualitative Research*. Mill Valley, CA: Sociology Press.
Gleeson, Shannon. 2010. 'Labor Rights for All? The Role of Undocumented Immigrant Status for Worker Claims Making'. *Law & Social Inquiry* 35, no. 3: 561–602.
Gleeson, Shannon, and Gonzales, Roberto G. 2012. 'When Do Papers Matter? An Institutional Analysis of Undocumented Life in the United States'. *International Migration* 50, no. 4: 1–19.

Golden, Lonnie, and Appelbaum, Eileen. 1992. 'What Was Driving the 1982–88 Boom in Temporary Employment?'. *American Journal of Economics and Sociology* 51, no. 4: 473–93.
Gonzales, Roberto G. 2011. 'Learning to Be Illegal: Undocumented Youth and Shifting Legal Contexts in the Transition to Adulthood'. *American Sociological Review* 76, no. 4: 756–76.
González, Carlos R., Mesanza, Ricardo B., and Mariel, Petr. 2011. 'The Determinants of International Student Mobility Flows: An Empirical Study on the Erasmus Programme'. *Higher Education* 62, no. 4: 413–30.
Gordon David. M. 1996. *Fat and Mean: The Corporate Squeeze of Working Americans and the Myth of Managerial 'Downsizing'*. New York: Kessler Books Free Press.
Gordon, Jean, and Jallade, Jean-Pierre. 1996. '"Spontaneous" Student Mobility in the European Union: A Statistical Survey'. *European Journal of Education* 31, no. 2: 133–51.
Gray, Mia. 2004. 'The Social Construction of the Service Sector: Institutional Structures and Labour Market Outcomes'. *Geoforum* 35, no. 1: 23–34.
Greene, Karen S., and Alys, Lilian. 2016. *Missing Persons: A Handbook of Research* Milton Park, Oxfordshire: Taylor & Francis.
Gribble, Cate. 2008. 'Policy Options for Managing International Student Migration: The Sending Country's Perspective'. *Journal of Higher Education Policy and Management* 30, no. 1: 25–39.
Griffith, Alison I. 1998. 'Insider/Outsider: Epistemological Privilege and Mothering Work'. *Human Studies* 21, no. 4: 361–76.
Griffiths, Anne. 2011. 'Pursuing Legal Pluralism: The Power of Paradigms in a Global World'. *Journal of Legal Pluralism and Unofficial Law* 43, no. 64: 173–202.
Griffiths, John. 1986. 'What Is Legal Pluralism?'. *Journal of Legal Pluralism and Unofficial Law* 18, no. 24: 1–55.
———. 2017. 'What Is Sociology of Law? (On Law, Rules, Social Control and Sociology)'. *Journal of Legal Pluralism and Unofficial Law* 49, no. 2: 93–142.
Grimshaw, Damien, Ward, Kevin G., Rubery, Jill, and Beynon, Huw. 2001. 'Organisations and the Transformation of the Internal Labour Market'. *Work, Employment and Society* 15, no. 1: 25–54.
Groger, Lisa, Mayberry, Pamela S., and Straker, Jane K. 1999. 'What We Didn't Learn because of Who Would Not Talk to Us'. *Qualitative Health Research* 9, no. 6: 829–35.
Groth, Markus, Goldman, Barry M., Gilliland, Stephen W., and Bies, Robert J. 2002. 'Commitment to Legal Claiming: Influences of Attributions, Social Guidance and Organizational Tenure'. *Journal of Applied Psychology* 87, no. 4: 781–88.
Guild, Elspeth. 2004. 'The Legal Elements of European Identity: EU Citizenship and Migration Law'. *International Migration Review* 41, no. 2: 549–50.
Guissé, Ibrahima, and Bolzman, Claudio. 2015. *Etudiants du Sud et Internationalisation des Hautes écoles: Entre Illusions et Espoirs; Un Parcours du Combattant vers la Qualification et l'emploi*. Geneva, Switzerland: Editions IES.
Gunawardena, Harshi, and Wilson, Rachel. 2012. *International Students at University: Understanding the Student Experience*. New York: Peter Lang.
Gupta, Tania. 2015. 'The Perils of Commercialization of Higher Education'. *International Journal of Research in Engineering, IT and Social Sciences* 5: 1–8.
Guruz, Kemal. 2011. *Higher Education and International Student Mobility in the Global Knowledge Economy*, 2nd ed. New York: Suny Press.
Habermas, Jürgen. 1996. *Between Facts and Norms: Contributions to a Discourse Theory of Law and Democracy*. Translated by William Rehg. Cambridge, MA: MIT Press.

Hagan, Jacqueline, Castro, Brianna, and Rodriguez, Nestor. 2010. 'The Effects of U.S. Deportation Policies on Immigrant Families and Communities: Cross-Border Perspectives'. *North Carolina Law Review* 88, no. 5: 1799–823.
Hakim, Catherine. 2000. *Research Design: Successful Designs for Social and Economic Research*. Hove, East Sussex: Psychology Press.
Hall, Sarah. 2011. 'Educational Ties, Social Capital and the Translocal (Re)production of MBA Alumni Networks'. *Global Networks* 11, no. 1: 118–38.
———. 2015. 'Geographies of Marketisation in English Higher Education: Territorial and Relational Markets and the Case of Undergraduate Student Fees.' *Area* 47, no. 4: 451–58.
Halliday, Simon. 2019. 'After Hegemony: The Varieties of Legal Consciousness Research'. *Social & Legal Studies* 28, no. 6: 859–78.
Halliday, Terence C., and Carruthers, Bruce G. 2007. 'The Recursivity of Law: Global Norm Making and National Lawmaking in the Globalization of Corporate Insolvency Regimes'. *American Journal of Sociology* 112, no. 4: 1135–202.
Harding, Rosie. 2012. *Regulating Sexuality: Legal Consciousness in Lesbian and Gay Lives*. Milton Park, Oxfordshire: Taylor & Francis.
Handmaker, Jeff, and Matthews, Thandiwe. 2019. 'Analysing Legal Mobilisation's Potential to Secure Equal Access to Socioeconomic Justice in South Africa'. *Development Southern Africa* 36, no. 6: 889–904.
Harding, Rosie. 2006. 'Dogs Are "Registered," People Shouldn't Be: Legal Consciousness and Lesbian and Gay Rights'. *Social & Legal Studies* 15, no. 5: 11–33.
Harrington, Christine, and Yngvesson, Barbera. 1990. 'Interpretive Sociolegal Research'. *Law & Social Inquiry* 15, no. 1: 135–48.
Harris, Philip. 1986. 'Curriculum Development in Legal Studies'. *The Law Teacher* 20, no. 2: 110–23.
Haugen, Heidi Østbø. 2013. 'China's Recruitment of African University Students: Policy Efficacy and Unintended Outcomes.' *Globalisation, Societies and Education* 11: 315–34.
Hawthorne, Lesleyanne. 2010. 'Demography, Migration and Demand for International Students'. In Christopher Findley and William. G. Tierney, eds. *Globalisation and Tertiary Education in the Asia-Pacific*. Hackensack, NJ: World Scientific.
Hayfield, Nikki, and Huxley, Caroline. 2015. 'Insider and Outsider Perspectives: Reflections on Researcher Identities in Research with Lesbian and Bisexual Women'. *Qualitative Research in Psychology* 12, no. 2: 91–106.
Hays Recruitments UK. 2009. https://www.hays.co.uk/.
Hazen, Helen D., and Alberts, Heike C. 2006. 'Visitors or Immigrants? International Students in the United States'. *Population, Space and Place* 12, no. 3: 201–16.
He, Xin. 2005. 'Why Do They Not Comply with the Law? Illegality and Semi-Legality among Rural-Urban Migrant Entrepreneurs in Beijing'. *Law and Society Review* 39, no. 3: 527–62.
Healey, Nigel. 2017. *Reflections on the Value of Insider Research as a Qualitative Research Methodology*. London: Sage Research Methods Cases.
Hein, Jeremy, and Beger, Randall R. 2001. 'Legal Adaptation among Vietnamese Refugees in the United States: How International Migrants Litigate Civil Grievances During the Resettlement Process'. *International Migration Review* 35, no. 2: 420–48.
Henry, Stuart. 2015. *Private Justice: Towards Integrated Theorising in the Sociology of Law*. United Kingdom: Taylor & Francis.
Henson, Kevin D. 1996. *Just a Temp*. Philadelphia, PA: Temple University Press.

Herrmann, Andrea W. 1989. 'The Participant Observer as 'Insider': Researching Your Own Classroom'. Paper presented at the Annual Meeting of the Conference on College Composition and Communication (40th, Seattle, WA, March 16–18, 1989). https://files.eric.ed.gov/fulltext/ED303835.pdf.

Hertogh, Marc. 2004. 'European Conception of Legal Consciousness: Rediscovering Eugen Ehrlich'. *Journal of Law and Society* 31, no. 4: 457–81.

———. 2009. 'What's in a Handshake? Legal Equality and Legal Consciousness in the Netherlands'. *Social & Legal Studies* 18, no. 2: 221–39.

Hewitt, Guy. 2020. 'The Windrush Scandal an Insider's Reflection.' *Caribbean Quarterly* 66, no. 1: 108–28.

Hewitt-Taylor, Jaquelina. 2002. 'Inside Knowledge: Issues in Insider Research'. *Nursing Standard* 16, no. 46: 33–35.

Higher Education Funding Council for England (HEFCE). 2004. *International Student Mobility*. HEFCE Issues Paper 30: London. https://dera.ioe.ac.uk/5155/1/04_30.pdf.

———. 2009. *Attainment in Higher Education: Erasmus and Placement Students*. HEFCE Issues Paper 44: London.

Higher Education Statistics Authority (HESA). 2016. *Students in Higher Education Institutions, 2015–2016*. Cheltenham: HESA.

Hillyard, Paddy, and Sim, Joe. 1997. 'The Political Economy of Socio-Legal Research'. In Philip Thomas, ed. *Socio-Legal Studies*. Aldershot: Dartmouth Press.

Hira, Anil. 2003. 'The Brave New World of International Education'. *World Economy* 26, no. 6: 911–31.

Hirsch, Barry, and Macpherson, David. 2015. 'Union Membership, Coverage, and Earnings from the CPS'. Available at: http://www.unionstats.com

Hirsh, Elizabeth, and Lyons, Christopher J. 2010. 'Perceiving Discrimination on the Job: Legal Consciousness, Workplace Context, and the Construction of Race Discrimination'. *Law & Society Review* 44, no. 2: 269–98.

Hobson's International Students Survey. 2015. https://www2.hobsons.com/resources/entry/2015-international-student-survey-sheds-light-on-the-competitive-global-rec.

Hockey, John. 1993. 'Research Methods - Researching Peers and Familiar Settings'. *Research Papers in Education* 8, no. 2: 199–225.

Hoffmann, Elizabeth A. 2003. 'Legal Consciousness and Dispute Resolution: Different Disputing Behaviour at Two Similar Taxicab Companies'. *Law & Social Inquiry* 28, no. 3: 691–716.

———. 2005. 'Dispute Resolution in a Worker Cooperative: Formal Procedures and Procedural Justice'. *Law & Society Review* 39, no. 1: 51–82.

Home Office. 2013. *Tackling Illegal Immigration in Privately Rented Accommodation: Consultation Document*. London: Home Office.

———. 2017a. 'Check Your UK Visa'. https://www.gov.uk/check-uk-visa.

———. 2007. 'Managing Global Migration: A Strategy to Ensure and Enforce Compliance with our Immigration Laws'. https://webarchive.nationalarchives.gov.uk/20100406101254/http://www.bia.homeoffice.gov.uk/sitecontent/documents/managingourborders/internationalstrategy/strategy-2007.pdf?view=Binary.

———. 2020. *Nationality: Good Character Requirement*. https://assets.publishing.service.gov.uk/government/uploads/system/uploads/attachment_data/file/923656/good-character-guidance-v2.0-gov-uk.pdf.

Hooker, M. Barry. 1975. *Legal Pluralism: An Introduction to Colonial and Neo-Colonial Laws*. Oxford: Oxford University Press.

Hooper, Kate, Desiderio, Maria V., and Salant, Brian. 2017. *Improving the Labour Market Integration of Migrants and Refugees: Empowering Cities through Better Use of EU Instruments*. Brussels: Migration Policy Institute.

Hora, Peggy F., and Chase, Deborah J. 2003/2004. 'Judicial Satisfaction When Judging in a Therapeutic Key'. *Contemporary Issues in Law* 7: 8–38.

Hora, Peggy F., Schma, William G., and Rosenthal, John T. 1999. 'Therapeutic Jurisprudence and the Drug Treatment Court Movement: Revolutionizing the Criminal Justice System's Response to Drug Abuse and Crime in America'. *Notre Dame Law Review* 74: 439–537.

Howe, Joanna. 2019. 'A Legally Constructed Underclass of Workers? The Deportability and Limited Work Rights of International Students in Australia and the United Kingdom'. *Industrial Law Journal* 48, no. 3: 416–46.

Hull, Kathleen E. 2003. 'The Cultural Power of Law and the Cultural Enactment of Legality: The Case of Same-Sex Marriage'. *Law & Social Inquiry* 28, no. 3: 629–57.

———. 2006. *Same-Sex Marriage: The Cultural Politics of Love and Law*. Cambridge: Cambridge University Press.

———. 2016. 'Legal Consciousness in Marginalized Groups: The Case of LGBT People'. *Law & Social Inquiry* 41, no. 3: 551–72.

Hünefeld, Lena, Gerstenberg, Susanne, and Hüffmeier, Jachim. 2020. 'Job Satisfaction and Mental Health of Temporary Agency Workers in Europe: A Systematic Review and Research Agenda'. *Work & Stress* 34, no. 1: 82–110.

Hunt, Alan. 1978. *The Sociological Movement in Law*. London: Palgrave Macmillan.

The Independent. 2010. 'Tories Would Seek £2,000 Bond from Foreign Students'. https://www.independent.co.uk/news/education/education-news/tories-would-seek-163-2-000-bond-from-foreign-students-1862403.html.

———. 2018. 'Benefits of International Students to UK Are "10 Times Greater than Costs", Shows Study.' https://www.independent.co.uk/news/uk/politics/international-students-uk-brexit-costs-benefits-non-eu-university-immigration-figures-a8152151.html.

International Conference on Population and Development (ICPD). 1994. 'Cairo Declaration on Population & Development'. https://www.unfpa.org/pcm/node/13920.

International Labour Organisation (ILO). 2010. 'Racial Discrimination in the World of Work'. https://www.ilo.org/wcmsp5/groups/public/---ed_norm/---declaration/documents/newsitem/wcms_104989.pdf.

International Monetary Fund (IMF) Annual Report. 2019. *Our Connected World*. https://www.imf.org/external/pubs/ft/ar/2019/eng/assets/pdf/imf-annual-report-2019.pdf.

International Organization for Migration (IOM). 2008. *World Migration Report; Managing Labour Mobility in the Evolving Global Economy*. https://publications.iom.int/system/files/pdf/wmr_1.pdf.

———. 2018. *World Migration Report*. https://www.iom.int/sites/default/files/country/docs/china/r5_world_migration_report_2018_en.pdf.

———. 2020. *World Migration Report*. https://publications.iom.int/system/files/pdf/wmr_2020.pdf.

Jacob, Herbert. 1969. *Debtors in Court*. Chicago: Rand-McNally.

Jayaweera, Hiranthi, and Anderson, Bridget. 2008. 'Migrant Workers and Vulnerable Employment: A Review of Existing Data'. Centre on Migration, Policy and Society. https://www.compas.ox.ac.uk/project/migrant-workers-and-vulnerable-employment-a-review-of-existing-data/.

Jefferson, Rachara. 2018. *Intrinsic and Extrinsic Job Motivators Predicting Likelihood of Employee Intent to Leave*. Doctoral Dissertation, Walden University.
Jolly, S. 1997. 'Family Law'. In Philip A. Thomas, ed. *Socio-Legal Studies*. Aldershot: Dartmouth.
Judge, Lindsay. 2017. 'Unwrapping the Agency Worker Pay Penalty'. Resolution Foundation. https://www.resolutionfoundation.org/comment/unwrapping-the-agency-worker-pay-penalty/.
———. 2018. *The Good, the Bad and the Ugly: The Experience of Agency Workers and the Policy Response*. London: Resolution Foundation.
Judge, Lindsay, and Tomlinson, Daniel. 2016. *Secret Agents. Agency Workers in the New World of Work*. London: Resolution Foundation.
Jürges, Hendrik, and Schneider, Kerstin. 2004. 'International Differences in Student Achievement: An Economic Perspective'. *German Economic Review* 5, no. 3: 357–80.
Kahn-Freund, Otto. 1951. 'Servants and Independent Contractors'. *Modern Law Review* 14, no. 4: 504–9.
Kaiser, Cheryl R., and Miller, Carol T. 2001. 'Stop Complaining! The Social Costs of Making Attributions to Discrimination'. *Personality and Social Psychology Bulletin* 27, no. 2: 254–63.
———. 2003. 'Derogating the Victim: The Interpersonal Consequences of Blaming Events on Discrimination'. *Group Processes & Intergroup Relations* 6, no. 3: 227–37.
Kalleberg, Arne L. 2008. 'The State of Work (and Workers) in America'. *Work and Occupations* 35, no. 3: 243–61.
Kalleberg, Arne. 2011. *Good Jobs, Bad Jobs: The Rise of Polarized and Precarious Employment Systems in the United States, 1970s–2000s*. United Kingdom: Russell Sage Foundation.
Kalleberg, Arne L., and Sorensen, Aage B. 1979. 'The Sociology of Labour Markets'. *Annual Review of Sociology* 5, no. 1: 351–79.
Kalleberg, Arne L., and Vallas, Steven P. 2017. *Precarious Work*. Bingley: Emerald.
Kallin, Walter. 2003. 'Human Rights and the Integration of Migrants'. In T. Alexander Aleinikoff and Vincent Chetail, eds. *Migration and International Legal Norms*. The Hague: TMC Asser Press.
Kalman, Laura. 2016. *Legal Realism at Yale, 1927–1960*. United States: University of North Carolina Press.
Kamerāde, Daiga, and Richardson, Helen. 2018. 'Gender Segregation, Underemployment and Subjective Well-Being in the UK Labour Market'. *Human Relations* 71, no. 2: 285–309.
Kawachi, Ichiro, and Kennedy, Bruce P. 1997. 'Health and Social Cohesion: Why Care about Income Inequality?'. *British Medical Journal* 314: 1037–40.
Kawalek, Anna. 2020. 'A Tool for Measuring Therapeutic Jurisprudence Values during Empirical Research'. *International Journal of law and Psychiatry* 71, no. 1: 1–16.
———. 2021. *Problem-Solving Courts, Criminal Justice, and the International Gold Standard: Reframing the English and Welsh Drug Courts*. London: Routledge.
Kawulich, Barbara. 2005. 'Participant Observation as a Data Collection Method'. *Forum Qualitative Sozialforschung / Forum: Qualitative Social Research* 6, no. 2 Art. 43. http://nbn-resolving.de/urn:nbn:de:0114-fqs0502430.
Kelley, Harold H., and Michela, John L. 1980. 'Attribution Theory and Research'. *Annual Review of Psychology* 31, no. 1: 457–501.
Kelly, Philip F. 2011. 'Filipino Migration and the Spatialities of Labour Market Subordination'. In Susan McGrath-Champ, Andrew Herod and Al Rainnie. *Handbook of Employment and Society: Working Space*. Cheltenham: Edward Elgar.

Kessler, Mark. 1990. 'Legal Mobilization for Social Reform: Power and the Politics of Agenda Setting'. *Law & Society Review* 24, no. 1: 121–43.
Keune, Maarten, and Marginson, Paul. 2013. 'Transnational Industrial Relations as Multi-Level Governance: Interdependencies in European Social Dialogue'. *British Journal of Industrial Relations* 51, no. 3: 473–97.
Khadria, Binod. 2006. 'Migration between India and the UK'. *Public Policy Research*, 13: 172–84.
———. 2009. 'Adversary Analysis and the Quest for Global Development: Optimizing the Dynamic Conflict of Interest in Transnational Migration'. *Social Analysis* 53: 106–22.
Khan, Aqeel, Hamdan, Abdul R., Ahmad, Roslee, and Mustaffa, Mohammed S. 2015. 'International Student's Academic Achievement: Contribution of Gender, Self-Efficacy and Socio-Cultural Adjustment'. *Asian Social Science* 11, no. 10: 153–58.
Kidner, Richard. 2019. *Blackstone's Statutes on Employment Law 2020–2021*. Oxford: Oxford University Press.
Kim, Ann, and Kwak, Ming-Jung. 2019. *Outward and Upward Mobilities: International Students in Canada, Their Families, and Structuring Institutions*. Toronto: University of Toronto Press.
King, Russell, and Raghuram, Parvati. 2013. 'International Student Migration: Mapping the Field and New Research Agendas'. *Population, Space and Place* 19: 127–37.
King, Nigel. 2004. 'Using Templates in the Thematic Analysis of Text'. In Catherine Cassell and Gillian Symon. *Essential Guide to Qualitative Methods in Organizational Research*. London: Sage.
King, Russell, Findlay, Allan, and Ahrens, Jill. 2010. *International Student Mobility Literature Review*. Project Report. Higher Education Funding Council for England (HEFCE), Bristol. http://www.hefce.ac.uk/media/hefce/content/pubs/2010/rd2010/rd20_10.pdf.
Kirk, Eleanor. 2020. 'Contesting "Bogus Self-Employment" Via Legal Mobilisation: The Case of Foster Care Workers'. *Capital and Class* 44 no. 4: 531–39.
Kirkland, Anna. 2008. 'Think of the Hippopotamus: Rights Consciousness in the Fat Acceptance Movement'. *Law & Society Review* 42, no. 2: 397–432.
Knerr, Beatrice, Tlatlik, Rebecca, and Xi, Zhao. 2010. 'The Benefits of International Student Mobility. A Comparison Between Chinese and Indian Students in Germany'. Retrieved from https://iussp.org/sites/default/files/event_call_for_papers/Knerr-Tlatlik-Zhao.pdf.
Knox, Angela. 2014. 'Human Resource Management (HRM) in Temporary Work Agencies: Evidence from the Hospitality Industry'. *Economic and Labour Relations Review* 25, no. 1: 81–98.
Korzeniewicz, Roberto P., and Moran, Timothy P. 2009. *Unveiling Inequality; A World-Historical Perspective*. New York: Russell Sage Foundation.
Kostiner, Idit. 2003. 'Evaluating Legality: Toward a Cultural Approach to the Study of Law and Social Change'. *Law & Society Review* 37, no. 2: 323–68.
———. 2006. 'Truth, Justice, and the Legal Consciousness'. In Laura Beth Nielson, ed. *The New Civil Rights Research: A Constitutive Approach*. London: Routledge.
Kritz, Mary M. 2006. 'Globalisation and Internationalisation of Tertiary Education'. International Symposium on International Migration and Development. Population Division, Department of Economic and Social Affairs (United Nations Secretariat, Turin, Italy, June 28–30).
———. 2013. 'Sending Country Determinants of International Student Mobility'. *Development Sociology Cornell University*: https://iussp.org/sites/default/files/event_call_for_papers/KritzBusanEducationStudent_textChartsTables.pdf.

———. 2015. 'International Student Mobility and Tertiary Education Capacity in Africa'. *International Migration* 53, no. 1: 29–49.

Kritzer, Herbert M. 2010. 'Claiming Behaviour as Legal Mobilization'. In Peter Cane and Herbert Kritzer, eds. *The Oxford Handbook of Empirical Legal Research*. Oxford: Oxford University Press.

Kubal, Agnieszka M. 2009. 'Why Semi-Legal? Polish Post-2004 EU Enlargement Migrants in the United Kingdom'. *Journal of Immigration, Asylum and Nationality Law* 23, no. 2: 148–64.

———. 2012a. 'Conceptualizing Semi-Legality in Migration Research'. *Law & Society Review* 47, no. 3: 555–87.

———. 2012b. *Socio-Legal Integration. Polish Post-2004 EU Enlargement Migrants in the United Kingdom*. London: Ashgate.

———. 2015. 'Legal Consciousness as a Form of Social Remittance? Studying Return Migrants' Everyday Practices of Legality in Ukraine'. *Migration Studies* 3, no. 1: 68–88.

———. 2016. *Socio-Legal Integration: Polish Post-2004 EU Enlargement Migrants in the United Kingdom*. United Kingdom: Taylor & Francis.

Larson, Erik W. 2004. 'Institutionalizing Legal Consciousness: Regulation and the Embedding of Market Participants in the Securities Industry in Ghana and Fiji'. *Law & Society Review* 38, no. 4: 737–68.

LaSala, Michael C. 2003. 'When Interviewing "Family" Maximizing the Insider Advantage in the Qualitative Study of Lesbians and Gay Men'. *Journal of Gay & Lesbian Social Services* 15, no. 1–2: 15–30.

Lavrakas, Paul J. 2008. *Encyclopedia of Survey Research Methods*. Thousand Oaks, CA: Sage.

Law Society. 2018. 'Failures in UK Immigration and Asylum Undermine the Rule of Law'. https://www.lawsociety.org.uk/en/contact-or-visit-us/press-office/press-releases/failures-in-uk-immigration-and-asylum-undermine-the-rule-of-law.

Lee, Kiong H., and Tan, Jee P. 1984. 'The International Flow of Third Level Lesser Developed Country Students to Developed Countries: Determinants and Implications'. *Higher Education* 13, no. 6: 687–707.

Lehoucq, Emilio, and Taylor, Whitney. 2020. 'Conceptualizing Legal Mobilization: How Should We Understand the Deployment of Legal Strategies?'. *Law & Social Inquiry* 45, no. 1: 166–93.

Leighton, Patricia, and Wynn, Michael. 2011. 'Classifying Employment Relationships – More Sliding Doors or a Better Regulatory Framework?'. *Industrial Law Journal* 40, no. 1: 5–44.

Levatino, Antonina, Eremenko, Tatiana, Molinero Gerbeau, Yoan, Consterdine, Erica, Kabbanji, Lama, Gonzalez-Ferrer, Amparo, and Beauchemin, Cris. 2018. 'Opening or Closing Borders to International Students? Convergent and Divergent Dynamics in France, Spain and the UK'. *Globalisation, Societies and Education* 16, no. 3: 366–80.

Levitsky, Sandra R. 2008. '"What Rights?" The Construction of Political Claims to American Health Care Entitlements'. *Law & Society Review* 42, no. 3: 551–90.

Lindahl, Hans. 2010. 'A-legality: Post Nationalism and the Question of Legal Boundaries'. *Modern Law Review* 73, no. 1: 30–56.

Lingard, Helen. 2007. 'Conflict between Paid Work and Study: Does It Impact Upon Students' Burnout and Satisfaction with University Life?'. *Journal for Education in the Built Environment* 2, no. 1: 90–109.

Liu, Sida. 2015. 'Law's Social Forms: A Powerless Approach to the Sociology of Law'. *Law & Social Inquiry* 40, no. 1: 1–28.

Liu, Sida, Liang, Lily, and Michelson, Ethan. 2014. 'Migration and Social Structure: The Spatial Mobility of Chinese Lawyers'. *Law & Policy* 36, no. 2: 165–94.

Lodovici, Manuela S. 2010. 'Making a Success of Integrating Immigrants in the Labour Market'. https://ec.europa.eu/social/BlobServlet?docId=8218&langId=en.

Lomer, Sylvie. 2014. 'Economic Objects: How Policy Discourse in the United Kingdom Represents International Students'. *Policy Futures in Education* 12, no. 2: 273–85.

———. 2018. 'UK Policy Discourses and International Student Mobility: The Deterrence and Subjectification of International Students'. *Globalisation, Societies and Education* 16, no. 3: 308–24.

Lowell, B. Lindsay, and Khadka, Pramod. 2011. 'Trends in Foreign-Student Admissions to the U.S'. In Barry R. Chiswick, ed. *High-Skilled Immigration in a Global Labor Market*. Washington, DC: American Enterprise Institute.

Macaulay, Stewart. 1987. 'Images of Law in Everyday Life: The Lessons of School, Entertainment and Spectator Sports'. *Law and Society Review* 21, no. 2: 185–218.

MacKenzie, Robert, and Forde, Chris. 2009. 'The Rhetoric of the "Good Worker" versus the Realities of Employers' Use and the Experiences of Migrant Workers'. *Work, Employment and Society* 23, no. 1: 142–59.

MacBride, Jo, and Smith, Andrew. 2018. 'Forgotten Workers'.' Durham University Business School. Report available at https://www.dur.ac.uk/business/research/research-centres/forgotten-workers/.

Macready, Caroline, and Tucker, Clive. 2011. *Who Goes Where and Why: An Overview and Analysis of Global Educational Mobility*. New York: IIE and AIFS Foundation.

Madge, Clare, Raghuram, Parvati, and Noxolo, Pat. 2014. 'Conceptualizing International Education: From International Student to International Study'. *Progress in Human Geography* 39, no. 6: 681–701.

Major, Brenda, Kaiser, Cheryl R, and McCoy, Shannon K. 2003. 'It's Not My Fault: When and Why Attributions to Prejudice Protect Self-Esteem'. *Personality and Social Psychology Bulletin* 29, no. 6: 772–81.

Malet Calvo, Daniel. 2018. 'Understanding International Students beyond Studentification: A New Class of Transnational Urban Consumers. The Example of Erasmus Students in Lisbon (Portugal)'. *Urban Studies* 55, no. 10: 2142–58.

Manacorda, Marco, Manning, Alan, and Wadsworth, Jonathan. 2012. 'The Impact of Immigration on the Structure of Wages: Theory and Evidence from Britain'. *Journal of the European Economic Association* 10, no. 1: 120–51.

Mangum, Garth, Mayall, Donald, and Nelson, Kristin. 1985. 'The Temporary Help Industry: A Response to the Dual Internal Labour Market'. *ILR Review* 38, no. 4: 599–611.

Marginson, Simon. 2007. 'The Public/Private Divide in Higher Education: A Global Revision'. *Higher Education* 53: 307–33.

———. 2014. 'International Students: The United Kingdom Drops the Ball'. *International Higher Education* 76: 9–10.

Maroukis, Thanos. 2016. 'Temporary Agency Work, Migration and the Crisis in Greece: Labour Market Segmentation Intensified'. *Transfer: European Review of Labour and Research* 22, no. 2: 179–92.

Marshall, Anna-Maria. 2003. 'Injustice Frames, Legality, and the Everyday Construction of Sexual Harassment'. *Law & Social Inquiry* 28, no. 3: 659–89.

———. 2005. 'Idle Rights: Employees' Rights Consciousness and the Construction of Sexual Harassment Policies'. *Law & Society Review* 39, no. 1: 83–124.

———. 2006. 'Communities and Culture: Enriching Legal Consciousness and Legal Culture'. *Law & Social Inquiry* 31, no. 1: 229–49.

Marshall, Anna-Maria, and Barclay, Scott. 2003. 'In Their Own Words: How Ordinary People Construct the Legal World'. *Law and Social Inquiry* 28, no. 3: 617–28.

Marson, James. 2013. 'Anatomy of an Employee'. *Web Journal of Current Legal Issues* 19, no. 3.

———. 2014. *Beginning Employment Law*. United Kingdom: Taylor & Francis.

Massey, Douglas S. 1990. 'The Social and Economic Origins of Immigration'. *The ANNALS of the American Academy of Political and Social Science* 510, no. 1: 60–72.

Marx, Karl. 1887. *Capital: A Critical Analysis of Capitalist Production*. London: Swan Sonnenschein, Lowrey.

———. 1931. *The Essentials of Marx; the Communist Manifesto, by Karl Marx and Frederick Engels. Wage-labor and Capital. Value, Price and Profit, and other Selections by Karl Marx, with Introduction and Notes by Algernon Lee*. New York: Vanguard Press.

———. 1968. *The German Ideology*. Moscow: Progress.

Mather, Lynn. 2011. *Law and Society*. Oxford: Oxford Handbook of Political Science.

Maxwell, Joseph A. 2012. *Qualitative Research Design: An Interactive Approach*, Volume 41. Los Angeles, CA: Sage.

Mayhew, Leon, and Reiss, Albert. 1969. 'The Social Organization of Legal Contacts'. *American Sociological Review* 34: 309–18.

Mayhew, Leon H. 1975. 'Institutions of Representation: Civil Justice and the Public'. *Law & Society Review* 9, no. 3: 401–29.

Mazzarol, Tim W. 1998. 'Critical Success Factors for International Education Marketing'. *International Journal of Educational Management* 12, no. 4: 163–75.

Mazzarol, Tim, and Soutar, Geoffrey. 2002. '"Push-Pull" Factors Influencing International Student Destination Choice'. *International Journal of Educational Management* 16: 82–90.

Mazzarol, Tim, Kemp, Steven, and Savery, Lawson. 1997. *International Students Who Choose Not to Study in Australia: An Examination of Taiwan and Indonesia*. Canberra: Australian International Education Foundation.

McBride, Jo, Smith, Andrew, and Mbala, Marcell. 2017. '"You End Up with Nothing": The Experience of Being a Statistic of "In-Work Poverty" in the UK'. *Work, Employment and Society* 32, no 1: 210–18.

McBurnie, Grant, and Ziguras, Christopher. 2003. 'Remaking the World in Our Own Image: Australia's Efforts to Liberalise Trade in Education Services'. *Australian Journal of Education* 47, no. 3: 217–34.

McCann, Michael W. 1994. *Rights at Work: Pay Equity Reform and the Politics of Legal Mobilization*. Chicago: University of Chicago Press.

McCrudden, Christopher. 2006. 'Legal Research and the Social Sciences'. *Law Quarterly Review* 122/ Oxford Legal Studies Research Paper No. 33/2006. https://ssrn.com/abstract=915302.

McGovern, Patrick, Smeaton, Deborah, and Hill, Stephen. 2004. 'Bad Jobs in Britain: Nonstandard Employment and Job Quality'. *Work and Occupations* 31, no. 2: 225–49.

McGregor, Alan, and Sproull, Alan. 1992. 'Employers and the Flexible Workforce'. *Employment Gazette* 100, no. 5: 225–34.

McMahon, Mary E. 1992. 'Higher Education in a World Market'. *Higher Education* 24, no. 4 465–82.

Menjívar, Cecilia. 2000. *Fragmented Ties: Salvadoran Immigrant Networks in America*. Berkeley: University of California Press.

Menjívar, Cecilia. 2006. 'Liminal Legality: Salvadoran and Guatemalan Immigrants' Lives in the United States'. *American Journal of Sociology* 111, no. 4: 999–1037.

Menski, Werner F., and Rahman, Tahmina. 1988. 'Hindus and the Law in Bangladesh'. *South Asia Research* 8, no. 2: 111–31.

Merry, Sally. 1985. 'Concepts of Law and Justice Among Working-Class Americans: Ideology as Culture'. *Legal Studies Forum* 9, no. 1: 59–70.

———. 1988. 'Legal Pluralism'. *Law & Society Review* 22, no. 5: 869–96.

———. 1990. *Getting Justice and Getting Even: Legal Consciousness Among Working-Class Americans*. Chicago: University of Chicago Press.

———. 1994. 'Complete Publications'. *Political and Legal Anthropology Review* 17, no. 2: 151–57.

———. 1995. 'Resistance and the Cultural Power of Law'. *Law & Society Review* 29, no. 1: 11–26.

Merton, Robert K. 1972. 'Insiders and Outsiders: A Chapter in the Sociology of Knowledge'. *American Journal of Sociology* 78, no. 1: 9–47.

Mezzadra, Sandro, and Neilson, Brett. 2008. *Border as Method, or the Multiplication of Labour*. Durham, NC: Duke University Press.

Migration Advisory Committee (MAC). 2018. 'Impact of International Students in the UK'. https://assets.publishing.service.gov.uk/government/uploads/system/uploads/attachment_data/file/739089/Impact_intl_students_report_published_v1.1.pdf.

Migration Observatory. 2020. 'International Student Migration to the UK'. https://migrationobservatory.ox.ac.uk/resources/briefings/international-student-migration-to-the-uk/.

Migration Watch. 2019. 'Jobs and Welfare'. https://www.migrationwatchuk.org/briefing-paper/428/jobs-and-welfare.

Miles, Robert. 1986. 'Labour Migration, Racism and Capital Accumulation in Western Europe Since 1945: An Overview'. *Capital & Class* 10, no. 1: 49–86.

Milkman, Ruth, González, Ana L., and Narro, Victor. 2010. *Wage Theft and Workplace Violations in Los Angeles: The Failure of Employment and Labour Law for Low-Wage Workers*. Los Angeles, CA: UCLA, Institute for Research on Labor and Employment. https://escholarship.org/uc/item/5jt7n9gx.

Miller, Audrey K., Markman, Keith D., and Handley, Ian M. 2007. 'Self-Blame among Sexual Assault Victims Prospectively Predicts Revictimization: A Perceived Sociolegal Context Model of Risk'. *Basic and Applied Social Psychology* 29. no. 2: 129–36.

Miller, Richard E., and Sarat, Austin. 1980. 'Grievances, Claims, and Disputes: Assessing the Adversary Culture'. *Law & Society Review* 15, no. 3: 525–66.

Mitlacher, Lars W. 2008. 'Job Quality and Temporary Agency Work: Challenges for Human Resource Management in Triangular Employment Relations in Germany'. *International Journal of Human Resource Management* 19, no. 3: 446–60.

Moore, Sally F. 1973. 'Law and Social Change: The Semi-Autonomous Social Field as an Appropriate Subject of Study'. *Law & Society Review* 7, no. 4: 719–46.

Morgan, David L. 1996. *Focus Groups as Qualitative Research*. Newbury Park, CA: Sage.

Mosneaga, Ana, and Winther, Lars. 2013. 'Emerging Talents? International Students before and after Their Career Start in Denmark'. *Population, Space and Place* 19, no. 2: 181–95.

Moss, Phillip, and Tilly, Chris. 2001. *Stories Employers Tell; Race, Skill, and Hiring in America*. New York: Russell Sage Foundation.

Moustakas, Clark. 1994. *Phenomenological Research Methods*. Newbury Park, CA: Sage.

Mulley, Sarah, and Sachrajda, Alice. 2011. Student Migration in the UK. London: Institute for Public Policy Research.

Munkres, Susan A. 2008. 'Claiming "Victim" to Harassment Law: Legal Consciousness of the Privileged'. *Law & Social Inquiry* 33, no. 2: 447–72.

Murphy-Lejeune, Elizabeth. 2002. *Student Mobility and Narrative in Europe: The New Strangers*. United Kingdom: Routledge.
National Health Service (NHS). 2020. *Personal Social Services: Staff of Social Services Departments, England*. https://digital.nhs.uk/data-and-information/publications/statistical/personal-social-services-staff-of-social-services-departments/england-2020.
Neill, Neill, Mulholland, Gwyneth, Ross, Villanda, and Leckey, Janet. 2004. 'The Influence of Part-Time Work on Student Placement'. *Journal of Further and Higher Education* 28, no. 2: 123–37.
Nelken, David. 2009. *Law, Liability and Culture*. In David M. Engel and Michael McCann, eds. *Fault Lines: Tort Law as Cultural Practice*. Stanford, CA: Stanford University Press.
Nielsen, Laura Beth. 2000. 'Situating Legal Consciousness: Experiences and Attitudes of Ordinary Citizens About: Law and Street Harassment'. *Law and Society Review* 34, no. 4: 1055–90.
———. 2004. 'The Work of Rights and the Work Rights Do: A Critical Empirical Approach'. In Austin Sarat, ed. *The Blackwell Companion to Law and Society*. Malden, MA: Blackwell, Chapter 4.
Neilson, Brett. 2009. 'The World Seen from a Taxi: Students-Migrants-Workers in the Global Multiplication of Labour'. *Subjectivity* 29, no. 1: 425–44.
Neilson, Brett, and Rossiter, Ned. 2008. 'Precarity as a Political Concept, or, Fordism as Exception'. *Theory, Culture & Society* 25, nos. 7–8: 51–72.
Nelken, David. 1998. 'Blind Insights? The Limits of a Reflexive Sociology of Law'. *Journal of Law and Society* 25, no. 3: 407–26.
Noy, Chaim. 2008. 'Sampling Knowledge: The Hermeneutics of Snowball Sampling in Qualitative Research'. *International Journal of Social Research Methodology* 11, no. 4: 327–44.
Nyland, Christopher, Forbes-Mewett, Helen, Marginson, Simon, Ramia, Gaby, Sawir, Erlenawati, and Smith, Sharon. 2009. 'International Student-Workers in Australia: A New Vulnerable Workforce'. *Journal of Education and Work* 22, no. 1: 1–14.
O'Brien, Charlotte. 2021. 'Between the Devil and the Deep Blue Sea: Vulnerable EU Citizens Cast Adrift in the UK post-Brexit.' *Common Market Law Review* 58, no. 2: 431–70.
Organisation for Economic Co-operation and Development (OECD). 2013. *Education Indicators in Focus*. https://www.oecd.org/education/skills-beyond-school/EDIF%202013--N%C2%B014%20(eng)-Final.pdf.
Office of National Statistics. 2018. *Labour Market Economic Commentary: November 2018*. https://www.ons.gov.uk/employmentandlabourmarket/peopleinwork/employmentandemployeetypes/articles/labourmarketeconomiccommentary/november2018.
———. 2019. *UK Labour Market: December 2019*. https://www.ons.gov.uk/releases/uklabourmarketdecember2019.
———. 2020. *UK and Non-UK People in the Labour Market*. February https://www.ons.gov.uk/employmentandlabourmarket/peopleinwork/employmentandemployeetypes/articles/ukandnonukpeopleinthelabourmarket/february2020.
Olds, Kris. 2007. 'Global Assemblage: Singapore, Foreign Universities, and the Construction of a "Global Education Hub"' *World Development* 35: 959–75.
Olofsdotter, Gunilla. 2012. 'Workplace Flexibility and Control in Temporary Agency Work'. *Vulnerable Groups & Inclusion* 3, no. 1: 18913.
Oucho, John. 2008. 'African Brain Drain and Gain, Diaspora and Remittances: More Rhetoric than Action'. In Aderanti Adepoju, Ton van Naerssen and Annelies Zoomers, eds. *International Migration and National Development in sub-Saharan Africa*. Leiden, The Netherlands: Brill.

Oung, Camille, Schlepper, Laura, and Curry, Natasha. 2020. *What Does the Social Care Workforce Look like across the Four Countries?* London: Nuffield Trust.

Owen, Joe, Thimont Jack, Maddy, Iacobov, Adela, and Christensen, Elliott. 2019. *Managing Migration after Brexit.* Institute for Government. https://www.instituteforgovernment.org.uk/publications/managing-migration-after-brexit.

Oxenbridge, Sarah, and Moensted, Maja L. 2011. 'The Relationship between Payment Systems, Work Intensification and Health and Safety Outcomes: A Study of Hotel Room Attendants'. *Policy and Practice in Health and Safety* 9, no. 2: 7–26.

Özden, Çaglar, and Schiff, Maurice, eds. 2006. *International Migration, Remittances and Development.* New York: Palgrave Macmillan.

Pandit, Kavita. 2009. 'Leading Internationalization'. *Annals of the Association of American Geographers* 99, no. 4: 645–56.

Paoli, Pascal, and Merllié, Damien. 2001. 'Third European Survey on Working Conditions 2000'. Report, Eurofound. https://www.eurofound.europa.eu/publications/report/2001/working-conditions/third-european-survey-on-working-conditions-2000.

Paret, Marcel, and Gleeson, Shannon. 2016. 'Precarity and Agency through a Migration Lens'. *Citizenship Studies* 20, nos. 3–4: 277–94.

Park, YoungAh, and Sprung, Justin M. 2013. 'Work–School Conflict and Health Outcomes: Beneficial Resources for Working College Students'. *Journal of Occupational Health Psychology* 18, no. 4: 384–94.

———. 2015. 'Weekly Work–School Conflict, Sleep Quality, and Fatigue: Recovery Self-Efficacy as a Cross-Level Moderator'. *Journal of Organizational Behavior* 36, no. 1: 112–27.

Partington, Richard. 2019. 'Gig Economy in Britain Doubles, Accounting for 4.7 Million Workers'. *The Guardian* https://www.theguardian.com/business/2019/jun/28/gig-economy-in-britain-doubles-accounting-for-47-million-workers.

Parvati, Raghuram. 2013. 'Theorising the Spaces of Student Migration'. *Population, Space and Place* 19, no. 2: 138–54.

Patton, Michael Q. 2002. 'Two Decades of Developments in Qualitative Inquiry: A Personal, Experiential Perspective'. *Qualitative Social Work* 1, no. 3: 261–83.

Perkins, Anne, and Quinn, Ben. 2018. 'May's Immigration Policy seen as "Almost Reminiscent of Nazi Germany"'. *The Guardian* https://www.theguardian.com/uk-news/2018/apr/19/theresa-may-immigration-policy-seen-as-almost-reminiscent-of-nazi-germany.

Perkins, Richard, and Neumayer, Eric. 2014. 'Geographies of Educational Mobilities: Exploring the Uneven Flows of International Students'. *Geographical Journal* 180, no. 3: 246–59.

Perlin, Michael L. 1993. 'What Is Therapeutic Jurisprudence'. *New York Law School Journal of Human Rights* 10, no. 3: 623–36.

———. 2017. 'Have You Seen Dignity? The Story of the Development of Therapeutic Jurisprudence'. 27 *New Zealand Universities Law Review* 27: 1135. https://ssrn.com/abstract=2932149 or http://dx.doi.org/10.2139/ssrn.2932149.

———. 2019. '"Changing of the Guards": David Wexler, Therapeutic Jurisprudence, and the Transformation of Legal Scholarship'. *International Journal of Law and Psychiatry* 63: 3–7.

Perlin, Michael L., and Lynch, Alison J. 2015. 'How Teaching about Therapeutic Jurisprudence Can Be a Tool of Social Justice, and Lead Law Students to Personally and Socially Rewarding Careers: Sexuality and Disability as a Case Example'. *Nevada Law Journal* 16, no. 1, Article 8. https://scholars.law.unlv.edu/nlj/vol16/iss1/8.

Petersen, Rebecca D., and Valdez, Avalardo. 2005. 'Using Snowball-Based Methods in Hidden Populations to Generate a Randomized Community Sample of Gang-Affiliated Adolescents'. *Youth Violence and Juvenile Justice* 3, no. 2: 151–67.

Pieraccini, Margherita, and Cardwell, Emma. 2016. 'Divergent Perceptions of New Marine Protected Areas: Comparing Legal Consciousness in Scilly and Barra, UK'. *Ocean & Coastal Management* 119: 21–29.
Piore, Michael J. 1979. *Birds of Passage: Migrant Labour and Industrial Societies*. Cambridge: Cambridge University Press.
Pole, Chrsitopher J., and Lampard, Richard. 2002. *Practical Social Investigation: Qualitative and Quantitative Methods in Social Research*. London: Pearson Education.
Polivka, Anne E. 1996. 'Contingent and Alternative Work Arrangements, Defined'. *Monthly Labour Review* 119, no. 10: 3–9.
Polivka Anne E., and Nardone, Thomas. 1989. 'On the Definition of "Contingent Work"'. *Monthly Labour Review* 112, no. 12: 9–16.
Porteli, John. 2008. 'Researching a Secondary School in Malta'. In Pat Sikes, ed. *Researching Education from the Inside*. New York: Routledge, 80–94.
Portes, Jonathan. 2016. 'Immigration after Brexit.' *National Institute Economic Review* 238, no. 1: R13–R21.
Pospisil, Leopold J. 1971. *Anthropology of Law a Comparative Theory*. New York: Harper & Row.
Pound, Roscoe. 1910. 'Law in Books and Law in Action'. *American Law Review* 44: 12–36.
Practical Law. 2019. 'Employment Status: Employee, Worker or Self-Employed'. https://uk.practicallaw.thomsonreuters.com/6-200-4244.
Quak, Evert-Jan, and van de Vijsel, Annemarie. 2014. 'Low Wages and Job Insecurity as a Destructive Global Standard'. *The Broker* https://www.thebrokeronline.eu/low-wages-and-job-insecurity-as-a-destructive-global-standard-d46/.
Raghuram, Parvati. 2013. 'Theorising the Spaces of Student Migration'. *Population, Space and Place* 19, no. 2: 138–54.
Riaño, Yvonne, Van Mol, Christof, and Raghuram, Parvati. 2018a. 'New Directions in Studying Policies of International Student Mobility and Migration'. *Globalisation, Societies and Education* 16, no. 3: 283–94.
———. 2018b. 'Policies of International Student Mobility and Migration: Theoretical and Empirical Insights'. *Globalisation, Societies and Education* 16, no. 3: 283–380.
Riaño, Yvonne, and Piguet, Etienne. 2016. *International Student Migration – An Annotated Review*. Oxford: Oxford University Press.
Richman, Kimberly D. 2006. 'LGBT Family Rights, Legal Consciousness, and the Dilemma of Difference'. In Benjamin Fleury-Steiner and Laura Beth Nielsen, eds. *The New Civil Rights Research: A Constitutive Approach*. New York: Routledge.
———. 2010. 'By Any Other Name: The Social and Legal Stakes of Same-Sex Marriage'. *University of San Francisco Law Review* 45: 357.
———. 2014. *License to Wed; What Legal Marriage Means to Same-Sex Couples*. New York: NYU Press.
Riggert, Steven C., Boyle, Mike, Petrosko, Joesph M., Ash, Daniel, and Rude-Parkins, Carolyn. 2006. 'Student Employment and Higher Education: Empiricism and Contradiction'. *Review of Educational Research* 76, no. 1: 63–92.
Ritchie, Jane, and Lewis, Jane. 2003. *Qualitative Research Practice – A Guide for Social Science Students and Researchers*. Thousand Oaks, CA: Sage.
Robertson, Shanthi. 2011. 'Cash Cows, Backdoor Migrants, or Activist Citizens? International Students, Citizenship, and Rights in Australia'. *Ethnic and Racial Studies* 34, no. 12: 2192–211.
Rodgers, Gerry, and Rodgers, Janine. 1989. *Precarious Jobs in Labour Market Regulation*. International Institute for Labour Studies. Geneva: United Nations Digital Library.

Rogers, Jackie K. 2000. *Temps: The Many Faces of the Changing Workplace*. Ithaca, NY: Cornell University Press.
Rodriguez, Nestor. 2004. ' "Workers Wanted": Employer Recruitment of Immigrant Labour'. *Work and Occupations* 31, no. 4: 453–73.
Rooney, Pauline. 2005. 'Researching from the Inside – Does it Compromise Validity: A Discussion'. *Level3*, 3, May.
Rosenzweig, Mark. R. 2006. 'The Circulation Migration of the Skilled and Economic Development'. *Proceedings Federal Reserve Bank of Dallas*, 147–70.
Roser, Max. 2013. 'Global Economic Inequality'. OurWorldInData.org. https://ourworldindata.org/global-economic-inequality.
Ross, E. Wayne, and Gibson, Rich. 2007. *Neoliberalism and Education Reform*. Cresskill, NJ: Hampton Press.
Rubery, Jill, Ward, Kevin, Grimshaw, Damian, and Beynon, Huw. 2005. 'Working Time, Industrial Relations and the Employment Relationship'. *Time & Society* 14, no. 1: 89–111.
Ruhs, Martin. 2010. 'Numbers versus Rights in Low-Skilled Labour Immigration Policy? A Comment on Cummins and Rodríguez'. *Journal of Human Development and Capabilities* 11, no. 2: 305–9.
———. 2014. *Immigration and Labour Market Protectionism: Protecting Local Workers' Preferential Access to the National Labour Market*. Oxford: Oxford University Press.
Ruhs, Martin, and Anderson, Bridget. 2010. 'Semi-Compliance and Illegality in Migrant Labour Markets: An Analysis of Migrants, Employers and the State in the UK'. *Population, Space and Place* 16, no. 3: 195–211.
Ruhs, Martin, and Vargas-Silva, Carlos. 2012. 'The Labour Market Effects of Immigration'. *Migration Observatory Briefing*, COMPAS. Oxford: University of Oxford.
Ruhs, Martin, and Vargas-Silva, Carlos. 2020. 'The Labour Market Effects of Immigration'. *Migration Observatory Briefing*, COMPAS. Oxford: University of Oxford.
Ruiz, Neil G. 2014. *The Geography of Foreign Students in US Higher Education: Origins and Destinations*. Washington, DC: Brookings Institution.
Rutherglen, George. 2006. 'Disparate Impact, Discrimination, and the Essentially Contested Concept of Equality'. *Fordham Law Review* 74, no. 4: 2313–38.
Rytter, Mikkel. 2012. 'Between Preferences: Marriage and Mobility among Danish Pakistani Youth'. *Journal of the Royal Anthropological Institute* 18, no. 3: 572–90.
Saidin, Khaliza. 2017. 'Insider Researchers: Challenges & Opportunities'. *Proceedings of the ICECRS*, 1: 849–54.
Salter, Michael, and Mason, Julie. 2007. *Writing Law Dissertations: An Introduction and Guide to the Conduct of Legal Research*. Essex: Pearson/Longman.
Samek, Robert A. 1974. *The Legal Point of View*. New York: Philosophical Library.
Sanchez-Gelabert, Albert, Figueroa, Mijail, and Elias, Marina. 2017. 'Working Whilst Studying in Higher Education: The Impact of the Economic Crisis on Academic and Labour Market Success'. *European Journal of Education* 52, no. 2: 232–45.
Sandefur, Rebecca. 2015. 'Bridging the Gap: Rethinking Outreach for Greater Access to Justice'. *University of Arkansas at Little Rock Law Review* 37, no. 4: 721–40.
Sarat, Austin. 1985. 'Legal Effectiveness and Social Studies of Law: On the Unfortunate Persistence of a Research Tradition'. *Legal Studies* 9, 23–31.
———. 1986. 'Access to Justice: Citizen Participation and the American Legal Order'. In Leon Lipson and Stanton Wheeler, eds. *Law and the Social Sciences*. New York: Russell Sage Found.
———. 1990. ' "…The Law Is All Over": Power, Resistance and the Legal Consciousness of the Welfare Poor'. *Yale Journal of Law and the Humanity* 2, no. 2: 343–79.

———. 1998. *Cause Lawyering: Political Commitments and Professional Responsibilities*. Oxford: Oxford University Press.

———. ed. 2004. *The Blackwell Companion to Law and Society*. Malden, MA: Blackwell.

Sarat, Austin, and Felstiner, William L. 1989. 'Lawyers and Legal Consciousness: Law Talk in the Divorce Lawyer's Office'. *Yale Law Journal* 98: 1663–88.

———. 1995 *Divorce Lawyers and their Clients*. Oxford: Oxford University Press.

———. 1997. *Divorce Lawyers and Their Clients: Power and Meaning in the Legal Process*. Oxford: Oxford University Press on Demand.

Sarat, Austin, and Garth, Bryant. 1998. *Justice and Power in Sociolegal Studies*. Evanston, IL: Northwestern University Press.

Schiff, David N. 1976. 'Socio-Legal Theory: Social Structure and Law'. *Modern Law Review* 39, no. 3: 287–310.

Schlegel, Alice. 1995. 'Introduction'. *Ethos* 23, no. 1: 3–14.

Schopp, Robert F. 2016. 'Therapeutic Jurisprudence, Coercive Interventions, and Human Dignity'. *Queensland University of Technology Law Review* 16: no. 3: 68–84.

Schuck, Peter. 1998. *Citizens, Strangers, and In-Betweens: Essays on Immigration and Citizenship*. London: Routledge.

Schuetz, Alfred. 1971. In B. R. Cosin, I. R. Dale, G. M. Esland, and D. F. Swift eds. *School and Society*. London: Routledge and Kegan Paul in association with The Open University Press.

———. 2000. 'Law and the Study of Migration'. In Caroline Brettell and James F. Hollifield, eds., *Migration Theory: Talking Across the Disciplines*. Rochester, NY: Routledge.

Scott, James C. 1989. 'Everyday Forms of Resistance'. *Copenhagen Journal of Asian Studies* 4: 33–62.

Seidman, Irving. 2006. *Interviewing as Qualitative Research: A Guide for Researchers in Education and the Social Sciences*. New York: Teacher's College Press.

Sennett, Richard. 1998. *The Corrosion of Character: The Personal Consequences of Work in the New Capitalism*. United Kingdom: W. W. Norton.

Sewell, William H. 1992. 'A Theory of Structure: Duality, Agency, and Transformation'. *American Journal of Sociology* 98, no. 1: 1–29.

Sexsmith, Kathleen. 2016. 'Exit, Voice, Constrained Loyalty, and Entrapment: Migrant Farmworkers and the Expression of Discontent on New York Dairy Farms'. *Citizenship Studies* 20, nos. 3–4: 311–25.

Sherer, Peter D. 1996. 'Toward an Understanding of the Variety in Work Arrangements: The Organization and Labour Relationships Framework'. *Journal of Organizational Behaviour*. https://search.proquest.com/docview/228796519/abstract/1B490D919CE94024PQ/1.

Shumar, Wesley. 1997. *College for Sale: A Critique of the Commodification of Higher Education*. Basingstoke: Falmer Press.

Silbey, Susan S. 2005. 'After Legal Consciousness'. *Annual Review of Law and Social Science* 1, no. 1: 323–68.

Silverman, David. 2017. *Doing Qualitative Research*. London: Sage.

Simmel, Georg. 1950. 'The Stranger'. In *The Sociology of Georg Simmel*. New York: Simon and Schuster.

Slaughter, Sheila, and Cantwell, Brendan. 2012. 'Transatlantic Moves to the Market: The United States and the European Union'. *Higher Education* 63, no. 5: 583–606.

Slobogin, Christopher. 1995. 'Therapeutic Jurisprudence: Five Dilemmas to Ponder'. *Psychology, Public Policy and Law* 1, no. 1: 193–219.

Smith, Andrew. 2016. '"The Magnificent 7 (am)"? Work-Life Articulation beyond the 9 (am) to 5 (pm) "Norm"'. *New Technology Work and Employment* 31, no. 3: 209–22.
Smyth, Anne, and Holian, Rosalie. 2008. *Credibility Issues in Research from within Organisations*. London: Routledge.
Snyder, Francis. 1999. 'Governing Economic Globalisation: Global Legal Pluralism and European Law'. *European Law Journal* 5, no. 4: 334–74.
Spilimbergo, Antonio. 2009. 'Democracy and Foreign Education'. *American Economic Review* 99, no. 1: 528–43.
Spring, Joel. 2009. *Globalization of Education: An Introduction*. New York: Queens College & Graduate Centre, City University of New York.
Stabile, Mark, and Apouey, Benedicte. 2019. *The effects of self and temporary employment on mental health: the role of the gig economy in the UK.* INSEAD Report, June https://www.insead.edu/newsroom/2019-new-study-gig- economy-boosts-mental-health-for- self-employed.
Stainback, Kevin, and Tomaskovic-Devey, Donald. 2009. 'Intersections of Power and Privilege: Long-Term Trends in Managerial Representation'. *American Sociological Review* 74, no. 5: 800–820.
Standing, Guy. 2011. *The Precariat: The New Dangerous Class*. London: Bloomsbury.
Stanworth, Celia, and Druker, Janet. 2004. 'Mutual Expectations: A Study of the Three-Way Relationship between Employment Agencies, Their Client Organisations and White-Collar Agency "Temps"'. *Industrial Relations Journal* 35, no. 1: 58–75.
Storrie, Donald. 2002. *Temporary Agency Work in the European Union*. Dublin, Ireland: European Foundation for the Improvement of Living and Working Conditions.
———. 2003. 'The Regulation and Growth of Contingent Employment in Sweden'. In Ola Bergström and Donald W. Storrie, eds. *Contingent Employment in Europe and the United States*. Cheltenham: Edward Elgar.
———. 2004. 'The Increase in Fixed-Term Employment in Sweden'. *Spotlight on the Labour Market* 21: 161.
———. 2007. 'Temporary Agency Work in the European union – Economic Rationale and Equal Treatment'. In Bengt Furåker, Kristina Håkansson and, Jan C. Karlsson, eds. *Flexibility and Stability in Working Life*. London: Palgrave Macmillan.
Summers, Clyde W. 1997. 'Contingent Employment in the United States'. *Cornell Labor Law Journal* 18, no. 4: 503–22.
Syed, Moin, Azmitia, Margarita, and Phinney, Jean S. 2007. 'Stability and Change in Ethnic Identity among Latino Emerging Adults in Two Contexts'. *Identity: An International Journal of Theory and Research* 7, no. 2: 155–78.
Szelényi, Katalin. 2006. 'Students without Borders? Migratory Decision-Making among International Graduate Students in the U.S.'. *Knowledge, Technology & Policy* 19: 64–86.
Takeda, Kasumi. 2005. 'The Excruciating Job Hunt'. *Global: Magazine of the Overseas Students Association*, University of Adelaide.
Tamanaha, Brian Z. 2000. 'A Non-Essentialist Version of Legal Pluralism'. *Journal of Law and Society* 27, no. 2: 296–321.
———. 2001. *A General Jurisprudence of Law and Society*. Oxford: Oxford University Press.
Tang, Denise T. S. 2007. 'The Research Pendulum: Multiple Roles and Responsibilities as a Researcher'. *Journal of Lesbian Studies* 10, no. 3–4: 11–27.
Tapinos, G. 1999. *Clandestine Immigration: Economic and Political Issues*. Part III in SOPEMI, Trends in International Migration–1999 Annual Report, OECD: 229–51.
Taylor, Stephen, and Emir, Astra. 2019. *Employment Law: An Introduction*, 5th ed. Oxford: Oxford University Press.

Teichler, Ulrich, Ferencz, Irina, and Wätcher, Bernd, eds. 2011. *Mapping Mobility in European Higher Education: Overview and Trends*, Volume 1. Brussels: Directorate General for Education and Culture (DGEAC), European Commission.

The Telegraph. 2010. 'Students Who Break Visa Rules Can Stay in UK'. https://www.telegraph.co.uk/news/uknews/immigration/7109967/Students-who-break-visa-rules-can-stay-in-UK.html.

Thomas, Philip. 1997. *Socio-Legal Studies*. Aldershot: Dartmouth.

Tienda, Marta, Findley, Sally, Tollman, Stephen, and Preston-Whyte, Eleanor. 2006. *Africa on the Move: African Migration and Urbanisation in Comparative Perspective*. Johannesburg: Wits University Press.

Tomaskovic-Devey, Donald, Zimmer, Catherine, Stainback, Kevin, Robinson, Corre, and Tomusk, Voldemar. 2004. *The Open World and Closed Societies: Essays on Higher Education Policies 'in Transition'*. New York: Springer.

Toms, Simon. 2012. 'The Impact of the UK Temporary Employment Industry in Assisting Agency Workers Since the Year 2000'. PhD Thesis, University of Gloucestershire.

Trades Union Congress. 2017. *Insecure Work and Ethnicity*. https://www.tuc.org.uk/sites/default/files/Insecure%20work%20and%20ethnicity_0.pdf.

Travis, Alan, and Weale, Sally. 2016. 'Amber Rudd Announces Crackdown on Overseas Students and Work Visas'. *The Guardian*. https://www.theguardian.com/uk-news/2016/oct/04/rudd-announces-crackdown-on-overseas-students-and-new-work-visas.

Tremblay, Karine. 2005. 'Academic Mobility and Immigration'. *Journal of Studies in International Education* 9, no. 3: 196–228.

Trubek, David M. 1984. 'Where the Action Is: Critical Legal Studies and Empiricism'. *Stanford Law Review* 36, no. 1: 575–622.

Tuckett, Anna. 2019. 'Managing Paper Trails after Windrush: Migration, Documents and Bureaucracy'. *Journal of Legal Anthropology* 3, no. 2: 120–23.

Tushman, Michael L., and Katz, Ralph. 1980. 'External Communication and Project Performance: An Investigation into the Role of Gatekeepers'. *Management Science* 26, no. 11: 1071–85.

Twining, William. 2009. 'Normative and Legal Pluralism: A Global Perspective'. *Duke Journal of Comparative & International Law* 20: 473–518.

UK Border Agency (UKBA). 2010. *The Student Immigration System A Consultation*. https://assets.publishing.service.gov.uk/government/uploads/system/uploads/attachment_data/file/268985/student-consultation.pdf.

UK Council for International Student Affairs (UKCISA). 2004a. *Broadening Our Horizons Survey*. https://www.ukcisa.org.uk/Research--Policy/Resource-bank/resources/90/Broadening-Our-Horizons-Survey-2004.

———. 2004b. *International Students in UK Universities and Colleges: Broadening our Horizons – Report of the UKCISA Survey, 2004*. http://www.ukcosa.org.uk/files/pdf/BOHreport.pdf.

———. 2006. *New horizons: The experiences of international students in UK further education colleges – Report of the UKCISA Survey 2006*. http://www.ukcosa.org.uk/files/pdf/new_horizons_report.pdf.

———. 2018. *The UKCISA Tier 4 Student Survey 2018*. https://www.ukcisa.org.uk.

Underhill, Elsa, and Quinlan, Michael. 2011. 'How Precarious Employment Affects Health and Safety at Work: The Case of Temporary Agency Workers'. *Relations Industrielles/Industrial Relations* 66, no. 3: 397–421.

University of Cambridge. 2014. 'Working While You Study'. https://www.cambridgestudents.cam.ac.uk/your-course/graduate-study/your-student-status/working-while-you-study.

United Nations Department of Economic and Social Affairs. 2021. *World Security Report 2020. Inequality in a Rapidly Change World*. United Nations Publication. https://www.un.org/development/desa/dspd/wp-content/uploads/sites/22/2020/01/World-Social-Report-2020-FullReport.pdf.
United Nations Educational, Scientific and Cultural Organization (UNESCO). 2018. 'Global Flow of Tertiary-Level Students'. http://uis.unesco.org/en/visualisation/global-flow-tertiary-level-students.
United Nations, Development Programme. 1993. *Human Development Report 1993*. Oxford University Press. https://books.google.co.uk/books?id=DpaOaJ4qvB4C.
Unluer, Sema. 2012. 'Being an Insider Researcher while Conducting Case Study Research'. *Qualitative Report* 17, no. 29: 1–14.
van Meter, Karl M. 1990. 'Sampling and Cross-Classification Analysis in International Social Research'. In Else Øyen, ed. *Sage Studies in International Sociology, Volume 40. Comparative Methodology: Theory and Practice in International Social Research*. London: Sage.
Van Mol, Chirstof, and Timmerman, Christiane. 2014. 'Should I Stay or Should I Go? An Analysis of the Determinants of Intra-European Student Mobility'. *Population, Space and Place* 20, no. 5: 465–79.
van Riemsdijk, Micheline. 2014. 'International Migration and Local Emplacement: Everyday Place-Making Practices of Skilled Migrants in Oslo, Norway'. *Environment and Planning A: Economy and Space* 46, no. 4: 963–79.
Vanhala, Lisa. 2018. 'Shaping the Structure of Legal Opportunities: Environmental NGOs Bringing International Environmental Procedural Rights Back Home'. *Law & Policy* 40, no. 1: 110–27.
Vick, Douglas W. 2004. 'Interdisciplinarity and the Discipline of Law'. *Journal of Law and Society* 31, no. 2: 163–93.
Vogt, Paul W. 1999. *Dictionary of Statistics and Methodology: A Non-Technical Guide for the Social Sciences*, 2nd ed. London: Sage.
Wächter, Berd. 2014. 'Recent Trends in Student Mobility in Europe'. *Internationalisation of Higher Education and Global Mobility* 23: 87–98.
Waite, Louise. 2009. 'A Place and Space for a Critical Geography of Precarity?'. *Geography Compass* 3, no. 1: 412–33.
Waldinger, Roger, and Lichter, Michael I. 2003. *How the Other Half Works: Immigration and the Social Organization of Labor*. Berkeley: University of California Press.
Waring, Teresa, and Wainwright, David. 2008. 'Issues and Challenges in the Use of Template Analysis: Two Comparative Case Studies from the Field'. *Electronic Journal of Business Research Methods*, 6, no. 1: 85–94.
Waters, Johanna L. 2006. 'Emergent Geographies of International Education and Social Exclusion'. *Antipode* 38, no. 5: 1046–68.
Waters, Johanna, and Brooks, Rachel. 2010. 'Accidental Achievers? International Higher Education, Class Reproduction and Privilege in the Experiences of UK Students Overseas'. *British Journal of Sociology of Education* 31, no. 2: 217–28.
Waters, Johanna, and Leung, Maggi. 2013. 'A Colourful University Life? Transnational Higher Education and the Spatial Dimensions of Institutional Social Capital in Hong Kong'. *Population, Space and Place* 19, no. 2: 155–67.
Watts, Jacqueline. 2006. '"The Outsider Within": Dilemmas of Qualitative Feminist Research within a Culture of Resistance'. *Qualitative Research* 6, no. 3: 385–402.
Weber, Max. 1978. *Economy and Society: An Outline of Interpretive Sociology*. Edited by Guenther Roth and Claus Wittich. Berkeley: University of California Press.

Wexler, David B. 1990. *Therapeutic Jurisprudence: The Law as a Therapeutic Agent*. Durham, NC: Carolina Academic Press.

———. 1999. 'Therapeutic Jurisprudence Forum: The Development of Therapeutic Jurisprudence: From Theory to Practice'. *Revista Juridica Universidad de Puerto Rico* 68: 691–705.

———. 2011. 'From Theory to Practice and Back Again in Therapeutic Jurisprudence: Now Comes the Hard Part'. *Monash University Law Review* 37, no. 1: 33–42.

Wexler, David B., and Winick, Bruce J. 1991. *Essays in Therapeutic Jurisprudence*. Durham, NC: Carolina Academic Press.

———. 1996. *Law in a Therapeutic Key: Developments in Therapeutic Jurisprudence*. Durham, NC: Carolina Academic Press.

Wheatley, Abby C., and Gomberg-Muñoz, Ruth. 2015. 'Keep Moving: Collective Agency Along the Migrant Trail'. *Citizenship Studies* 20, nos. 3–4: 396–410.

Wilkinson, Richard, and Pickett, Kate. 2009. *The Spirit Level: Why Greater Equality Makes Societies Stronger*. London: Bloomsbury.

Williams, Colin C. 2009. 'Formal and Informal Employment in Europe: Beyond Dualistic Representations'. *European Urban and Regional Studies* 16, no. 2: 147–59.

Winick, Bruce. J. 1991. 'Harnessing the Power of the Bet: Wagering with the Government as a Mechanism of Social and Individual Change'. In David. B. Wexler and Bruce J. Winick, eds. *Essays in Therapeutic Jurisprudence*. Durham, NC: Carolina Academic Press, 219–90.

———. 1997. 'The Jurisprudence of Therapeutic Jurisprudence'. *Psychology, Public Policy, and Law* 3, no. 1: 184–206.

World Bank. 2010. *Financing Higher Education in Africa*. http://documents1.worldbank.org/curated/en/497251467990390368/pdf/544410PUB0EPI01BOX0349416B01PUBLIC1.pdf.

Wu, Tina. 2016. 'More than a Paycheck: Nannies, Work, and Identity'. *Citizenship Studies* 20, nos. 3–4: 295–310.

Xiang, Biao, and Wei, Shen. 2009. 'International Student Migration and Social Stratification in China'. *International Journal of Educational Development* 29, no. 5: 513–22.

Yamada, David C. 2021. 'Therapeutic Jurisprudence: Foundations, Expansion, and Assessment', *University of Miami Law Review* 75, no. 3: 660.

Yin, Robert K. 2017. *Case Study Research and Applications: Design and Methods*. London: Sage.

Ying, Yu-Wen, Lee, Peter A., and Tsai, Jeanne L. 2007. 'Attachment, Sense of Coherence, and Mental Health Among Chinese American College Students: Variation by Migration Status'. *International Journal of Intercultural Relations* 31, no. 5: 531–44.

Yngvesson, Barbara. 2006. 'Backed by Papers: Undoing Persons, Histories, and Return'. *American Ethnologist* 33, no. 2: 177–90.

Young, Kathryne M. 2014. 'Everyone Knows the Game: Legal Consciousness in the Hawaiian Cockfight'. *Law & Society Review* 48, no. 3: 499–530.

Zemans, Frances K. 1983. 'Legal Mobilization: The Neglected Role of the Law in the Political System'. *American Political Science Review* 77, no. 3: 690–703.

Ziguras, Christopher, and Law, Siew-Fang. 2006. 'Recruiting International Students as Skilled Migrants: The Global Skills Race as Viewed from Australia and Malaysia'. *Globalisation, Societies and Education* 4, no. 1: 59–76.

Zou, Mimi. 2016. 'Migrants at Work: Immigration and Vulnerability in Labour Law'. *Industrial Law Journal* 45, no. 4: 565–69.

INDEX

20-hour (work) 155, 156, 203

abuse 4, 9, 45, 50, 82, 90, 93–94, 97–98, 108–9, 123–24, 137–38, 139–40, 141, 163–64, 165, 169, 179, 192, 201–2, 205–6
agency work 8–9, 11–12, 95, 102–6
Agency Workers (Amendment) Regulations 2019 116
Agency Workers Regulations 2010 115–16
atypical employment 8–9, 20–21, 95, 100–1, 102–3, 123–24, 151

consciousness 2–3, 7, 8, 9–10, 11–12, 18, 19, 22, 40–41, 54, 55–56, 61–62, 63–71, 72–74, 76, 77–78, 79–81, 82–83, 86, 92–94, 108–9, 167, 174–75, 176, 183–84, 187, 188–90, 192, 193–94, 195, 196–97, 198, 202–3, 204–5, 206–7

degrees of harm 8, 91, 174, 199
discrimination 4, 9, 17–18, 32–33, 46–47, 51–52, 106–7, 108–9, 115–16, 123–24, 137–38, 139–40, 141, 143, 147, 176, 202
dispute transformation pyramid 55–56,
  blaming 22, 55–56, 77–78, 82, 178, 181
  claiming 22, 55–56, 77–78, 79, 82, 179–80, 181
  naming 22, 55–56, 77–78, 82, 176, 178, 181, 197, 204

education 1–2, 14–15, 29–33, 34–39, 41–42, 43–45, 46, 48–49, 52–53, 75, 83, 86, 91, 93–94, 95–96, 120–21, 124, 189–91
Employment Rights Act 1996 (ERA 1996) 107

equality Act 2010 113–14, 115–16
Ewick and Silbey 8, 17, 18, 19, 21, 22, 55–56, 57, 61, 62–64, 65–67, 68, 69, 70–71, 72–73, 80–81, 82–83, 175, 184, 192, 193
  against the law 9–10, 63–64, 66–67, 82, 93–94, 184, 193, 195, 198, 204–5, 207
  before the law 63–64, 184, 189, 195, 198, 204–5, 207
  with the law 2–3, 9–10, 63–64, 184, 187, 189–90, 192, 193, 195, 198, 204–5
exploitation 5, 6, 9, 93–94, 123–24, 137–39, 163–64, 165, 169, 192, 201–2

flexibility 9–10, 24, 59, 69, 87, 103–4, 105, 118–19, 125, 127, 130–31, 151–52, 153, 154–55, 164–65, 201

grievances 19, 22, 60, 77–78, 93–94, 175, 176, 178, 179–80, 197, 202, 204
Guy Standing 4, 98–99
  Precariat 3, 4, 98–99, 200

Health and Safety at Work Act 1974 113–14

immigration 4, 14, 38–39, 42, 46, 48–49, 50–51, 52, 53, 83–86, 87–90, 92, 93–94, 108–9, 119–21, 125, 135, 146, 148, 156, 162–64, 168, 174–75, 183, 184, 189–90, 198, 199, 207
Immigration Act 1971 50
Immigration Act 2016 50, 199
Immigration Rules 162–63, 174–75, 184, 189–90
Immigration, Asylum and Nationality Act 2006 50
independent contractor 1–2, 48–49, 50–51, 88, 90–91, 106–7, 108, 110–11, 113–14, 115–16, 120–21, 199;
inequality 7–8, 30, 38–40, 76, 108

INDEX

insecurity 3, 4, 5, 94, 95, 99, 101–2, 106, 118, 123–24, 132, 143, 147, 152–53, 172–73, 174–75, 187, 200, 206–7

legal hegemony 9–10, 65, 66, 67, 167, 194–95, 198, 204–5
legal mobilisation 2–3, 8, 9–10, 22, 40–41, 54, 55–56, 74–75, 76, 78, 80–81, 93–94, 167, 196–97, 202–3, 204
legal pluralism 55–56, 68, 70–73, 189–90, 195
lived experiences 14–15, 21, 24–25, 46–47, 59, 68, 94, 95–96, 99, 108–9, 161–62, 167, 198, 199, 200, 205
lived reality 24–25, 92, 94, 193
low pay 9, 100, 105, 126, 131, 138

methodology 7, 19, 21–22, 42, 58–59, 69, 79–80, 103, 114
   black letter 58
   doctrinal 58
   ethnographic 1, 4, 5, 7, 9–10, 11–12, 13, 14, 15, 16, 17, 19–20, 21, 24–25, 26, 38–39, 150, 152–53, 173, 196, 200
   insider research 12–13, 23, 25–26
   qualitative 11–12, 20, 21–22, 24, 25, 26, 38–39, 111, 134, 200
   snowball(ers) 15–17, 19, 20–21, 25
migrants 1–3, 4–5, 6, 8, 9, 16–17, 21, 30, 31–32, 35–36, 40–42, 44, 45–46, 47–49, 50, 51–52, 53–54, 55–56, 59, 68, 83–84, 85–91, 92, 93, 94, 95–96, 97–98, 99, 104, 108–9, 118–21, 124, 125–26, 127–28, 129–31, 132–33, 134, 137, 139, 142–43, 148, 151, 155, 158–60, 162–63, 168, 173, 174, 192, 196, 198, 199–201, 202–4, 205–6, 207

National Living Wage 113–14, 126, 138
National Minimum Wage (Amendment) Regulations 2016 113–14
nomads 167, 169, 172–73, 193

perceived injurious experiences 77–78, 180

precarity 3, 4–7, 8–9, 11–12, 22, 40–41, 85, 91–93, 94, 95, 98–99, 108–9, 118, 120–21, 123–24, 135–36, 152–53, 154–55, 164–65, 172–73, 196–97, 200, 203–4, 206
protectionism 7–8, 49
protectionist 46
pseudopreneurs 170–71, 172–73

racism 46–47, 139–40, 143
resistance 5–7, 9–10, 61, 63–64, 65–67, 81, 90, 93–94, 100, 167, 184, 189–90, 191, 192, 193, 194–95
rule of law 71

second-order consciousness 55–56, 68–69, 70
semi-legal employment 93–94, 174–75, 182–83, 192, 196, 197
semi-legality 2–3, 8, 9–10, 11–12, 22, 54, 55–56, 88–94, 167–69, 172–73, 174–75, 177–78, 180, 181, 184, 187, 191, 192–93, 194, 195, 196–97, 198, 202–5, 206–7
social network 25, 32–33, 92, 129–30, 148, 162–63
socio-legal 2–3, 7, 8, 9–10, 11–12, , 20, 21–22, 40–41, 54, 55–56, 57, 58–60, 61, 63–64, 65, 68, 69, 70, 71, 72–73, 74, 78, 80–81, 85–87, 90–91, 93, 94, 98, 99, 114, 148, 167, 175, 177–78, 189–90, 192, 194–95, 196–97, 198, 200, 202–3, 204–5, 206–7
socio-legal studies 2–3, 56–59
student visa 9, 18, 24–25, 35–36, 44–45, 52, 134, 151, 168, 169–70, 174, 175, 186, 189, 195
study visa 9–10, 20–21, 45, 46, 48–49, 124, 134, 146, 156, 185, 195, 199

therapeutic jurisprudence (TJ) 8–9, 108–9, 160–62
transnational mobility 29–30, 35–36, 37–38, 40–41, 42, 46, 86–87, 206

Working Time Regulations 1998 19, 113–14, 115–16

www.ingramcontent.com/pod-product-compliance
Lightning Source LLC
Chambersburg PA
CBHW021139230426
43667CB00005B/188